The VOLKSWAGEN Golf STORY

The VOLKSWAGEN Golf STORY

40 YEARS OF THE SECOND PEOPLE'S CAR

Russell Hayes

BEHEMOTH
PUBLISHING

Published in May 2014

ISBN 978-0-9928769-0-6

Published by Behemoth Publishing
59 High Street, Wincanton, Somerset BA9 9JZ, UK
www.behemothpublishing.co.uk

Printed and bound in the UK by Butler Tanner & Dennis
Caxton Road, Frome, Somerset BA11 1NF

Edited by Derek Smith
Designed by Richard Parsons

Cover pictures by the author, except rear centre
(yellow Golf 1) courtesy Volkswagen
Cover design by Lee Parsons

Contents

Preface

'I have a Golf,' we say, or 'It's a Golf,' and we know what that means. Few things in life are constant but the Volkswagen Golf appears to be one of them. Of course in another age the Volkswagen Beetle seemed eternal but the Golf's production has now outnumbered it and its influence has been far greater. It changes constantly under its surface but never changes much on the outside, bypassing car fashion yet somehow remaining modern and desirable to millions.

So it certainly merits serious examination in its fortieth year, and I hope this history does it justice. I make no claims that it's definitive, but I hope it's comprehensive without any major omissions and, of course, major errors.

Some points to bear in mind as you hopefully enjoy this book. Firstly, naming: Volkswagen never used the term Golf Mk1 and so on, but others have. The company has tended to go with 'generation', which I have also adopted, and the terms Golf 1 and 2 and so on. I have made occasional use of factory 'Type' codes (such as 1 and 2) and engine and platform designations. Internally the Golf was also referred to as the 'A-class' car.

Hatchbacks were unusual in 1974 and the Golf was referred to by the number of passenger doors – two and four. Nowadays the tailgate of a hatchback or estate is counted so I have used three- and five-door.

Unless specified, I quote mainland Europe launch dates. Apart from 1974 and 1997 a September launch has usually been followed by an October on-sale date and UK sale the following January. The two major European motor shows are Frankfurt and Paris, which alternate. American on-sale dates could come well after Europe.

On countries, money and measures, for the German market please read West German until reunification in 1990. Germany used the Deutsche Mark (DM) until 1999, then the Euro. Measurements are a mixture of metric and imperial. British readers will be more used to miles per gallon/per hour than litres per 100km or kph although where that is the only measure I have converted. Wheel sizes still seem to be always in inches.

From the Golf 5 onwards, car power outputs were much more often quoted in PS for Pferdestärke, the German measure. To convert to imperial brake horsepower (BHP) you divide by 1.0139, which reduces the figure slightly, thus 105 PS equals 103.56bhp. Some British magazines stuck with BHP as a descriptor even if the badge indicated a PS engine output. Otherwise a TDI 140 becomes the slightly less neatly named TDI 138.

Volkswagen and mainland Europe describe a convertible as a cabriolet, so I have followed that convention. Likewise, Volkswagen uses GTI all in capitals, even though some magazines do not. Some of the Volkswagen figures quoted (retired or current) use the prefix Dr. or Dr. Ing. This stands for *Doktor-Ingenieur*, awarded for a doctorate in engineering.

Russell Hayes, London, 2014

Peter Kogler/ZeitHaus, The Autostadt in Wolfsburg

WOB
PR 44

Beyond the Beetle

In spring 1967 Volkswagen was unable to see its own future. Many observers thought it didn't have one.

'We were a car company which had never designed a car,' said former boss Carl Hahn. It was true: the vast Wolfsburg factory had only been created to produce one model, commissioned by the Third Reich from Ferdinand Porsche in 1934, which became known as the Beetle. In 1967 the Porsche company still did most of Volkswagen's design work.

Since the end of the Second World War the Beetle had been in relentlessly increasing production and any derivatives were new bodies atop Beetle underpinnings. The original vehicle flew in the face of built-in obsolescence, only changing in detail year-on-year. Heinrich 'Heinz' Nordhoff (see panel on page 16), Volkswagen's inspirational leader since 1948 had laid down his philosophy that very year: 'In any sound design there are almost unlimited possibilities. I see no sense in starting anew every few years with the same teething troubles, making obsolete all of the past.'

And why be worried nearly twenty years later anyway? The symbol of Germany's post-war success, the Beetle had sold 96,918 vehicles in the first quarter of 1967 – a new sales record. The previous year Volkswagen had made a profit of £45 million and it was well on the way to a total production figure of 15 million vehicles since 1945.

Yet the once unassailable company seemed vulnerable. New economic measures in Germany at the end of 1966 such as higher petrol and insurance prices had seen domestic Beetle sales slump. Other carmakers were also hit, but the giant suffered the hardest blow. Nordhoff warned that spring 1967 sales might be 30% down on the previous year. Short-time working was introduced for Wolfsburg's 150,000 employees.

Then, as now, a company largely owned by the State of Lower Saxony, Volkswagen's prospects were of intense public and political interest. Very publicly Franz-Josef Strauss, the German finance minister accused Nordhoff of sitting on enormous financial reserves yet having done nothing to develop new products. Volkswagen, the newspapers said, had been sleeping. News monthly *Der Spiegel*'s article of May 1967 was headlined *Für Käfermüder* – 'tired of Beetles'. Comparisons were made with Ford, which had produced the Model T from 1908 to 1927 with very little change and lost its market lead when it failed to see customers wanted more choice.

In response Volkswagen would argue that it wasn't a one-model company after all, that Beetles made up around half the total number of annual sales. Apart from the van and the Karmann-Ghia coupe, it had been supplemented in 1961 by the Type 3 Volkswagen 1500/1600 saloon, later joined by estate and coupe variants. Its bodywork was far more contemporary than the Beetle and it sold nearly three million until 1973.

Not that effort hadn't been made on the original people's car, diligently modified from year to year, but the first major change only came in 1967 with the adoption of double-jointed rear driveshafts and trailing arms on automatic models (and all American Beetles), replacing the swing axles.

In 1967 Bosch fuel injection, highly unusual at the time, made its first appearance in a Volkswagen on Type 3 1600 models destined for the US market, and it would later make its way into European Volkswagens, albeit attached to an expensive additional model. The next radical Beetle change was the addition of the 1302 model in August 1970. It supplemented lower-powered models and had a redesigned front end with MacPherson strut suspension for increased boot capacity, better roadholding and through-flow ventilation.

➔ Volkswagen Beetles line up for export in 1962 at Bremen. The car that had created massive sales had also created massive risks as the company became reliant on foreign sales. (LAT)

➔ The 10,000th Volkswagen (not then known as Beetle and the sole model) produced in 1946 was inscribed by the workers '10,000 cars and too little to eat, could you stand it?'

← The 1961 Type 3 had a boot front and rear, made possible by a cooling fan positioned at the rear of the crankcase rather than sitting on top.

These developments did not satisfy the critics, and in spring 1967, to show that it had been far from idle in thinking about further models, Nordhoff took the extraordinary step of throwing open the doors of the company's secret development centre. Although design and development work was at the time largely contracted out to Porsche, 36 prototypes were dragged out of storage and shown to the press.

Since 1952 Volkswagen's engineers had in fact developed 70 different new models, none of which went into production. About half were scrapped and the rest were locked away. They may have had four doors or been coupes and convertibles, but they were all essentially re-bodied Beetles, with rear-mounted air-cooled engines. Some had got no further than styling mock-ups, but others were functional prototypes.

According to *Der Spiegel* the development work had taken up to five years for some models and cost up to 200 million dollars. As well as Porsche, the Italian styling houses Pininfarina and Ghia had also been contracted (Ghia's coupe design had been adopted for production as the VW Karmann-Ghia), with Pininfarina getting a maximum fee of $1m for each prototype. Its largest commission was a four-door touring car with a six-cylinder engine from 1963/64.

As an aside, there had been a revolutionary small car, EA48 (EA stood for *Entwicklungsauftrag* or development order) a 1955 tiny van-like car with an air-cooled twin-cylinder engine driving the front wheels and front suspension that echoed the MacPherson strut – something most cars would eventually adopt. In development between 1953 and 1955, the appetite for production was lost when the Beetle fully established itself and when the federal government warned Nordhoff away from smaller cars to protect the

continued on page 16

↓ This 1960 EA97 prototype almost came into German production as a smaller relative to the Type 3 but was halted at the last minute. (Stiftung AutoMuseum)

Wolfsburg: the factory, the town and the car

Wolfsburg was created in the 1930s to support the manufacture of one design of car. Then it was called the Stadt des KdF-Wagens – town for Kraft durch Freude cars, or 'strength through joy' cars. There are many histories which examine that car's beginnings in more detail, but it is worth a short account here.

The name volkswagen, or people's car, was in common use in Germany in the 1930s to describe a small cheap-to-run car. In 1934 BMW, Mercedes, Opel, Ford, Adler and Hanomag all presented volkswagens suitable for mass production, but in reality few people could afford them.

At the March 1934 Berlin Motor Show, Adolf Hitler called for a car to be developed for the masses by the National Socialist Party. In June the Reichsverband der Deutschen Automobilindustrie (RDA) commissioned Austrian engineer Ferdinand Porsche to design a volkswagen. Porsche's rear-engined designs were influenced by cars produced by the Czech company Tatra and a Porsche project abandoned by NSU the same year showed strong indications of what was to come.

Prototypes of the Porsche Type 60 were developed over the next four years and on 3 July 1938 the *New York Times* newspaper used the nickname 'Beetle' to refer to 'Porsche's People's Car' for the first time. Hitler, however, named it the KdF-Wagen Kraft durch Freude meaning strength through joy.

To give working people the prospect of actually owning this car a savings scheme was established by the Nazi Party so that every German, regardless of their standing would be entitled to purchase one. The response to this savings scheme was overwhelming – 270,000 savers by the end of 1938, but this was not quite enough. Up to the end of the Second World War a total of 336,638 German citizens continued to save hard for their cars but never got them. The funds were not enough to produce the planned number of cars and the war of course curtailed production. In 1945 the savers took the fledgling Volkswagen company to court and the action was only settled in 1961.

Production was expected to start in 1939 and the search for a place to build the car became urgent. The first seemingly acceptable site for the Stadt des KdF-Wagens emerged near the village of Fallersleben in Lower Saxony in the north-western part of the country. It was the wrong place for a car factory in many ways. Lower Saxony was a mainly agricultural area, but it had received some heavy-industry investments from the Third Reich such as a steelworks at Salzgitter and the factory became linked to it by the Mittelland canal. A further plant at Braunschweig was set up to produce panels and parts.

On 26 May 1938 the foundation stone of the plant was laid. It was conceived as a mainly self-sufficient factory closely based on Ford's River Rouge plant in Detroit, which was then considered the most modern automobile factory in the world.

As the factory and the town was under construction a shortage of domestic labour was supplemented by migrant workers from Italy, Belgium, Denmark and the Netherlands. As war broke out this became forced labour, a fact Volkswagen today commemorates with a memorial. The plant grew to an area of more than six square kilometres, with the factory buildings alone taking up a surface area of 1.6 square kilometres.

↓ A wartime Volkswagen sits amid the wreckage of the Wolfsburg factory.

Wolfsburg: the factory, the town and the car (continued)

A grid system of 75km of roads (with speed limits enforced by the factory's own police force) connects the factory buildings as well as 70km of railway tracks. In 2013 two power stations operated by Volkswagen Kraftwerk BmbH still generated power and heat for both the factory and the city with its population of around 123,000.

Only some 800 KdF-Wagens had been built by September 1939 when production was halted to make way for aircraft production and repairs. With parts of the facility not yet occupied, it struggled to justify its existence at first. During the war amphibious vehicles (VW Type 128 and 166 Schwimmwagen) and the Kübelwagen military car were built, all based on a Beetle chassis. From mid 1943, amid increased bombing raids, machinery was relocated to underground locations.

The end of hostilities saw the town renamed Wolfsburg on 25 May 1945, after a nearby castle owned by Count Werner von der Schulenberg, who had lost two-thirds of his land to the factory and new town. From June Major Ivan Hirst was the British Army officer and engineer instrumental in reviving production with his colleague, Colonel Charles Radclyffe.

The original intention was to scrap the factory and use the proceeds as war reparations, but Hirst found a pre-war prototype Volkswagen in a remote workshop on the site and realised that the factory could be used for producing cars for the British Army. It was no longer possible to bring in Kübelwagen or Beetle saloon bodies – supplied by Ambi-Budd in Berlin, which had been dismantled by the Russians – but the saloon car presses and dies were still at Wolfsburg, although some were badly damaged.

The ownerless company still existed on paper, but its management had dispersed and only a few of the remaining executives had returned to the factory under the former chief inspector Rudolf Brörmann, now appointed plant manager.

Production of the Volkswagen Type 1 saloon under the British administration began slowly with the assembly of 55 vehicles up until December 1945, and by March 1946 1,000 Beetles a month were being built. The impetus was an ambitious order for 20,000 cars for the Allies. Sizeable orders were received from the US army and the French armed forces, and cars were also supplied to essential German services and Allied private owners.

Given the after-effects of war, these early days of Volkswagen production were beset by multiple difficulties, from shortages of materials to labour and political problems. However, other German car factories for Ford, Opel and Daimler-Benz struggled to restart production and then only had ageing designs to fall back on. Unconventional though it may have been, the Beetle was still a new design. The British military government's directive to dismantle Volkswagenwerk GmbH was put on hold for four years from September 1946. One month later, the level of industry plan, which limited the number of German automobiles to 40,000 per year, was revised. The survival of Volkswagenwerk was guaranteed.

The design of the Volkswagen was of course famously dissected by the British and dismissed. Humber had received a sand-filled Kübelwagen in 1943 and a tired 'Volkswagen saloon Type 11' (Type 11 was what the British termed the civilian saloon) in 1946 and subjected them to a full range of tests while Ford bench-tested an engine. Both vehicles were famously rejected as a long-term product people might buy, although not as unequivocally as one might expect. The report published in 1947 and subsequently reprinted makes for interesting and contradictory reading. Humber body engineers thought that: 'From the body engineering point of view the design of this vehicle is exceptionally good, and shows a great advance on previous construction methods.'

However, Humber's overall verdict was: 'Looking at the general picture, we do not consider that the design represents any special brilliance.' Lord Rootes, the owner of Humber, rejected the offer of the factory and the car as war reparations and Ford and General Motors took even less interest, according to historian Karl Ludvigsen.

In January 1948 former Opel manager Heinrich Nordhoff was appointed General Director of the Volkswagenwerk GmbH (see separate panel) and the workforce stood at 8,400 producing nearly 20,000 vehicles a year as planned. On 8 October 1949 Colonel Radclyffe signed the protocol to turn over Volkswagenwerk GmbH to the trusteeship of the federal German government, the State of Lower Saxony.

The only way to invest in production facilities, especially American pressing machinery, was with hard currency, so exports became vital from a very early stage.

The first civilian foreigner to buy Volkswagens was Ben Pon, a Dutch motor trader who had even tried to get the first VW franchise in 1938 before the war intervened, returning in 1947 to buy Beetles for resale in Holland. Pon was also the inspiration behind the Volkswagen van (see separate panel on page 22). Other European countries followed and the foreign currency flowed in – vital as nobody would provide loans. Volkswagen's early drive for exports proved crucial.

By 1951 a quarter of a million Volkswagens had been built, and half a million achieved by 1953, based on the Type 1 (export) Volkswagen 1200 saloon and the Type 2 Transporter van. Volkswagen's market share in the German Federal Republic was 42.5%. As a comparison, the British Morris Minor, itself a much-praised design seen as having Beetle-like qualities, sold 176,000 from 1948 to 1953 but took 13 years to reach its only million, a milestone the Beetle attained in 1955.

By the 1960s Wolfsburg was totally secure as the home of the Beetle and rocketing demand meant its maker's main problem was finding extra production capacity elsewhere, sparking takeovers later in the decade. Nearly 12 million Beetles were built there before European production moved to Emden in 1974.

Yet this industrial powerhouse remained isolated. 'We in Wolfsburg were at the end of the federal republic,' Carl Hahn recalls. 'The political and economic activity took place along the Rhine river and we were far away by the Iron Curtain. Going to Bonn [the home of government] was a big excursion so we went there a minimum.'

This changed dramatically when the map of Germany and Europe was redrawn after the fall of the Berlin wall in 1989. Wolfsburg suddenly found itself perfectly located to take advantage of new manufacturing capacity in the former East Germany.

Although the outer shells of its buildings were over 60 years old, the Volkswagenwerk at Wolfsburg adapted to every change of model and by 2013 was using the Modularer Querbaukasten (MQB) transverse-engined platform construction system. The world's largest single car manufacturing complex made the Golf, Golf Plus, Touran and Tiguan, plus components including drive shafts and injection moulded parts. It was still the primary home of the Golf and had produced about 40 million vehicles.

➔ The mighty Wolfsburg factory in 2010. The office block with the VW symbol houses management and the town is beyond the Mittelland canal in the lower part of the picture.

Nordhoff: the great leader

Heinrich or 'Heinz' Nordhoff was born in 1899 and became the architect of Volkswagen's post-war success. In January 1948 he took office as General Director of Volkswagenwerk GmbH, run by the British administration. Nordhoff was 40 years old and a former Opel manager.

He quickly became an inspirational figure for the demoralised workforce – for six months he lived in the factory, sleeping in a room near his office. He recalled: 'I had to start from scratch in the real sense of the word. Seven thousand workers were painfully producing at the rate of a mere 6,000 a year – provided it did not rain too much. Most of the roof and all the windows had been destroyed. Pools of stagnant water were underfoot.'

The rapid rise in production has been attributed partly to Nordhoff's close and friendly relationship with the workforce, as attested by Carl Hahn who was appointed as his assistant in 1954 and was destined to play a major part in the company's future. 'He was absolutely loved by the workers as his rhetoric was superb,' he told the author in 2013. 'He knew how to sell and explain his strategies and his policies. He exercised a very great human quality of creating confidence and showing leadership and being capable of mastering the German language.'

To the envy of his competitors, Nordhoff was an enlightened patron in those dark days, convincing the Berlin Philharmonic orchestra to play in the vast works canteen kitchen and encouraging the showing of films and art. Being largely a state-owned company, the board of directors at the time was dominated by politicians including the prime minister of Lower Saxony. 'They didn't have much to say. Nordhoff was basically calling the shots,' says Hahn.

Furthermore, his influence soon stretched beyond Wolfsburg. The world's industrialists marvelled at Volkswagen's speed of development and it was seen as the engine of growth of the West German republic. Nordhoff soon diversified the product range (albeit all Beetle-based) and energetically travelled the globe setting up export partners, especially outside Europe. His work on developing an efficient sales and service organisation around the Beetle was an integral part of the car's success, especially in North America.

Nordhoff very soon became a statesman for the German motor industry whose annual press conference at the Geneva Motor Show was a significant event. The philosophy of taking a car that didn't resemble any other and espousing change for change's sake in favour of small year-on-year improvements

livelihoods of Goliath and Lloyd. One car survives today at Volkswagen's museum.

Also still to be seen in the Wolfsburg museum is a 1960 prototype of EA97, another last-minute cancellation. Developed alongside the Type 3 since 1957, this 1,100cc car had evolved into a boxy two-door saloon with an estate version, cabriolet and hatchback in prospect. It would have been a natural competitor to the likes of the NSU Prinz, Simca 1100, Renault 8, Fiat 850 and Hillman Imp – all of them rear-engined 'three box' cars. However, in May 1965 even while the production line was being assembled and 100 pilot vehicles were built, Volkswagen got cold feet. It was too close to the Type 3 and the newly acquired Audi 60, the strategists decided, and it was cancelled. 'It wasn't a big blow for us because we were so profitable in those days,' Hahn told the author in 2013. 'We were in good shape.' EA97 was not quite abandoned though. All the production tools were shipped to Volkswagen Brazil – delayed for a year after the transporter ship sank and the machinery had to be recovered – and EA97 was restyled to become the popular Brasilia series.

Even though he was cemented to the Beetle concept, from the mid-1960s Nordhoff had been laying the foundations for the way out, even if it was still unclear in 1967. He assured the press that none of the DM 870 million scheduled for 1967 investment would be used to expand capacity. Instead it would be used to improve and streamline Volkswagen production and more than half of it would be spent on development.

Since 1964 a new development centre had been built next to the Mittellandkanal in Wolfsburg, bringing together all the engineering departments (some 2,000 people), and a climatic wind tunnel – at the time the largest facility of its kind in Europe – opened in 1966.

Work began on a vast test-and-development centre near Ehra-Lessien, 15 miles north of Wolfsburg in April 1967 and was largely completed by 1970. The facility was dominated by a 13-mile long high-speed circuit and a further 60 miles of tracks of all

confounded the notion of built-in obsolescence and became Volkswagen's ethos, but by the late 1960s Nordhoff was clearly aware that major change had to come. Giving a lecture in London in 1967 he said: 'Previously, products were developed, produced and sold for many years with few changes ... Today, if we are to compete, the emphasis must be on innovation.'

He pointed to American-owned companies building in Europe as having access to the 'best brains and data'.

One of his last and most far-reaching actions was to create the *Ausschuss für Produktplanung* or product planning committee (APP) – also known as the PSK – in 1967, which would come up with the post-Beetle plan. The same year he announced that he would retire by the end of the following year, and that Dr Kurt Lotz would succeed him as managing director. Sadly Nordhoff suffered heart failure that summer, and died on 12 April 1968 aged 69. At the time Volkswagen was the world's fourth largest car manufacturer.

➔ This famous image had Heinrich 'Heinz' Nordhoff standing on a platform in front of his 30,000 Wolfsburg workers in August 1955 as one million Volkswagens had been built. (LAT)

surfaces and gradients. All this was impressive, but the cost was immense.

During Nordhoff's final days his successor Kurt Lotz (see panel) was well aware that the Beetle was still bringing in the biggest share of profit and refrained from saying anything in public to imply that it would shortly be superseded by another model. In full agreement with the ill Nordhoff he decided that it would be 'best' to say as little as possible on the future programme, although in private he had set work in train.

Eventually though, Volkswagen was obliged to say something about what the 'future Beetle' might be. Questioned by the press, engineers would be vague, refusing to dismiss the rear-engined air-cooled heritage, but they admitted that a new Beetle could be front-driven and water-cooled, although they told *Autocar* magazine in April 1970 that it probably wouldn't have a hatchback as that added weight and an estate car could always be added later. At more or less the same time the Golf was being styled by Giugiaro.

Audi benefits

Whilst making all this investment into its own research and development, Volkswagen under Nordhoff had largely ignored the potential of Auto Union GmbH – now better known as Audi – which it had bought from Daimler-Benz at the start of 1965.

Based in Ingolstadt, Auto Union had been rescued from financial problems by Daimler-Benz in 1958. Under the Audi name it produced a range of conservative medium-sized, front-wheel-drive saloons; the smallest, the DKW F102, was re-engineered for 1965 as the Audi 60, replacing its antiquated two-stroke engine with a more modern design from Mercedes.

Daimler-Benz offered Volkswagen a 50% share with an option on the plant at Ingolstadt while it retained one in Dusseldorf. In 1968 Volkswagen exercised its option and Audi became a fully owned subsidiary.

It gave Volkswagen a range of upmarket cars and increased market share, but the Wolfsburg giant viewed it largely in terms of extra manufacturing capacity (Beetle

continued on page 20

Nordhoff's inheritance

Volkswagen's painful transition to its new generation of cars claimed two chief executives in very public ways, yet both Kurt Lotz and Rudolf Leiding were crucial players in the Golf story.

Dr Kurt Lotz was elected to the board of management in June 1967 and came with extensive experience as an industrial manager, although not in the motor industry. He assumed control in April 1968 and called in management consultants McKinsey to set up a new organisation chart and brought in new, younger board members.

'The problem was to reduce the relative weight of the Beetle in our overall programme,' Lotz told journalist Edouard Seidler. 'But I found very few prototypes in Wolfsburg's research and development department which might have been put into production. I had to move fast, using whatever I could find, wherever I could find it.'

The chief model of his unhappy inheritance was the Volkswagen 411 saloon, which he had no option but to press ahead with. A more attractive part of the 1969 NSU takeover was the ready-made front-wheel-drive K70 saloon (and according to Seidler the way the takeover was effected infuriated NSU's shareholders). Although during the Audi and NSU mergers Lotz hinted that the identities of the new companies would be preserved, the view of most outsiders was that this would be short lived.

At the 1969 Frankfurt Show he outlined his plans for the new Volkswagen combine, which ranged from economy cars to luxury saloons and sports cars. There would be low-cost automatic transmissions and electronic fuel injection. The brands would compete with each other on the market and so would the internal divisions.

On the other hand the Volkswagen-Audi-NSU offer looked like a sprawling range of cars that seemed to share very few components with each other and spanned engine types from the air-cooled Beetle and 411 to the rotary Ro80 via the different water-cooled engines of the front-driven Audi 100 and Volkswagen K70 plus the mid-engined Volkswagen-Porsche 914. Compared with a giant such as Opel producing all front-engined rear-driven cars, it seemed chaotic.

Lotz was beset by critics and disastrous figures. To take but a few, there was a 42% fall in profits between 1969 and 1970 from £37m to £22m. Outside of Volkswagen's control, the Deutsche Mark was revalued in late 1969 by 9.3%, costing the company £22m because it couldn't pass the cost on to the customer, and a wiring fault and poor fuel consumption on the new Super Beetle 1302 meant over 200,000 had to be recalled in 1970.

An all-out domestic press campaign began to lay the blame on Lotz, simply not accepting that the poor sales of the K70 and the 411 were his inherited problems and that the new generation was at least four years away. All the same, reflecting problems in the wider German economy, Opel saw its profits fall by the same amount while Daimler-Benz and BMW were also affected.

Lotz's response was optimistic. 'I knew all along that 1971 and 1972 were going to be tough years. They are turning out to be even tougher than expected because of revaluation and inflation. But we have prepared for a brighter future, and results in the American market have confirmed our belief that Detroit's small cars will not affect our sales. On the contrary, they have aroused more interest in economy cars, and we are keeping our position despite growing competition.'

His struggle was also political, as nearly half of the board represented either government or unions. He was a Christian Democart (Liberal) while most of the federal and the state government of Lower Saxony (which owned 36% of VW's capital and controlled another 4%) were run by the Social Democratic Party.

Lotz opposed moves to increase organised labour's part in running the company and battled with the board over internal appointments. He went to Bonn to meet chancellor Willy Brandt armed with details of prototypes but to no avail. On 22 September 1971, three years and six months after taking control of Volkswagen, Kurt Lotz left after a great deal of negotiation. His rise and fall was remarkable at the time for its speed and he had in fact brought the board's attention to the man who was to oust him.

Rudolf Leiding took up post in October 1971 at the age of 56. His track record with Volkswagen was already formidable, having helped Heinz Nordhoff set up the first post-war assembly line and being sent to America to help organise the first US sales network.

Known as a mechanically minded troubleshooter he was sent into Auto-Union (Audi) in 1965 by Nordhoff to pull it into shape. Within a year he had pulled down its production costs by 34%. He was known for walking the factory floor at night and taking pictures of inefficient or untidy work areas.

In 1968 he was sent to Brazil as president of the local

subsidiary. In a preview of the pragmatic style he would adopt for Volkswagen's future, he rejected plans to merely assemble Wolfsburg designs but used the components to tailor models specifically for the Brazilian market such as the Brasilia and the P2 sports car.

Kurt Lotz called him back to Germany in 1970 to run the newly formed Audi-NSU grouping. He then offered him the chance to be vice chairman of Volkswagen to which he was said to have preferred to be number one at Ingolstadt (home of Audi) than number two at Wolfsburg. In the end the board demanded that he replace Lotz as he was considered politically neutral.

Faced with the slump in US sales in 1973/4 and rising costs of European assembly, Leiding believed that the only way sales could be regained would be by lowering the price of US Volkswagens by building them locally. However, the moment was simply not right to suggest such a thing, and when he put his proposals for a US plant to the board in September 1974, the financiers baulked at possible costs and the unions opposed the idea of creating foreign jobs while mass redundancies took place at home.

Thwarted by the board's refusal to countenance an American assembly plant (see Chapter 2) in December 1974 Rudolf Leiding asked for his contract to be terminated on health grounds and by February 1975 Toni Schmücker, a former sales director of Ford of Germany, was in the hot seat.

For Volkswagen to have its third chairman in seven years was enough of a shock and the refusal to back US manufacture was condemned in the British press. As he departed in December 1974 the *Sunday Times* said: 'Although German Chancellor Helmut Schmidt has so far rejected the growing pleas from management and unions for help for the crisis-ridden German car industry, the Government was strongly opposed to Leiding's plan to build a major Volkswagen assembly plant in America.'

Autocar was more forthright in January 1975: 'Were the Volkswagen pressure groups right to defeat the plan? No matter what the state of the industry at the moment, it seems incredibly short-sighted. We are short of European leaders as it is. There are few enough men who could have taken an ailing giant by the scruff of its neck and set it back on the right road, as Leiding did at Wolfsburg.'

So while Lotz and Leiding had to endure years of criticism while laying down the new generation of Volkswagens, it would be Schmücker who would reap the glory.

The advanced Ro80 with its rotary engine came with Kurt Lotz's purchase of NSU but it remained a curiosity in the Volkswagen stable.

sales had been booming). Audi vehicle development director at the time Ludwig Kraus knew exactly where his company stood, as he told the authors of *Audi 1965 – 1975 Die Entscheidenden Jahre:* 'VW was believed essentially to have bought a Beetle assembly plant and so it was in the beginning. We built up to 300 a day! Whenever the VW chief of operations came to the factory and saw the flags of the four rings on the roof, he said: "I'm just waiting for that to come down so I can see the VW logo."'

The once-proud manufacturer looked in danger of being swallowed by the mighty Beetle. Kraus continued: 'Immediately after the sale to VW I got a letter from Wolfsburg: In the future, Audi will no longer be developing new cars. VW was very sure. I was faced with the question: shall we stop? So we developed a secret.'

The secret was the Audi 100 executive saloon, which Nordhoff eventually signed off in November 1966 and entered production in 1969. It was an immediate success and its profits helped steer Volkswagen through its own troubles. Audi's technical expertise in front-wheel drive gradually came to the fore although in the early 1970s there was the real prospect the parent company would just sell it off to stem its own losses.

Publicly Volkswagen was clear its dealers were not about to start selling Audis, and vice-versa, saying in 1971: 'The directorate of Volkswagen AG affirm absolutely that the present programme of construction and sales of VW models will be adhered to without change. There cannot be, under any circumstances, a question of the eventual distribution of the Audi 100 or of any other Audi models by the Volkswagen organisation.'

The biggest Beetle

While the new generation of 1970s Volkswagens started to gestate behind closed doors, new introductions conspired to confuse the market and the transition of power from Nordhoff to Kurt Lotz was cut short by the great man's death in April 1968.

What proved to be the final development of the Beetle line, the 411 saloon or Type 4, was introduced in 1968 somewhat in a rush as photos and details were published prematurely. In development since 1962, as well as the largest Volkswagen to date the 4.52m-long 411 was also the first Volkswagen with unitary construction and, perhaps incredibly in retrospect, the first four-door car. It was marketed as *'Der Große aus Wolfsburg'* – the big one from Wolfsburg. The flat-four air-cooled engine was derived from the VW 1500, extended to 1,679cc and 68bhp.

MacPherson strut and coil suspension made its first Volkswagen appearance at the front of the 411, allowing for more luggage space, supplementing that behind the rear seats. Strut front suspension was later introduced on a new Beetle derivative, the 1302 in 1970. Another improvement, which had come through the development of automatic transmission for the Beetle, was rear suspension with double-jointed driveshafts and semi-trailing arms and struts, much reducing tendencies for wayward handling at the rear. At launch the American magazine *Road and Track* observed: 'It looks as if the 411 may have given a new lease of life to the rear-engine concept; by giving the car a large front overhang VW has achieved a weight distribution of only 45% front 55% rear (our last Beetle test car was 38/62 tail-heavy!).'

The 411 carried high hopes. In late summer 1968 Lotz forecast daily production of 500 cars yet by spring the following year it had fallen as low as 200, accompanied by an unexpected rise in Beetle sales at home and abroad. The paradox was that the 411 was supposedly what critics had been crying out for: a bigger and better Beetle.

Yet despite the space and interior comforts, the 411 had early clutch problems and was criticised for its lack of power, a tendency to wander in crosswinds and its awkward looks. *Auto Motor und Sport* found it lacking in many respects to its competitors and soon those were in-house. The front-wheel-drive, water-cooled Audi 100 went on sale from January 1969 and was an immediate hit, so much so that a four-month wait developed and its daily production soon eclipsed the 411.

A revised 411, the 411E (or LE in luxury trim) appeared in 1969 and was the first German car with standard Bosch electronic fuel injection, developed for US emissions regulations. Power was increased to 80bhp with the added benefits of better cold starting. The oblong headlamps were replaced by a pair of twin round units and a three-door variant was introduced. A further facelift and an extension to 1.8-litres brought the 1972 412, and production ended in the wake of the new Passat in 1974. Total Type 4 output had been a disappointing 370,000 units.

↑ **The 1968 Volkswagen 411 was essentially a large Beetle with four doors. Its initial headlamps were likened to TV screens.**

NSU and front-wheel drive

By 1970 yet another medium-sized Volkswagen-group car had been introduced into the 411's market, the Volkswagen K70, a hastily rebadged NSU and the first Volkswagen with a water-cooled engine and front-wheel drive.

It was the first fruit of Audi-NSU, formed by the merger with Auto Union in 1969, in which Volkswagen had an initial share of 59.5% rising to 99% a few years later.

NSU was a small but highly innovative company, which in 1964 had put the Wankel rotary engine into production in the Prinz coupe and convertible, and in 1967 stunned the world with the Ro80 luxury saloon. However, the development costs of the Ro80 had crippled the company and it was ripe for takeover, especially attractive for the value of licensing its rotary engine technology (before its durability and fuel consumption problems became apparent).

But above all, VW wanted to lay claim to the NSU K70 (K for *Kolbenmotor* – piston engine), conceived in 1967 as a mid-sized saloon to fill the chasm between NSU's small rear-engined Prinz models and the Ro80. Furthermore, it was ready for production at the time of the merger. Kurt Lotz saw it as a ready-made tester for the new generation of Volkswagens. With its additional research and development facilities Volkswagen was set to use NSU as Fiat had used Autobianchi to test front-wheel drive before the introduction of the Fiat 128.

Using some Ro80 body parts, the K70 was a plain-looking four-door saloon with a long wheelbase, large boot and short overhangs front and rear. Similar in design to the Audi unit, the chain-driven 1,605cc single-overhead-cam engine was mounted longitudinally and drove the front wheels through a four-speed gearbox. Suspension was to echo the future Volkswagen range with MacPherson struts at the front and semi-trailing arms with wishbones at the rear, and the front disc brakes were mounted inboard. Plans to give it a rotary engine in due course failed to materialise.

NSU was set to launch the K70 at the March 1969 Geneva Motor Show, but Volkswagen withdrew it shortly before the merger that month, re-engineered it to suit its manufacturing techniques (the most major change was

continued on page 25

The Volkswagen van

The Volkswagen van, a box with wheels, was unveiled at the 1949 Geneva Motor Show, destined to become as famous as the Beetle it was based on and exceed its production run.

Post-war Europe was not just starved of cars but commercial vehicles. Whilst negotiating the first export deal to buy five Volkswagen saloons in 1947, Dutch importer Ben Pon sketched the box-shaped outline of a delivery vehicle, which enclosed a Beetle engine at the rear and had the driver positioned over the front wheels. The inspiration is also said to have been the *Plattenwagens*, rear-engined open vehicles built to carry parts around the factory.

Within a year the design was taken up by Heinz Nordhoff and intensively developed over the next two years. Its outline was refined through wind-tunnel experiments at the University of Braunschweig and the chassis developed to take the necessary payload on the flat floor between the axles. This was not a heavy van. The kerb weight of the first very basic versions was settled at 850kg and when it was exceeded the bumpers were simply left off.

On sale from March 1959 as an 1,100cc panel van, its wide-opening side doors and flat floor provided a model copied ever since. A Kombi (for *Kombinationskraftwagen*) with side windows and various combinations of seating was a prototype people carrier. Before long numerous commercial bodies were offered, but it was the camper van conversions by outside companies that gave it an enduring cult following as carefree transport for good times, known by names such as the Bulli.

The model's internal code was T2 to 1967 when it was substantially redesigned as the T2a. While the shape never varied the series received all the developments afforded to the Beetle but with engines up to two litres, which was about the limit of the design's efficiency. Some competitors copied both its cab and engine layout.

Built principally in Hannover until 1979, the T2a gave way to the squared-off T3, which retained the rear-mounted engine, albeit water-cooled from 1983. However, like the original Beetle, when it no longer met European emissions and safety legislation the air-cooled original continued in Brazilian production. The final version had water-cooled engines, exhaust catalysts and fuel injection, and was produced until December 2013, with total production over 3.5 million.

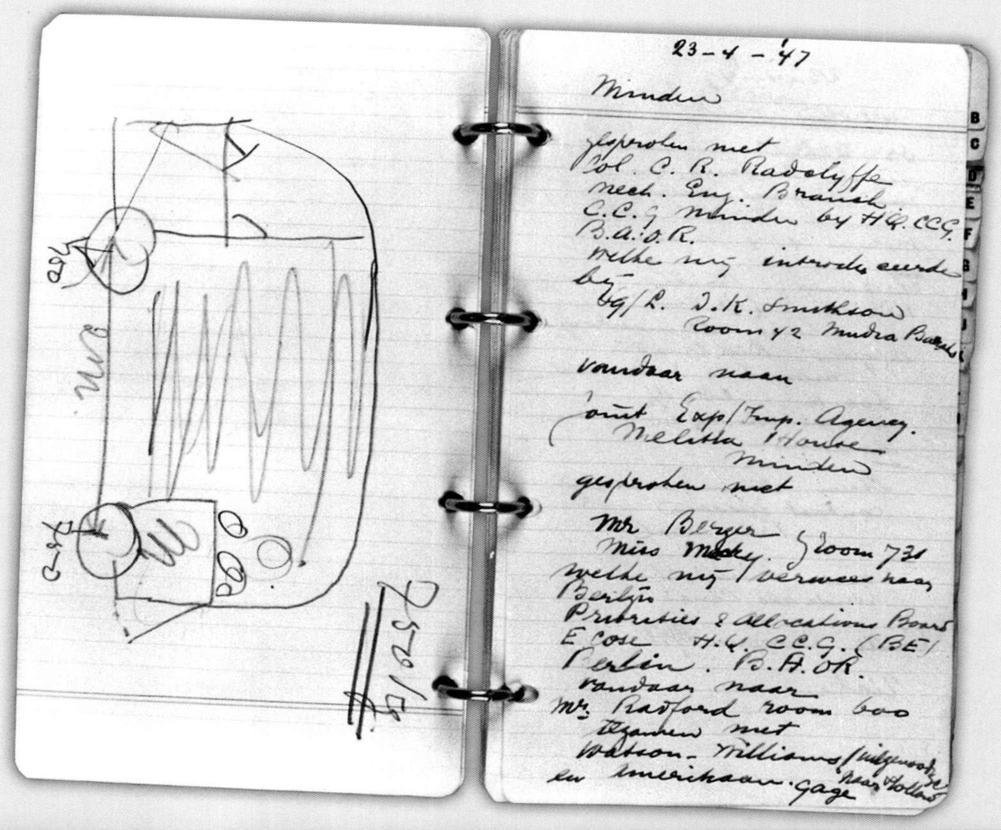

➔ Ben Pon's 1947 Beetle-based van sketch showed exactly the layout which would become a best-seller.

↙ This beautifully restored 1954 Type 2 Transporter has double doors at the side opening to floor level, and was one of many configurations available.

↓ The van was a best-seller but the kombi can be argued to be the first people carrier. It remains a symbol of good times.

Volkswagen and Karmann

In 1901 Wilhelm Karmann took over coachbuilder Klases and named it after himself. Up until the advent of the Second World War in 1939 it designed and manufactured for the Adler company and enabled Ford to launch its Eifel Roadster cabriolet. To this day Karmann is based in Osnabrück, Lower Saxony, 220km west of Wolfsburg.

Together with Hebmüller, Karmann won the contract to build the first convertible Beetle in 1948 and it was launched the following year. However Hebmüller went bankrupt in 1952 and the Karmann Beetle cabriolet stayed in manufacture until 1980. Karmann also added production of a DKW cabriolet for Auto Union and Ford delivery vans to its output.

However, it was Wilhelm Karmann junior's friendship with Luigi Segre, owner of coachbuilder Ghia in Turin, that joined the two companies to Volkswagen. In the early 1950s Volkswagen had shown an interest in Karmann building a sports car on a Beetle chassis, but Segre took the initiative and bodied his own car in 1953. The resulting Volkswagen Karmann Ghia coupe was launched in 1955 to immediate success, especially in America. Although the handsome shape hid standard Beetle engines it also sold at a handsome premium. It was very much a hand-finished car, which Volkswagen played upon in its advertising, stating it took 185 men to make the body alone. Joined by a convertible in 1957 and a more contemporary-styled 2+2 version in 1961, it was manufactured to 1974 when it gave way to Scirocco production after some 445,000 classic-shaped coupes and convertibles had been built.

While Volkswagen production was Karmann's lifeblood it was also a major supplier of tooling and equipment to other manufacturers, mostly domestic but with some notable exceptions such as the Triumph TR6 and Jaguar XJ-S convertible. It undertook body manufacture for the Volkswagen-Porsche 914 and an offshoot company was set up to produce BMW coupes in 1965.

In 1979 the Golf cabriolet proved an instant hit and Karmann took on the design and manufacture of the rival Ford Escort soft top. In 1998 when Karmann junior died Wilhelm Karmann GmbH employed 6,400 people in Germany and 2,600 in operations in Brazil, Portugal and Plymouth, Michigan from 1996.

In the following decade it added Renault, Mercedes and Chrysler to its list of clients but in 2009 filed for bankruptcy and was bought by Volkswagen to expand its own production and take on specialist projects.

↑ A 1959 Volkswagen Karmann-Ghia, the glamorous Beetle which made the designer and builder household names.

← A 1970s Volkswagen Beetle Cabriolet. For many years the lifeblood of Karmann, it was costly to build and had many unique parts.

from an alloy to cast-iron cylinder block) and launched it with its own badge at the September 1970 Paris Motor Show. To avoid internal competition, planned estate and hatchback versions were halted.

Through the NSU merger, yet another plant, at Nekarsulm, was added to the Volkswagen empire, but a new £40m factory was constructed for the K70 at Salzgitter near Brunswick, close to Wolfsburg, with an optimistic capacity for 500 K70s a day. It was now competing with both the Volkswagen 411 and Audi 100 in the same family, although priced slightly higher than the 411 and 412.

Like the 411, K70 sales projections proved over-optimistic and the K70 developed an early reputation for rust. In the UK it was considered interesting but too expensive, and its economics were disastrous – it was said to share not a single nut and bolt with another Volkswagen. A sporty 1800 variant was added in 1973 but as with the 411/2 the Passat sounded the K70's death knell in January 1975 after 211,127 had been built.

The small rear-engined NSUs lasted until 1972 with the Ro80 retained as a top-line addition to the Volkswagen range until 1977. The NSU name disappeared in 1985 when Audi NSU Auto Union AG was renamed Audi AG.

↑ The Volkswagen K70 started life as an NSU and failed to sell well despite revisions such as this sports-trimmed version. It was, however, the first front-driven Volkswagen.

The surprising sports car

By 1970 Volkswagen group saloons came with front- and rear-wheel drive and air-cooled, rotary and water-cooled engines. To most observers it looked like Volkswagen had no model strategy at all, throwing out short-term models until something stuck while in the background Beetles continued to pop off production lines across the world at the rate of around 4,000 a day.

Buyers could also choose Volkswagen's first sports car, the Volkswagen-Porsche 914 (or Vo-Po as some writers had it). One of Nordhoff's stillborn prototypes

← The Volkswagen-Porsche 914 seemed like a folly to most observers but was a successfully packaged mid-engined car. (Author)

W - 22

had been an open-topped sports car, cancelled when the market took a downturn, but the idea persisted. In the mid 1960s the European market for small affordable sports cars continued to expand: the Fiat 124 Spider, Alfa Romeo Duetto and assorted MGs and Triumphs were especially popular in the USA and Opel developed its GT coupe for 1968. So why not a Volkswagen sports car? It also happened that Porsche was looking to replace its entry-level four-cylinder 912. An agreement was struck between Dr Ferry Porsche and Nordhoff in 1966, Porsche designing the car and Volkswagen taking care of assembly (thus building in such volume that the cost would come down). Volkswagen would have a lower-powered car with its own engine, Porsche a more expensive one with its own. The two-seater mid-engined design mirrored current race-car thinking and the successful Porsche 904. The steel body had a built-in roll-over bar and the open part was covered by a removable fibreglass roof. It was a strong structure, well able to meet US safety requirements, and if the boxy style was not to all tastes it offered good space for the occupants with two luggage compartments.

The first prototype had barely run when Nordhoff died, but after reportedly wavering on the whole idea Lotz honoured what had been a 'gentlemen's agreement', even though his critics accused him of playing with an 'expensive toy'. Launched at the 1969 Frankfurt Motor Show the 914 initially featured the Volkswagen 411's 1,679cc fuel-injected engine with 80bhp. The agreement between the two companies allowed for a certain number of cars with a Porsche six-cylinder engine, and the 110bhp 914/6 appeared the following February.

The 914 was assembled by Karmann in Osnabrück (entirely in the case of VW-engined cars and minus engine for the Porsche versions), but Lotz priced the cost of the bodyshells far higher than Porsche had anticipated, meaning it was no longer an affordable entry-level car.

A joint company was set up to sell the car, VW-Porsche Vertriebsgesellschaft (distribution) and it was known in the USA only as a Porsche. Buyers found it intriguing, but despite detail improvements sales of both cars proved disappointing, the four-cylinder at 115,631 and the Porsche six at only 3,351. Production ended in 1976.

A product plan and EA266

What the public couldn't see was the seismic shift taking place around the board table in Wolfsburg. By the middle of March 1968 Lotz and the product-planning committee had developed a radical long-term plan in response to Nordhoff's wishes – that Volkswagen products would switch to water-cooled engines within five to ten years.

The model programme set out four basic types of car with three engine sizes: a small car with a 1.1- to 1.3-litre engine and a possible Beetle successor was

← A group of EA266 prototypes at rest in the late 1960s. It was one more costly aborted project on the way to the Golf. (Porsche)

↓ The Porsche-designed EA266 could have been the world's first mid-engined hatchback. (Porsche)

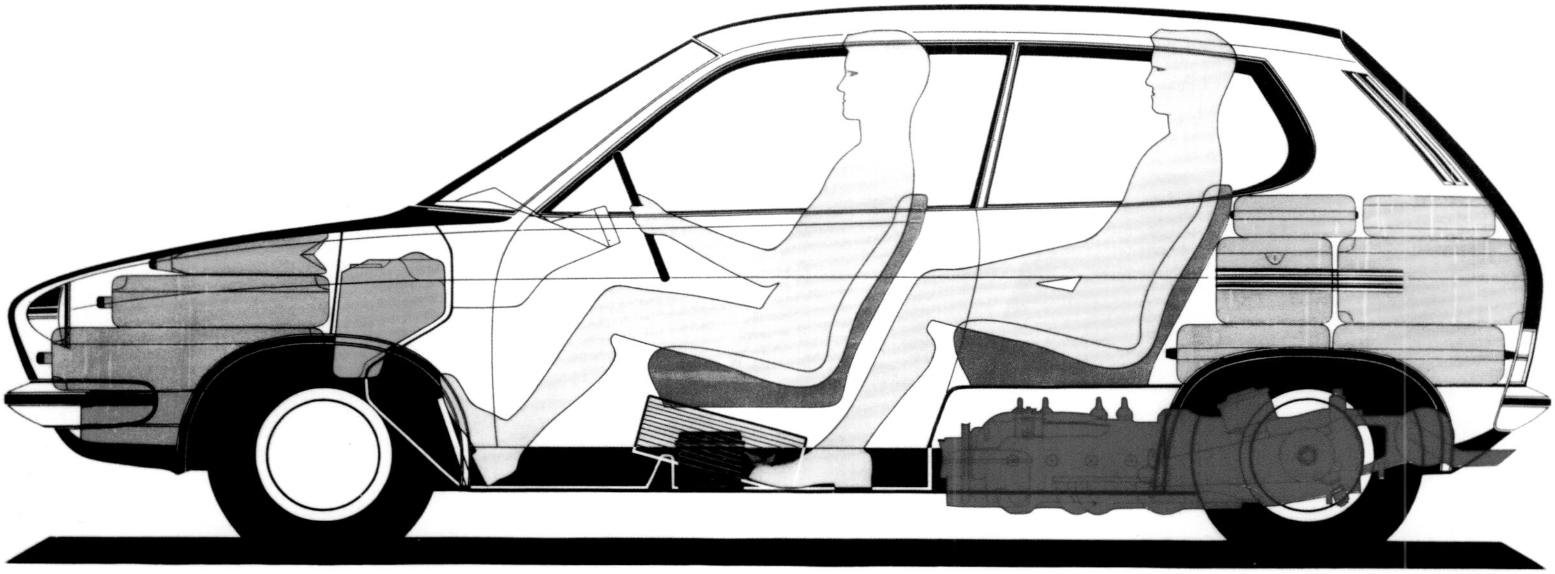

the absolute priority. The arguments in favour were well rehearsed, not least in comparison to the Beetle engine, which with its two cylinder heads and use of magnesium was expensive to build (although the long production run and vast numbers produced lessened this effect), difficult to service, not that economical and produced very little interior heat at low speeds.

By better exploiting development capacities in Wolfsburg and Auto Union in Ingolstadt, and ending the agreement with Porsche as an external development service provider, the VW board believed it could push through three engine variations – mid engine, front engine with front-wheel drive and front engine with rear-wheel drive. All this of course would demand a vast investment budget.

There was, however, one final contract already in progress with Porsche. Whilst Volkswagen had opened its doors in 1967 to reveal a somewhat bare development cupboard, Kurt Lotz had instructed Porsche to start work on 'Property 1966' or, to give it its internal codes, EA266 or Type 266, for mass production. In the minutes of meetings EA266 was called the *Käfer-Nachfolger* or Beetle successor and had it come to market would have been a unique small car. Details only emerged after the project was cancelled in 1971.

Inspired by the Porsche 914, this Beetle-sized hatchback had a water-cooled four-cylinder engine laid flat under the rear seat and driving the rear wheels, so strictly speaking here was a mid-engined family car. Developed from scratch by Porsche's engineering department with little help from Wolfsburg, it was such a significant contract that Porsche reorganised its management structure to speed up development and one Ferdinand Piëch, Ferry Porsche's nephew, was put in charge of client projects development. Much later, of course, Piëch would become chairman of the Volkswagen Group and oversee the merger with Porsche.

EA266's engine was a water-cooled, four-cylinder, overhead-camshaft design and had a basic capacity of 1.3 litres but was said to be capable of being stretched to 2 litres or reduced to a two-cylinder version. According to later reports, the engine was tested in the K70 and was intended to be used much more widely in the group. It was not intended as a direct Beetle replacement but as a supplement, because the Beetle still had prospects in underdeveloped countries. It would also have complied with 1975 US safety legislation, which the Beetle was not anticipated (in 1971) to be able to do. It was said to have been planned for production at a rate of 3,000 a day from 1973 but was complicated, expensive to build and there were problems with noise and smells. Some Wolfsburg engineers, notably Hans-Georg Wenderoth, objected to the layout because it would be difficult to service (the rear seat would have to have been removed by oily hands) and the design was suffering problems with crosswind stability. Yet the project moved steadily on and Lotz ordered the tooling.

'I liked the 266 very much,' Hahn recalls. 'I don't know if it would have been a success as it was, that was hard to predict. With its central engine it had some problems in handling but apart from this it had very good looks, very good space. The prototypes did not give us reason to be concerned.'

All changed with the management shake-up of 1971. In October 1971, after only having taken up post on 24 September, Rudolf Leiding cancelled EA266 because it could not be built profitably. There was also nervousness about how it would be received in the USA. News of the decision was public very soon, covered in quite some detail by *Der Spiegel*'s 8 November edition, complete with a prototype EA266 on test.

According to *Der Spiegel* 50 cars had been completed and a pilot build was scheduled to start in May 1972. It was said that the decision cost the company £21 million in written-off research and development. This came against an increasing background of trouble: from 1969 to 1970 the value of VW shares fell from £38m to around £22m.

In November 1971 the same very-well-informed journal stated that Audi-NSU would now be providing the Beetle successor, a 1300cc car to be marketed both as a hatchback and a saloon, which could supplant the ageing Type 3 1600 (E272, the Passat, see Chapter 2). In fact there was rather more in prospect. The Audi 80-derived Passat would replace the Type 3 and 4, and EA266 would in turn be replaced by what would become the Audi 50 and eventual Volkswagen Polo. Their available engines would be under 1.3 litres as the 50/Polo would be part of a two-pronged Beetle-replacement strategy, the other component being the 1.1- and 1.5-litre.

Meanwhile EA337, the eventual Golf, was making its own steady progress. However, neither would arrive quite as quickly as expected by the press; there would be more pain to come for Volkswagen bosses and workers.

↑ An EA266 prototype viewed from behind shows the large cooling vents for its mid-mounted engine and wide rear track. Accessibility and noise problems bedevilled the programme. (Porsche)

→ This 1969 EA276 prototype in the AutoMuseum (wearing Golf wheels) bears a similarity to the Porsche project but has a front-mounted Beetle engine. It was the final stage before Giugiaro gave the Golf its style. (Author)

Boom and bust in America

Volkswagen's post-war success was due in no small part to its conquest of the American market, on which it became so dependent that it threatened to sink the parent company.

As production restarted in the 1940s, exports from Wolfsburg were vital for the fledgling company. 'Wherever there was an automobile company you had that country's protection of the domestic industry, so our market share in all the big markets which had an auto company like France, Great Britain and Italy was not much more than 1%,' Carl Hahn explained to the author in 2013. 'We were prospering in all the small markets with high market share but the populations being small we had to go overseas.'

Some Volkswagens had made their way to the US in the hands of returning servicemen (who were allowed to buy them for $645), but the first Beetles shown officially in the United States of America were at the German industrial exhibition in New York in 1949.

Initial sales were unsurprisingly low: two in 1949 but then 328 in 1950. If it seemed a curiosity to European eyes, this strange little car was the polar opposite of the direction in which American cars were heading on a wave of prosperity. Every year they grew bigger in all directions and manufacturers became masters of built-in obsolescence.

Slow, small and odd-looking, the Beetle seemed to be everything that US buyers would have appeared not to desire, but the car struck a note with a growing group of well-educated consumers who didn't buy a Beetle because it was cheap but because it was modest, well made and would not go out of fashion the following year (VW boasted that most parts were interchangeable from one year to the next). It became an anti-car statement. Its air-cooled engine wouldn't boil or freeze and although not fast it was low-stressed and would run happily at its top speed for long distances. In 1953 only 1,139 Beetles were sold, but a strong dealership network was established and this was as important as the virtues of the car itself. Whether you were in a city or a small town you could expect high standards of service and a minimum level of spare parts was mandatory.

Volkswagen of America was founded in 1955. The following year it sold 42,884 Beetles and the Karmann-Ghia coupe added a dash of style. By 1958 sales topped 61,507 Beetles (and 24,478 Type 2 Transporters) and by 1959 there was a six-month waiting list.

All of this had been done without advertising and, as recounted in *Remember those great Volkswagen ads?* Carl Hahn, newly arrived from Germany, concluded that sales would not surpass 160,000 a year by word of mouth and reputation alone. He decided to appoint Volkswagen's first US advertising agency.

After a three-month search a young agency composed of Bill Bernbach, Ned Doyle and Maxwell Dane was recommended to him, Doyle Dane Bernbach or DDB. Its campaigns became an advertising legend, stripping away the pretence of other carmakers and speaking to the Volkswagen customer as an intelligent adult, often using self-deprecating humour. Some didn't even show the car at all.

Meanwhile domestic carmakers brought out their answer to the Beetle and other small imported cars. Initially known as a 'compact' car they were nearer the size of larger European saloons. The most astonishing Volkswagen-esque and subsequently notorious compact was Chevrolet's 1959 air-cooled, rear-engined Corvair.

While new compacts from Ford, General Motors and Chrysler hastened the exit of European manufacturers such as Renault or Austin – which were already failing through rust, unreliability or poor service – Volkswagen was unaffected. Some of this was certainly due to its talked-about advertising. Volkswagen was still a major client of DDB in 2014.

Volkswagen's American success continued in the 1960s with improved Beetles, Transporters and the Type 3 saloons and Variant. German products were gaining a reputation as a byword for quality. The Beetle's place in the American landscape was cemented in the 1969 Disney film *The Love Bug*. At a time when the German press was getting weary of the Volkswagen, Hahn took a group to see the Beetle in an American setting: 'I showed them how the Beetle was a member of the American family who went to live in the garage,' he recalled. 'And this member of the family was loved, admired and a symbol for many positive things. When they returned these German journalists knew that the Beetle was admired by the most motorised nation in the world, so I think that helped just a little bit.'

Volkswagen's dependency on the US imports market was remarkable and dangerous. Towards the end of the 1960s sales were over half a million cars a year – over a third of production – despite rising antipathy towards imported cars. Meanwhile in Europe Fiat and Renault were making inroads into Volkswagen's territory.

As Kurt Lotz took over from Nordhoff, Japanese carmakers

were making gains in the USA (Toyota sales went from 16,000 in 1966 to 110,000 in 1969) and a new breed of domestic cars much closer to the Beetle in size was under development. Ford was about to launch the Maverick, the Pinto was in prototype form and VW was now potentially vulnerable. The 411 was met with bemusement and the Beetle seemed to be falling out of favour, labelled as 'hopelessly outdated' by US car magazines.

The five millionth Beetle reached the USA in 1971 but faced the strong-selling and almost exactly Beetle-sized Ford Pinto, the Chevrolet Vega, AMC Gremlin and cars from Datsun, Toyota and Mazda.

The heavily revised (for a Beetle) 1302 with its MacPherson-strut front suspension sold alongside a stripped-down standard Beetle at a premium as the Super Beetle. *Car & Driver* called it 'durable but antique.' Volkswagen's image was harmed even further by a 200-page report from safety campaigner Ralph Nader's Center for Auto Safety in September 1971: 'The Volkswagen Beetle is the most hazardous car currently in use in significant numbers in the United States. The VW Microbus or Van is so unsafe that it should be removed from the roads entirely.' This argument had been raging for some time, and Volkswagen itself had commissioned its own research into Beetle accidents from Cornell University in 1964 and published in 1968.

Lemon.
This Volkswagen missed the boat.
The chrome strip on the glove compartment is blemished and must be replaced. Chances are you wouldn't have noticed it; Inspector Kurt Kroner did.
There are 3,389 men at our Wolfsburg factory with only one job: to inspect Volkswagens at each stage of production. (3000 Volkswagens are produced daily; there are more inspectors than cars.)
Every shock absorber is tested (spot checking won't do), every windshield is scanned. VWs have been rejected for surface scratches barely visible to the eye.
Final inspection is really something! VW inspectors run each car off the line onto the Funktionsprüfstand (car test stand), tote up 189 check points, gun ahead to the automatic brake stand, and say "no" to one VW out of fifty.
This preoccupation with detail means the VW lasts longer and requires less maintenance, by and large, than other cars. (It also means a used VW depreciates less than any other car.)
We pluck the lemons; you get the plums.

↑ Doyle Dane Bernbach's 1960 'Lemon' advertisement became a classic. At first it appeared to mock its subject but was really about quality.

At the same time Volkswagen was struggling in its home market to renew its product range and this over-reliance on the US began to threaten its very survival, a scenario other carmakers feared. In November 1971 a Fiat spokesman was quoted in *Autocar* saying: 'If Volkswagen collapse in the USA they will just have to flood the European market with cars. Competition is a good thing but a price war could be murderous. On the other had a recession at VW would have side effects which would hurt everybody.'

Severely affected by the falling value of the dollar, which made its cars more expensive, US sales continued to fall even as the Dasher (Passat) was introduced. Total annual American VW sales went from 476,295 in 1973 to 334,515 in 1974. Nonetheless VW was still in first place, with Toyota second at 171,196 having also suffered a decline as the US compact cars flourished in the fuel crisis. Before the Golf, scheduled for a January 1975 introduction as the Rabbit, it truly seemed as if the good times were over.

D
WOB GO 501
Volkswagen Classic

Golf 1 1974–1983

Revolution

The 13th of May 1969 was a pivotal day in Golf evolution. As detailed in Jens Meyer's book *Kult Klassiker VW Golf 1*, Volkswagen assembled a group of its development prototypes within the walls of the Wolfsburg test track to be viewed by the Product Strategy committee and senior management in the open air. Most were running cars and all could have their doors and bonnets opened. For comparison a Beetle 1300 and Fiat's just-launched 128 saloon were also present.

From Porsche the mid-engined EA266 prototype was the nearest car to production and from Audi in Ingolstadt came the water-cooled front-wheel drive (engine mounted longitudinally) EA267, considered to be in the Beetle class, so possibly an ancestor of the future Audi 50/Polo.

The Wolfsburg development department fielded three different versions of a small car prototype called EA235. During a good part of the Porsche project it had been working on a similar-sized three-door car. In response to Lotz's plan the head of technical development, Helmut Orlich, developed EA235 between 1968 and 1969. It was a neat hatchback with front-wheel drive, strut front suspension and trailing-arm rear suspension but with a Beetle flat-four air-cooled engine driving the front wheels. EA235 is the car that starts to have some of the elements of what was to become the Golf, the packaging is very similar, with the long roof and short tail with hatchback. One survivor, EA276, is held by the Volkswagen AutoMuseum.

Long discussions followed that meeting in May. While EA266, the Porsche prototype, continued, Wolfsburg nonetheless made the decision to go with the front-engined water-cooled layout for its other models, although the debate continued as to whether the engines would be mounted across the car (transversely) instead of north to south (longitudinally).

Finding a style

By the end of 1969 the package of what would later become the Golf (the A-class car) had been decided, but there was a feeling that Wolfsburg's own styling would not offer the simple attractive looks the marketers were calling for. Kurt Lotz looked to Italy.

In the 1960s every carmaker sooner or later beat a path to Italian styling houses. Volkswagen had already made the link with Ghia and Pininfarina. In 1967 it had been announced that Volkswagen had signed up for co-operation in the development of car bodies with Pininfarina, and it had started work on the Passat (see panel on page 47) yet in 1969 the next Volkswagen went to the much younger and much smaller firm of Ital Design. It had only been founded the previous year by Giorgio (Giorgetto) Giugiaro who had graduated from the Academy of Fine Arts in Turin and been persuaded by Dante Giacosa to work for the Fiat styling centre 'Centro Stile'.

By the age of 21 Giugiaro had moved to the Italian coachbuilder Bertone and under the guidance of Nuccio Bertone he designed the Iso Grifo and the Alfa Romeo Giulia GT. In 1966, he moved to Ghia's styling house where he helped design the De Tomaso Mangusta and the Maserati Ghibli. In 1967 he left and started his own company 'Ital Styling', which in 1968 became Ital Design.

Unbeknown to Giugiaro, on the direction of Kurt Lotz the Italian VW importer Gerhard Gumpert had toured the 1969 Turin motor show held in late October/early November (while Giugiaro remembers the venue as Turin, some histories have this as the Frankfurt show, held earlier in October 1969) and had been asked to identify six of the best-looking cars at the show. Four of them turned out to be Giugiaro designs; the Maserati Ghibli, De Tomaso Mangusta, Iso Rivolta and Grifo.

'True,' Giugiaro told the author in 2012. 'I had a meeting with the importer because the importer was keen to have me take a look at the possibilities of developing a family of cars in terms of style. I was surprised at the time because Bertone and Pininfarina were already well established and I had only just opened up my own firm. And so I asked why me? I had certainly less experience than the others. Together with my partner Mr Mantovani, who is an engineer, I had set up a company that specialised in designing for series production. We had just completed work on the Alfasud, so I think the choice also depended on whether the candidate had a sound engineering background, given the fact that it was necessary to deal with a range of aspects, the architectural design related elements (but also the ergonomics, technology). But actually maybe this aspect isn't the most important because there was no shortage of engineering skills in Volkswagen!'

In January 1970 Ital Design was contracted to rapidly style a family of cars for Volkswagen: a medium-sized saloon it already had under development (which became the Passat), a smaller family car (the Golf) and a Golf-based coupe (the Scirocco). Work started on the Passat (see panel on page 47) but the priority then shifted to the Golf. Kurt Lotz was clear that he wanted a Beetle successor, drawn around the same dimensions.

By opting for an in-line four-cylinder engine and gearbox mounted transversely, more room could be devoted to passenger and luggage space. The 1959 Mini and 1962 BMC 1100 had popularised the space-saving virtues of the transverse-engined layout, but their gearboxes were below the engine. Fiat pioneered the more straightforward layout and eventual industry standard of a gearbox inline with the engine across the car with the 1964 Autobianchi Primula – also a hatchback – and later applied it to the Fiat 128.

So the eventual Volkswagen Golf was not the first front-wheel drive, five-door hatchback but a thoroughly analysed combination of a trend that had matured in the 1960s. By the end of that decade Renault could boast a three-car range of hatchbacks, but the nearest proto-Golf was the 1967 Simca 1100, which had five doors plus a transverse-mounted engine and according to Wikipedia (thus unverified) was studied by Volkswagen during Golf development. However, the Alfa Romeo Alfasud, coming so soon before the Golf commission, cannot be discounted as a major influence – according to Giugiaro it only escaped being a hatchback because the company's chief designer believed a tailgate would be too heavy.

In any case, Volkswagen's own EA235/276 design had been a hatchback and Giugiaro told the author it was an inevitable choice: 'Volkswagen gave us specifications only in terms of length and wheelbase with the driving position. It had to be two volumes, it would have been ridiculous otherwise.'

Not that Volkswagen was giving any such detail publicly. During 1970 it told the motoring press that a fifth door would add around 20kg to the weight of a car, thus making it more expensive and less torsionally rigid. Engineers conceded that the option was attractive to small car buyers, but an estate car could always be added to the range.

With nothing to draw on from Volkswagen's own experience, the only packaging reference points were the competition and Giugiaro confirms the Fiat 128 was one of the templates: 'I remember the 2nd of January 1970 seeing this young 30-year-old in a room with 20 engineers and there was a Fiat 128 which had been taken completely apart bit by bit. They showed me the sketch [of the Golf dimensions] with the seats and the pedals. I looked at the measurements and I said this is going to be far more uncomfortable to drive than a Fiat 128, because I had all the measurements, and they said to me "we'll never succeed in making a product that is as functional, as cost effective and as comfortable, we'll have to be smaller like the Beetle."'

In March 1970 the car was given its official designation, EA337. During 1970 German engineers would head over to Turin in the company jet or Giugiaro would travel to Wolfsburg.

Just one styling model was produced to arrive at the Golf style in three-door form. On 12 August 1970, the Ital Design model was presented internally at Volkswagen and, although he was not present, Giugiaro recalls that

↑ The Alfa Romeo Alfasud (top) came from Ital Design before the Golf, and the Fiat 128 (above) influenced its packaging. Both became Golf rivals at launch. (Alfa Romeo and Fiat)

↑ The original proposal for frontal styling did not survive as the rectangular lights and the three-part bumper unit were deemed too expensive for production. (J. Meyer, Bremen)

← This side profile of the 1970 styling clay by the designer Giugiaro shows the key proportions, which were to be carried through generations of production. (Italdesign Giugiaro)

it was up against the Porsche-developed EA266. That afternoon he received a call in Turin to tell him his was the chosen design. Only small modifications were made to arrive at a production version. To comply with the recently introduced American safety standards, the angle of the windscreen was adjusted and an extra 70mm was added to the front.

Like the Passat prototype, the Golf study featured rectangular headlamps with integrated indicators at the edges. However, for cost reasons these were replaced by round headlamps, the indicators placed alongside them and a modified styling model produced. The rear light cluster was also reduced in width for cost reasons. 'My concern was the fact that the Alfa Romeo GT had the same kind of design,' Giugiaro recalls. 'The round headlamps in a rectangular grille, but obviously cost was a factor. Everything else was along the lines of what I had designed.' For final production Volkswagen moved the indicators out of the grille down to the front bumper and the headlamps outwards, to make the Golf appear wider.

In autumn 1970, equipped with Giugiaro's styling, production work began at a cost of some DM 1.2 million. According to author Joachim Kuch's 2007 *Schrader-Typen Chronik* book, the project involved 5,200 new parts and around 1,400 technicians and engineers were assigned to prototype work, headed by Hans-Georg Wenderoth, who had come from NSU.

The new running gear was tested in Audi 60s and under Fiat 127 bodies, modified to sometimes strange proportions in the eyes of spy photographers. Three generations of prototype were subjected to functional

↑ Giugiaro's rear styling of EA337 was largely translated into production minus the air vents, with smaller tail lamps, recession for the number plate and a simpler bumper design. (J. Meyer, Bremen)

➔ The rectangular lamps were first replaced by round units with indicators alongside, and these were fitted to prototype cars but for production the headlamps moved outwards and the indicators down into the bumper. (Italdesign Giugiaro)

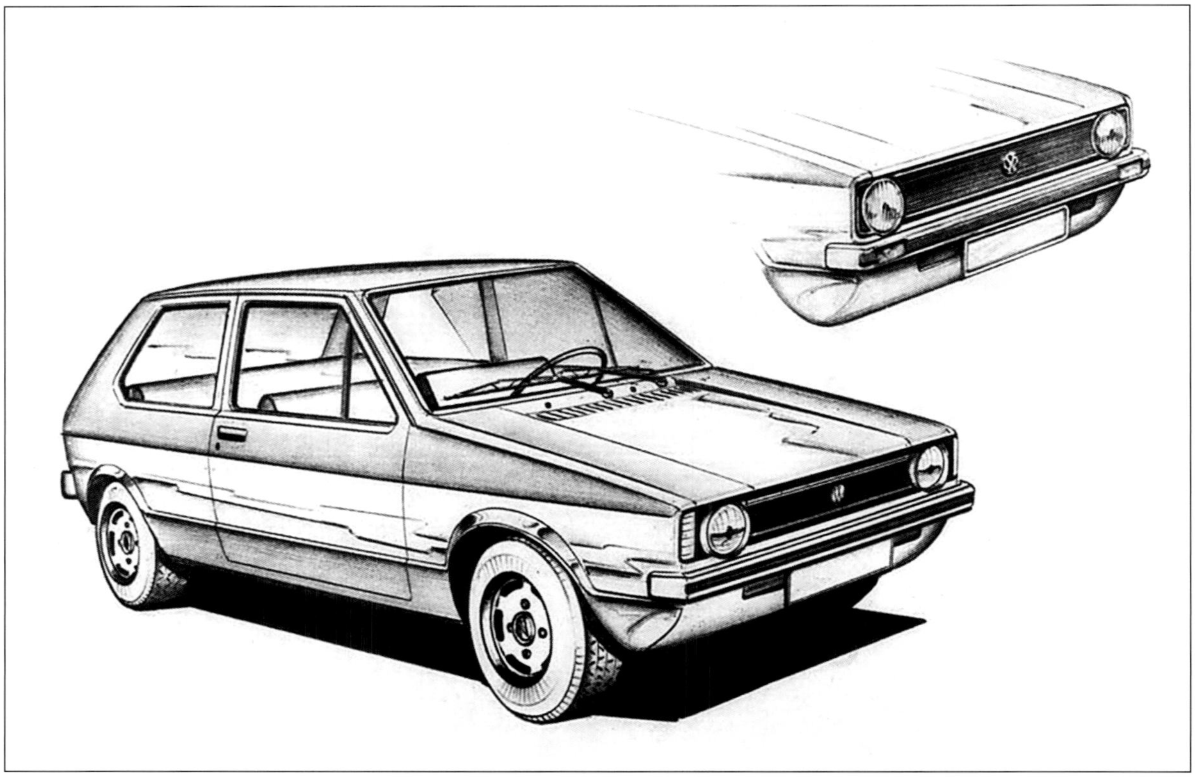

➔ This sketch for gear levers shows the golf-ball idea was around before the GTI used it. (Italdesign Giugiaro)

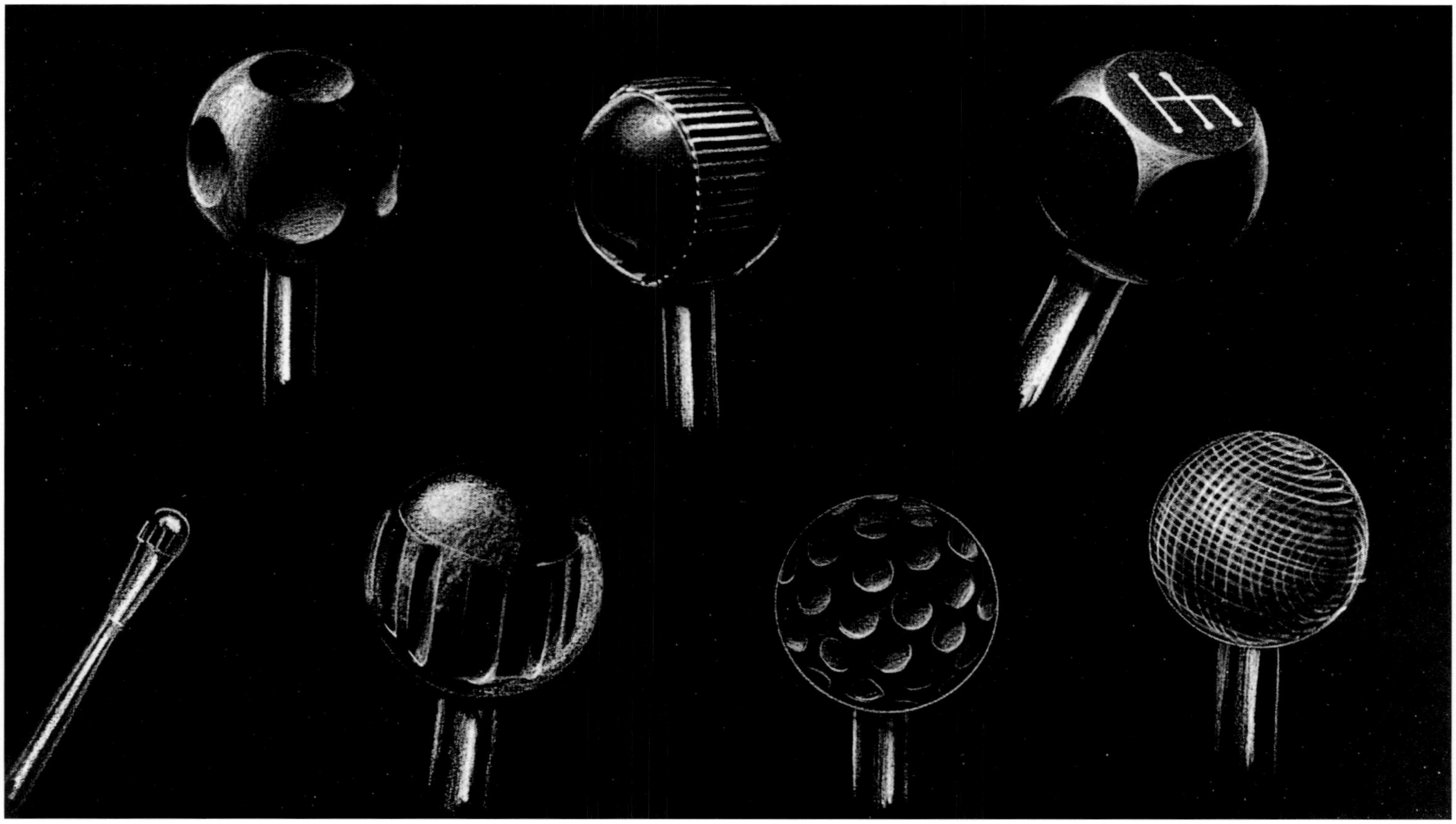

and endurance tests. At launch Dr Friedrich Goes, Volkswagen's head of passenger car development stated that no fewer than 100 prototypes were built for development purposes, and 4,000,000 kilometres were covered in preliminary testing. The Golf and Scirocco took exactly 200 weeks to complete.

Golf under the skin

With decades of only building air-cooled boxer engines it was inevitable that Volkswagen would turn to Audi to power its new generation. There was one ready-made engine, the 1,471cc Audi 80 four-cylinder (EA827), but those versions would be the top of the range cars sold in smaller volumes. To capture the Beetle clientele a smaller engine was needed and EA111 was initially designed at Ingolstadt by Franz Hauk for the Audi 50 and the basic Golf.

'A decision was made that Volkswagen would take over the development of the small engine,' Peter Hofbauer told the author in 2014. From 1969 he had been head of advanced propulsion systems research and from 1978 worldwide power-train development. 'Audi

↑ **Giorgio Giugiaro poses behind his most reproduced design at Lake Constance in 1974 as the Golf is launched. Volkswagen knew Italian styling had cachet. (Italdesign Giugiaro)**

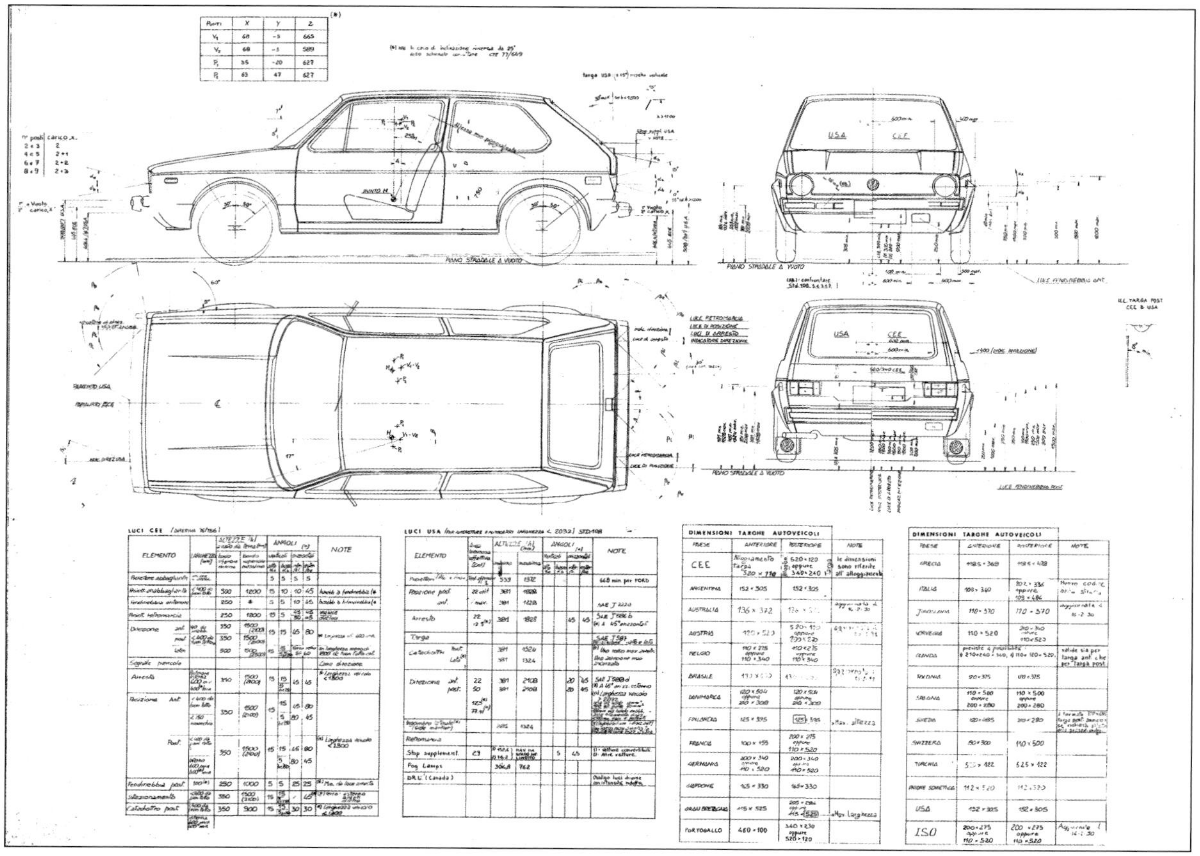

← **These final production drawings are sectioned so that one side is a European Golf, the other American specification with side marker lights and bigger bumpers. (Italdesign Giugiaro)**

↑ **Developed for the Golf and Audi 50/Polo, the 1.1-litre engine was inclined forwards for balance and accessibility. (LAT)**

said it was busy with the EA827 and we cannot do this little one, so management decided we should do it.'

The thoroughly contemporary 1,093cc unit (69.5mm bore x 72mm stroke) had an iron block and aluminium cylinder head with an overhead camshaft driven by a rubber belt. The cylinder head was a cross-flow design (inlet ports on one side, exhaust on the other) for efficient combustion and the pistons operated a five-bearing crankshaft.

It differed from the Audi 80/Passat EA827 engine by having its valves operated by short rockers instead of bucket tappets, and the drive to the oil pump and distributor was direct from the left side of the overhead camshaft. It was specifically designed to be short enough for transverse installation and the four-speed gearbox was end-on. 'It had a finger follower valve train when we had it,' says Hofbauer. 'It created a lot of noise so we called it the singing dervish. We changed it to [what was] at that time the modern solution of tappets. It wasn't a super engine when we got it, we did a lot of modifications.'

The single downdraught carburettor had an electrically-operated choke for cold starts and for engine cooling an electric fan would cut in when needed. Service intervals were set at 9,000 miles – considered long for the day. Like the latest Beetles the Golf also had a diagnostic socket for garages to use to fault-find.

The 1.1-litre engine/gearbox assembly was inclined forwards by 15 degrees for balance and better service access while the 1.5-litre was inclined backwards by 20 degrees for balance. All service items such as the water pump, cylinder head and clutch were designed to be removed without having to take the engine out. The front wings were bolted on for ease of repair.

In this first installation the 1,093cc unit developed 50bhp at 6,000rpm, a complete contrast to the low-revving air-cooled engines – the 1,285cc Beetle engine developed its 44bhp at 4,100rpm. EA111 became the base engine for the Golf, the basic Scirocco and the top engine of the Audi 50 range and later Volkswagen Polos.

Before the first all-new transverse-engined Volkswagens arrived the company continued to keep observers guessing that a wholesale switch to water-cooled front-driven cars was imminent – after all it was still trying to sell the Volkswagen 1600 and the 412.

Ernst Fiala had been brought into Volkswagen in 1970 from Berlin technical university to develop the company's ESV safety cars, also being built by other manufacturers to showcase safety ideas for American legislators. The first Volkswagen ESV car shown in 1972 had an air-cooled rear-mounted engine and rear drive, but one front-engine/front-drive car was said to have been tested, ostensibly to measure crush properties. The latter car, *Road & Track* noted, had a transverse-mounted engine, which had been in development since 1970 and was not related to the Audi 80 or Volkswagen K70 unit.

Fiala told the author in 2013: 'Having in mind that this will be the future successor of the Beetle, for the presentation in Washington in 1972 I said we cannot present a car with a front engine when we have to sell the rear-engined ones, so we made an ESV with the 411's 2-litre in the rear but the concept was for a front-engined car. More than 50% of the experiments had been with a front engine.'

Simple but effective suspension

The Golf's MacPherson-strut front suspension was no longer a surprise, but at launch it was the rear suspension that drew immediate attention from the press and motor industry. Already seen on the Scirocco, each rear wheel was independently sprung on a trailing arm and coil spring with the trailing arms pivoting on a beam linking them across the car. Seen in profile this beam was a simple T section, which fitted neatly beneath the fuel tank.

It avoided the problem of other dead axles, which would transmit abrupt wheel movements from one side to the other, known as 'axle tramping', because it was located by rubber bushes and acted as an anti-roll bar to twist in corners, exerting powerful wheel control.

Der Speigel in 1974 revealed that Volkswagen engineers had tested approximately 450 rear axle designs

↓ After two years of development the Volkswagen ESV safety concept was first shown in June 1972. Never intended for production, it nevertheless showcased items such as anti-lock brakes, pre-tensioning seatbelts and all-round impact protection, which were decades ahead.

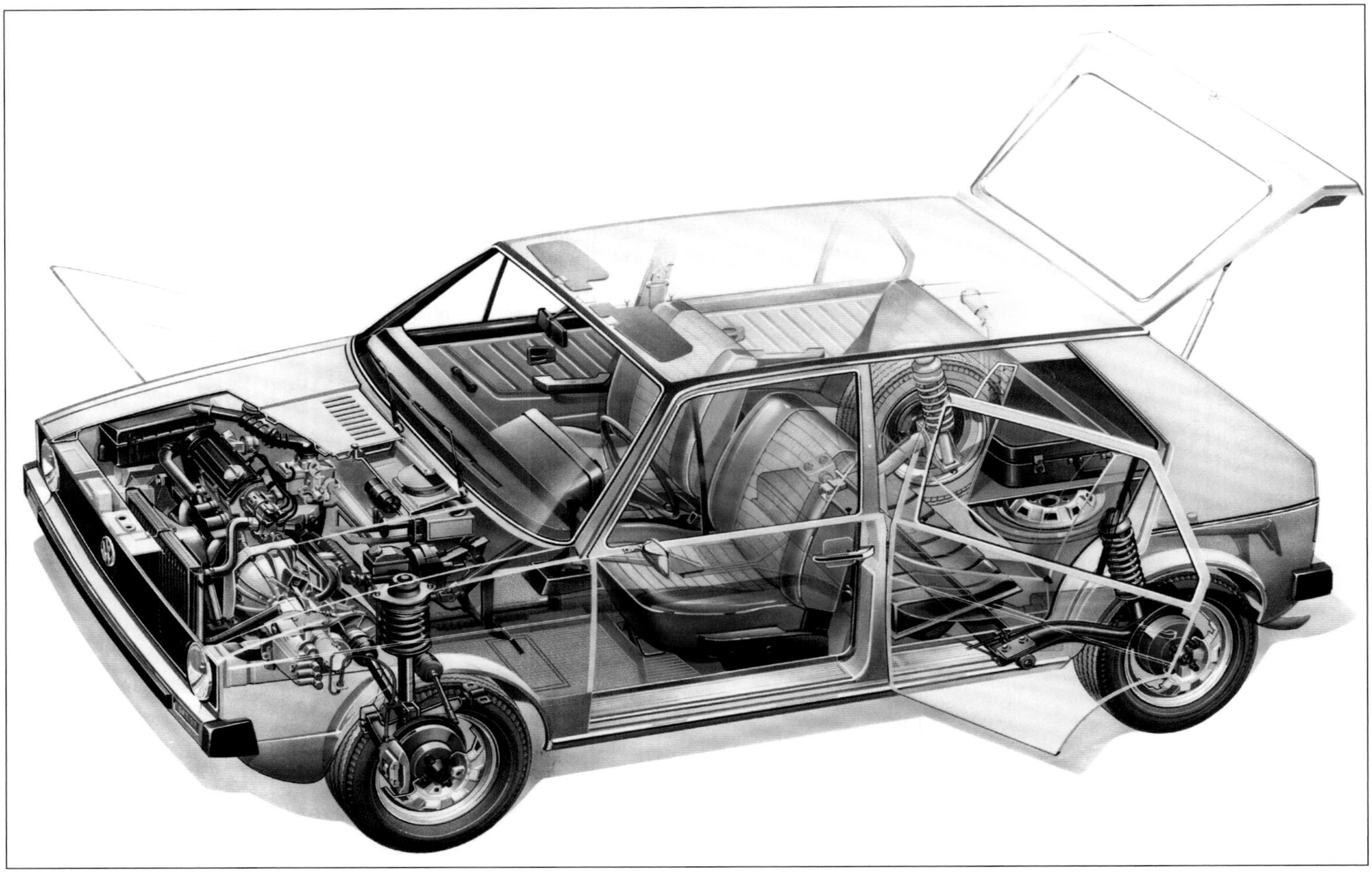

↑ **Cutaway drawings provided at launch illustrated the Golf's layout and the simplicity of the torsion-beam rear suspension.**

until this version, which they then patented. Friedrich Goes, quoted in the same article, called it so easy to manufacture that it was 'almost idiotically cheap'.

Autocar's technical editor Jeff Daniels wrote: 'Quite clearly, somebody got down to basics and worked out two simple and effective solutions which combine "proper" trailing arms with a light dead axle which assists in location and also functions as a rear anti-roll bar … to VW a large part of the attraction must have been the stunning simplicity and economy of the layout.' It went on to be much imitated by other carmakers.

Steering was by rack and pinion, including the negative offset geometry introduced on the Audi 80 and Passat, which kept the car stable in the event of a tyre blowout or a wheel locking up. Braking was by drums all round on basic models with front disc brakes and rear drums for the larger-engined Golfs. The braking circuit was split to maintain braking in the event of one side losing pressure.

Strong but light bodyshell

After decades of building Beetles using a separate chassis, Volkswagen was relatively new to designing its own chassis-less or unitary-construction bodyshells (the 411 was the first), which had to be internally stressed. The fact that the Golf was to have a hatchback, so a large area of its shell was 'open', was a particular challenge that had been alluded to in 1970. However, with its strong sills and computer-aided design the final bodyshell was considered to be a particularly rigid structure, although owners may not have appreciated the high lip over which they had to load luggage.

The work being done on the ESV safety cars also fed through into the design of the Golf's bodyshell. The scuttle and the firewall had two box sections, which were corrugated to form controlled crumple zones, extending forwards to provide the mounts for the front bumpers. As in all the new Volkswagens, the fuel tank

was located away from rear impacts ahead of the rear axle under the rear seats.

In European specification the 1974 Golf's final weights were 750kg dry for the 1100 three-door rising to 830kg for the automatic 1500 five-door. *Autocar* magazine considered this to be light while *Auto Motor und Sport* thought it to be heavy, but within the same weight range as the Beetle. At 3.7m long it was 33cm shorter than a Beetle but sat on the same 2.4m wheelbase.

It might have looked boxy but great attention had been paid to aerodynamics through testing in Volkswagen's own wind tunnel, especially to make sure the new generation suffered none of the rear-engined cars' tendency to wander in crosswinds and to help fuel economy.

There were, however, last-minute changes to the Golf's aerodynamic properties after Ernst Fiala took up his post as head of development in 1972, replacing Hans-Georg Wenderoth and given to understand that the drag coefficient (Cd) was a seemingly excellent 0.36. 'As we had the first prototypes it turned out we in fact had a Cd of 4.5 and so all the gearboxes were wrong because we had a false Cd number. We had to change the gearbox anyway, but we took some measures to reduce the air drag. One was a little upturn out of the sheet metal on the tailgate, then at the front we changed the radius of the front-end fender and the underbody at the rear end of the floor so we could reduce the number from 4.5 to 4.2.'

A name, not a number

And the Golf name? The Passat and Scirocco had used up the names of exotic winds (not used by Maserati) and a meeting note of September 1973 gives two possible names as Pampero for the world market and Rabbit for the USA: *'Weltweit = Pampero, USA = Rabbit'*. The minutes noted that the name Pampero had already been registered as a precaution, a winter wind blowing across South America.

↑ A pre-production Golf meets its end for safety tests. Volkswagen was confident that it set new standards. (Giles Chapman picture library)

↑ Just to make sure nobody confused it for a Beetle this showed the engine was at the front, the boot at the back.

However, EA337 was finally named after the German spelling for the perhaps less bleak-sounding Gulf Stream (*Golf Strom* in German), the Atlantic Ocean current that brings warmer temperatures to European waters, although as soon as it was on the market a lot of headlines about 'playing Golf' and 'Golf lessons' sprang up. German motor magazine *Auto Motor und Sport* quipped that it might also conjure up associations with a 'warm dollar stream which Volkswagen might hope to stimulate through exports'. Volkswagen itself was playing it both ways, to quote its 1974 press pack: 'But who on hearing the name GOLF thinks of the Gulf Stream which makes its way across the Atlantic. Golf is the game and the name suits. Golf stands for endurance, perfect technique and – drive.'

Between 1972 and 1975 Volkswagen had embarked on a massive investment programme, spending DM 2.5 billion to equip its factories for the new generation. The plants in Wolfsburg and Emden were equipped with a flexible suspension assembly system in 1973 and the production of air-cooled engines was reduced, while increasing capacity for water-cooled engines. The future was in unitary construction, allowing the use of the same parts for various models with essentially the same technology.

It was notable that despite the Golf being a completely different car to build, production at Wolfsburg never took a break, the newcomer moving in alongside the Beetle without any shutdown.

To illustrate the change of culture and manufacture Volkswagen was now finding it not only had to build a completely new type of engine in cast iron but also had to use radiators in massive quantities for the first time. In conjunction with Valeo, major investment was made to manufacture radiators in Hannover.

Golf to market

The first Volkswagen Golf came off the production line on 29 March 1974, two months after the Scirocco. Production was scheduled with the first derivative the 1.5 two-door, the 1.1 two-door in July and the 1.1 four-door in August 1974. The international press presentation was in Munich that May.

Volkswagen said the Golf was part of the 'new horizon' and 'planned diversification' of Volkswagens. The press material acknowledged that it had been a hard journey getting there. 'Again and again new solutions challenged our classical concept but keeping to our Beetle, despite strong pressure, brought us success. It is therefore natural that we hesitated to take a new course beside the proven line, but the critical pause proved to be creative.'

The Golf was described in forensic detail by European writers, *Auto Motor und Sport* devoting nine pages to it. 'When one considers the vast pool of Beetle drivers, who are accustomed to unpretentiousness and reliability but not however spoilt in relation to comfort, then this concept looks set for success. Luggage loading without dislocating body parts, heating even during short trips and good visibility were all things that millions of VW customers have willingly gone without.'

On every measure, from interior space to noise, comfort and roadholding the Golf was found to be far superior to the first people's car, but in bettering the Beetle the writers noted that Volkswagen had been careful not to lose one of its most important features, a feeling of independence from the status-seeking associated with cars. 'They were conscious of this in Wolfsburg and decided against building a "pretty" car, a blatant shrinking of current design, in the knowledge that small cars cannot be as beautiful as a Ferrari or a Jaguar.'

German market Golfs were launched in a basic and

L trim for the 1.1, and in S and LS designations for the 1.5-litre. While the base model was sparsely equipped with a rubber floor covering and no parcel shelf or boot floor cover, it did have fabric seats, while more expensive Golfs were finished in simulated leather. On all models the rear backrest could be dropped by a lever giving an overall loading length of 1.2m albeit over a high sill. L and S models added more soundproofing, seatbelts, extra instrumentation and metal trim embellishments. A blended air heater was common to all Golfs. German buyers had a copious options list including a laminated windscreen, heated rear window, rear wiper, sunroof and integrated head restraints. The 1.5-litre cars ran on 5in wide wheels with 155/13 radial tyres while the 1.1-litre was given 4.5in wide wheels with 145/13 cross-ply tyres. Although fitted to many competitor basic cars at the time, cross-plies were starting to be replaced by radials, which offered better grip and more stable cruising. Alloy wheels with 175/70SR13 tyres were available as an option. The most expensive choice was a three-speed automatic gearbox for the 1.5-litre engine.

Factory performance figures claimed a 0 to 100kph (62mph) of 16.5 seconds and a top speed of 140kph (87mph) for the 1.1-litre and 15.5sec/160kph (99mph) for the 1.5 manual, with a shorter set of gear ratios on the 1.1. Official fuel-consumption figures for the 1.1 ranged from 35.2 to 51.3mpg and from 33.2 to 47.8mpg for the 1.5 manual.

Before the first full test an initial drive was enough for the *Auto Motor Und Sport* writers to proclaim: 'Beetle drivers in particular will feel in the first few metres in a Golf the progress of 40 years of car development … we have here a handy, useful car. It is also a lively car as the 1.1-litre has a delightful temperament and the 1.5-litre

continued on page 52

← The Volkswagen Golf body assembly conveyor in the mid-1970s. It adopted the cheerful colours of the Beetle and of the time. (Giles Chapman picture library)

The supporting cast: Audi 80, Passat, Scirocco and Polo

Boss Rudolf Leiding took no chances that the failure of any one model in the new generation would drag the company down, perhaps mindful of the poor sales of the 411 and the K70. Between 1972 and 1975 the Golf was bracketed by cars that were just as important and, fortunately, just as accomplished. The Audi 80, Volkswagen Polo, Passat and Scirocco went on to become long-lasting series in their own right.

Audi 80

The building block of the new Volkswagen generation was the Audi 80 saloon, announced in July 1972 and produced both in Ingolstadt and Wolfsburg – the first time a water-cooled engine had been made within its walls. Under its neat conservative styling, its engine (code-named EA827), was a four-cylinder design with a cast-iron cylinder block and aluminium head with overhead valves actuated by a single overhead camshaft and bucket tappets. Introduced in 1,296cc and 1,470cc versions, most of Volkswagen's future range – with the exception of the Polo – was powered by EA827 derivatives running on petrol, diesel, methanol and alcohol. It was also the basis for the five-cylinder Audi engine, which became a company trademark and was used in the Quattro. In the Audi 80 and Passat it was mounted longitudinally driving the front wheels – in the Golf and Scirocco it became transverse-mounted.

While its styling was conservative, the 80 was the first car in the world to have negative steering scrub radius or offset steering as a safety feature. It was claimed the driver could brake hard with one wheel on a different type of surface to another and the car would still stop straight, or would remain stable if a tyre blew out – a feature advertised in the US market as 'the skidbreaker'. The 80 was an immediate success, taking Audi's share of the German market from 6.6% to over 10%, and was voted Car of the Year 1973. By 1975 half a million had been produced.

➔ This 1972 prototype Passat at the AutoMuseum resembles a big Golf and also had a transverse engine. (Author)

⬋ The 1973 Audi 80 GT had a new 1.6-litre engine which in fuel-injected form would find its way into the Golf GTI. (Audi)

Volkswagen Passat

In May 1973 Volkswagen's new mid-size front-driven saloon, the Passat, marked the true start of the new Volkswagen generation, rendering the K70 redundant and laying the ground for the Golf. Volkswagen public relations referred to it as 'the most important car since the Beetle'.

Work had started in 1968 when, under Lotz's direction, the PSK had settled on a range of new 'A' and 'B'-class cars. A became the Golf, B the Passat. A range of intermediate and strange solutions was discussed, such as a water-cooled boxer engine or a 411 with a front-mounted Audi engine, before management settled on the final layout of EA272. This could have been front-engined and rear-wheel drive, but Volkswagen management wanted strongly to follow the Audi front-drive route.

A range of three new engines was planned from 1.3 to 2.0 litres. They were to be transverse-mounted and while development prototypes were being built, the new engines were tested in Audis and Autobianchis.

Styling was initially entrusted to Pininfarina, with whom Volkswagen already had a contract, but was switched to Ital Design, newly founded by Giorgio Giugiaro, in 1970. Volkswagen agreed a fastback style for both the two- and four-door versions, an intentional resemblance to the 411 and 412 that it was replacing in the hope that it would attract the former's customers. Early prototypes had been hatchbacks, but this was not a feature of the Passat until the 1980s.

Looking like a larger version of the Golf, which was being styled alongside it, the design of EA272 took an abrupt change of course as it neared its on-sale date in 1972. Rudolf Leiding quickly realised after his arrival in 1971 that the company's finances could not support the development of two new engine lines, one for EA272 and one for EA337, the Golf. He looked across to Audi for a solution.

'In Ingolstadt we of course noticed that the Beetle had plunged sharply and the 1600 was also not doing well,' Audi's Ludwig Kraus recalled. 'Leiding saw the car and wanted it, but there were also voices in Volkswagen which argued for the Audi 80 to go on immediate sale as a notchback VW – it was then already finished and was about to start production.'

The Audi 80 boasted an engine range of virtually the same capacities as those planned for the Volkswagen, but they were longitudinally mounted. Thus the longer, flatter front end of the 80 was grafted onto the Ital Design fastback rear styling, delaying its launch until 1973.

The new car marked the start of a whole series of Volkswagen model names, rather than numbers, based on famous winds. Maserati had already laid claim to a number of these (Indy, Ghibli and so on), but the Passat was named after the trade wind that blew Columbus to America and a famous commercial sailing

The supporting cast: Audi 80, Passat, Scirocco and Polo (continued)

ship. In American markets the Passat became the Dasher while the Audi 80 was the Fox.

Although expected to be launched in fairly basic trim, the Passat arrived with a range of 17 different combinations of engine, trim and body shape, two- and four-door fastback saloons (a hatchback came later) and a four-door estate.

The three engines were now entirely Audi: a 55bhp 1.3 (or 60bhp export as 55bhp was a cut-off for German insurance) and a 75bhp and 85bhp 1.5-litre (early pre-launch cars still had Audi stamped on the cam covers). Compared with the 80 the biggest mechanical change was a relocated fuel tank and spare wheel plus separate spring and damper units in the rear suspension to improve accessibility on the estate.

Hours could be spent seeing which Passat was cheaper than which Audi 80, but the money went the same way. Volkswagen owned Audi and 35% of 80s were produced at Wolfsburg by 1973. The Passat design only split from the Audi 80 in 1988 when it adopted a transverse-engined layout to offer vastly increased interior space. The location of the Passat's engine remained changeable. In 1996 it was back to longitudinal, in 2005 transverse again.

Volkswagen Scirocco

It might have seemed odd that cash-strapped Volkswagen launched a three-door coupe in March 1974, months before the Golf, but it was made known from launch that this smart bodyshell clothed the mechanical basis of the '337', the much-rumoured Beetle replacement.

Internally known as EA398, the Giugiaro-styled Scirocco had been developed in parallel with the Golf. According to author James Ruppert, Karmann had been painfully aware that its Volkswagen Karmann-Ghia coupe was woefully out of date by even the mid-1960s, and Ghia would supply new designs which Volkswagen in turn was completely uninterested in (discounting the Volkswagen-Porsche 914/916 as an expensive diversion). Karmann styled its own coupes just for the Brazilian market. The Scirocco came into being as Giugiaro reckoned the Golf's packaging would be ideal for a shorter coupe and Karmann largely financed the development of the car it was eventually to build.

The Scirocco's bodyshell was light, efficiently made and clothed the future Golf's transverse-mounted engines, simple yet effective torsion beam rear suspension,

↗ The Scirocco as first announced in 1974. It was a pretty preview of the Golf.

← To save money and time the front section and running gear of the Audi 80 was grafted on at a very late stage. Round or square headlamps were fitted.

MacPherson-strut front suspension and rack-and-pinion steering.

Coming before the Golf the Scirocco now represented Wolfsburg's considered opinion of the optimum layout for the small car of the future.

These 1974 cars mirrored the engine choices of the first Golfs. The range started with its 1,093cc engine developing 50bhp – this model was not imported into the UK – and then the 1,471cc Passat/Audi 80 unit developing 70 or 85bhp.

Thus the Scirocco was the second new Volkswagen named after a wind, this time a hot desert one, and company records show that when market tested in 1973, the name 'Scirokko' had tested well as having 'exotic' associations, perhaps a car made by Alfa Romeo. Plans to call it the Blizzard in the US were not pursued.

Built by Karmann in Osnabrück, the Scirocco was introduced before the Golf to test its running gear and get the dealers used to servicing it on a low-volume model. It also enabled engine production to be brought on stream for the much higher Golf volumes. 'Intrinsically the Scirocco is much less important than its implications,' said *Motor*.

Audi 50

The final piece in the front-wheel-drive revolution was intended as back-up in case the Golf failed but instead became a household name in its own right. It started life as the Audi 50.

Styling studies of a neat three-door car – the essence of the forthcoming 'supermini' class of the 1970s – date back as far as 1968, but the Audi 50 truly got going with the merger with NSU in 1969. A replacement for the rear-engined NSU Prinz saloon had become the top priority. Now eager to raid the store cupboard of its new brands, Volkswagen stipulated that the new Audi had to also serve as a Volkswagen and potential Beetle successor.

'The Group's wish was to have a car beneath the planned Golf,' Ludwig Kraus recalled. 'VW wanted this vehicle from our company. They calculated that such a small car would only be cheap to produce from 2,000 units per day and at Audi we had no such capacity. We could not have had the money to invest to this magnitude, which is why the decision was made to develop the new car at Audi and finish with VW.'

A great deal of detail on the Audi 50 was public long before it went on sale as a replacement for the axed EA266 small car. *Autocar* mistakenly stated the car would begin production in 1972.

The supporting cast: Audi 80, Passat, Scirocco and Polo (continued)

Following the Passat, Scirocco and Golf, the Audi 50 was launched in September 1974 with the 1,093cc base Golf engine on the understanding that it would come to the UK in a lower-powered form and only as a Volkswagen.

'Will the true and worthy Beetle successor please come forward at long last? Thank you Audi 50,' wrote Jerry Sloniger having driven a pre-production version for *Motor* magazine. 'Audi wants to make it very clear that they designed this car, wherever it may be built, and that they are not simply using Golf parts...'

At 3.5m the 50 was 20cm shorter than a Golf and was offered only as a three-door. The crisp modern styling had also seen the hand of an Italian stylist. Although the official line was that the style was pure Ingolstadt, Nuccio Bertone and his then chief designer Marcello Gandini had been at work.

As was now the norm for Volkswagen-Audis, front suspension was by MacPherson struts/coil springs and the rear a simple torsion-beam axle with struts, trailing arms and no Panhard rod. At launch Audi engineers claimed their chassis was better developed having set spring and damper rates by testing on public roads as they didn't have a test track.

Steering was rack-and-pinion and slightly inclined struts were said to give lighter steering. The 1,093cc engine was offered in two states of tune, 50bhp as in the base Golf or 60bhp. Coming in LS and GL equipment levels, as befitting a small Audi it had carpets and a wood or mock-wood fascia. Servo assistance for the disc/drum brakes was optional on either trim and radial-ply tyres standard on the GL.

Volkswagen Polo

What seemed at last to be really the new Beetle, the Volkswagen Polo, was presented to the international press in March 1975. As expected, it was a lower specification Audi 50.

To position it below the Golf, Volkswagen stated that the Polo would never be produced with four doors, never with an engine of larger than 1,100cc or with automatic transmission. Pitched about 10% cheaper than the Golf it was intended to extend the range rather than overlap with it. It drew natural comparisons with the basic 1200 Beetle. In future, all of these constraints fell away.

The 895cc engine was identical in design to the Audi 50/Golf N 1,093cc unit but with its capacity reduced by shortening the stroke from 72 to 59mm, leaving the 69.5mm bore unchanged. It was considered a very free-revving and flexible unit for the time.

Lower-powered engine aside, the only differences between the Audi 50 and Polo were of trim – or lack of it. A base 1975 Polo had no brightwork, and featured rubber flooring, single-speed wipers and heater fan. Drum brakes were fitted all round on wheels with standard cross-ply tyres.

Set up against the Beetle, the Polo unsurprisingly came out ahead on all measures. Although 506mm (20in) shorter than a Beetle overall the Polo offered more internal space and although on paper the 895cc engine was smaller than the 1,192cc air-cooled Beetle it developed 40bhp as opposed to 34bhp, had a rev range up to 5,900rpm compared with 3,800rpm and at 700kg weighed about 70kg less than the kerb weight of a 1200 Beetle.

Praise was heaped upon the Polo, well able to compete with cars such as the Renault 5, Fiat 127 and the 1977 Ford Fiesta. It was number one in its class in Germany 16 months after launch. Contradicting its earlier position, Volkswagen continued to upgrade it, offering 1.1- and 1.3-litre engines, a short-lived sporty Polo GT and spinning off a two-door booted saloon, the Derby. The Audi 50 was destined for a short career. British Audi dealers declined to sell it at all, at the risk of confusing their upmarket customers. A 1300 engine was introduced in 1977 but production ended the following year at 188,000.

Aside from the Audis, between 1973 and 1975 Volkswagen had astonished industry watchers by rushing out four all-new model lines, with no relation to its previous cars, in less time than it took most manufacturers to develop one. It is still regarded as one of the great automobile turnarounds.

↑This group shot from 1974 seems to imply the Beetle is still dominant. The jeep-type vehicle back left is the Beetle-based 181 – named 'the thing' in America.

→ Golfs and Polos await dispatch onto trains at Wolfsburg. The Polo was a fallback in case the Golf failed but both became a huge success. (Giles Chapman picture library)

←The Polo was essentially an Audi 50 with a smaller engine and a lot less trim. It was almost as significant as the Golf.

leaps far ahead of the Beetle standard.' About the only criticisms were of a slightly rubbery gear change and over-firm suspension. It concluded that the Golf was indeed – subject to proving as reliable and cheap to run – capable of one day being a worthy Beetle successor.

There was an immense sales challenge to be waged with the new Volkswagens, especially the Golf, which was seen as the true heir to the Beetle. After decades of devotion to air-cooled engines and selling their virtues to the world, Wolfsburg had suddenly thrown it all in and put the engine at the other end. 'We were very concerned. The standard propaganda of VW was always "air doesn't freeze and you drive ahead of the engine, away from the noise" and it was difficult for people to understand,' Fiala recalls. 'Most of the supervisory board and politicians asked why we had come up with a front-driven car when nobody else seemed to make one; not the Japanese, the successful Opel and Ford in Germany had abandoned the front-drive P4 in favour of the rear-drive Escort. It was difficult to convince them to stay with the programme. And some of them thought this into 1975 when Opel overtook VW in the German market.'

➔ Germany's famous monthly magazine got straight to the point: this was a Käfer Nachfolger – Beetle successor. (Author's collection)

The Golf's European advertising strategy was as playful as ever, adopting a no-nonsense approach that listed the many virtues of the new car. There was no attempt to link the name with exotic winds, with the first brochures placing the car on a little patch of grass and a flag to introduce customers to the 'ABC of Golf.' Bertel Schmitt of advertising agency GGK Dusseldorf coined the phrase: *'Der neue Volkssport: Golf'* – the new national sport: Golf. The starting price for a Golf was DM 7,990, almost exactly where the Beetle range ended.

By happy accident it hit a market clamouring for small fuel-efficient cars. In the middle of 1974 the Western world was only just emerging from an energy crisis triggered the previous October when members of the Organization of Petroleum Exporting Countries (OPEC) launched an oil embargo in response to the Yom Kippur War. As well as far-ranging economic effects the price of petrol rocketed. This was felt most keenly in the US, but European countries had had to introduce fuel and energy rationing. It turned out to be just the right time for Volkswagen to be fielding not only the Golf but also the smaller 1975 Polo.

On the first day of July 1974 the last of 11 million Beetles built at Wolfsburg rolled off the line, and it continued in German production at Emden until 1978. On 8 July the first Golf was delivered to a German dealer. Golf production grew rapidly – numbers had to be increased after three months to meet demand – and by autumn 1974 was confidently set at 3,000 units a day. It became the best-selling car in West Germany, and by the end of 1974 production of the new generation was running at 69% Golf, 20% Audi 50 and 11% Passat. Yet in spite of this highly acclaimed product Volkswagen was once more in dire financial trouble.

It had spent DM 2.5bn on its new model range but had been running at a loss since autumn 1973. Production costs in Germany continued to rise and the fall in the value of the dollar relative to the mark was killing sales in the US (see panel on page 58), which fell by 30%. While its new cars were fuel-efficient the oil crisis and a stock-market crash had plunged the world's motor industry into recession and sales also slumped in Europe. The number of Volkswagen employees rose with the success of the Passat to 215,000 but had to be reduced in 1974 to 204,000 through early retirement, voluntary redundancy and transfers within the company.

Leiding's replacement from February 1975, Toni

← April 1974 and Volkswagen presents its newest model, the Golf, to the British press in a matter-of-fact way. Its promise of right-hand drive cars in October went adrift. (Giles Chapman Library)

Schmücker, finally agreed with the unions to lay off a further 25,000 people by the end of 1976 and close down Audi-NSU plants at Heilbronn and Nuenstein. Most workers returned as the company became profitable after August 1975. By 1977 Volkswagen employed 192,000 worldwide.

Golf in the UK

British buyers did not get hold of right-hand drive Golfs until early 1975, restricted to 1.1-litre versions until the second half of the year when the 1.5-litre arrived. British buyers were only offered the latter in five-door form in LS trim, sporting carpet throughout, a heated rear window, reclining seats, extra instrumentation, servo-assisted brakes and radial tyres as standard. Three-door 1.5 S and LS models were not available in the UK because the importers considered it to be a predominantly five-door market.

Launched with a six-model range in February 1975 prices started at £1,349 for the Golf N to the £1,756 four-door LS, although they soon went up. The N was a UK-specific base model with a slightly higher specification than the German equivalent, with an

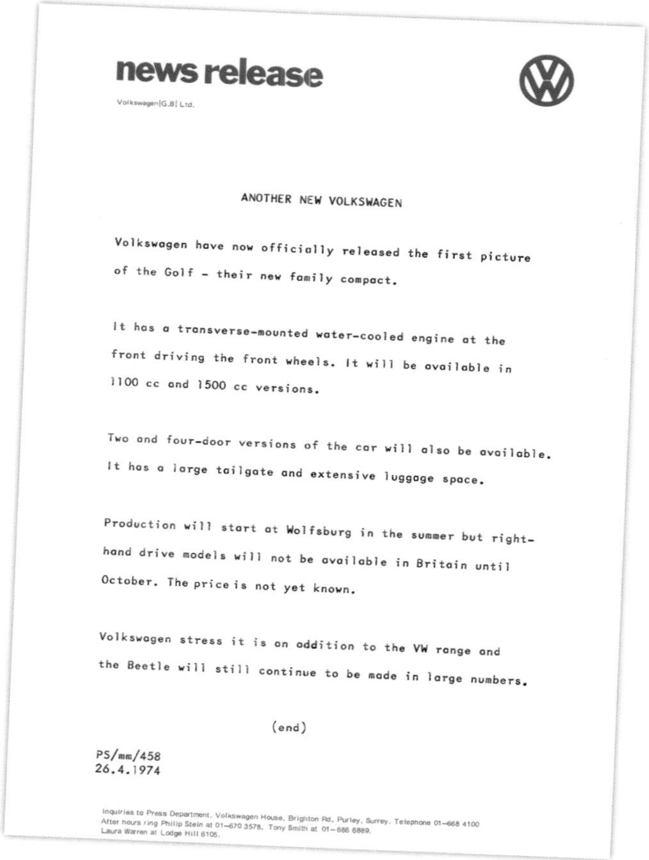

news release

Volkswagen(G.B.) Ltd.

ANOTHER NEW VOLKSWAGEN

Volkswagen have now officially released the first picture of the Golf – their new family compact.

It has a transverse-mounted water-cooled engine at the front driving the front wheels. It will be available in 1100 cc and 1500 cc versions.

Two and four-door versions of the car will also be available. It has a large tailgate and extensive luggage space.

Production will start at Wolfsburg in the summer but right-hand drive models will not be available in Britain until October. The price is not yet known.

Volkswagen stress it is an addition to the VW range and the Beetle will still continue to be made in large numbers.

(end)

PS/mm/458
26.4.1974

Inquiries to Press Department, Volkswagen House, Brighton Rd, Purley, Surrey. Telephone 01–668 4100
After hours ring Philip Stein at 01–670 3578. Tony Smith at 01–686 6889.
Laura Warren at Lodge Hill 6105.

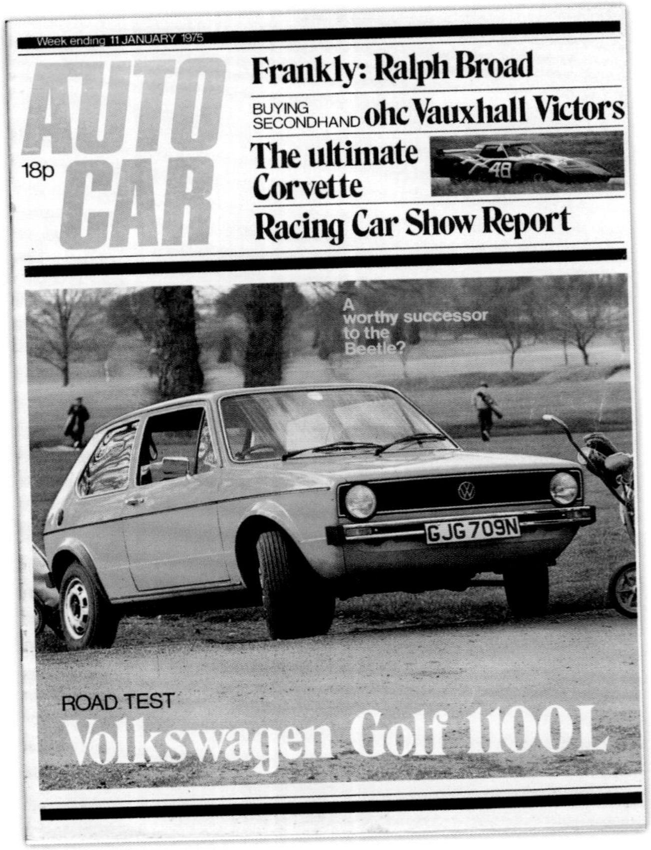

➔ **The British press had to wait over eight months for right-hand drive Golfs. *Autocar* took its 1100 to – of course – a golf course. (Author's collection)**

electric screen washer, a rear parcel shelf and disc front brakes (in Germany drums all round) but without servo assistance.

British magazine *Autocar* first tested an 1100 L in January 1975 and found it 'an outstandingly good example of what a second-generation front-drive east-west car ought to be', its designers having benefited from a later start on rivals such as the Fiat 128, Renault 5, Peugeot 104, Honda Civic, Datsun Cherry and Austin Allegro.

With the pound weak against the Deutsche Mark, a UK Golf 1100 L didn't present itself as good value at £1,538 but immediately impressed with its sophisticated handling: 'There is none of the tuck-in suffered by the Mini when the accelerator is released. Perhaps in panic, in mid-corner: the car stays on its line but the load on the steering wheel becomes less, encouraging the driver to haul the Golf into a tighter line. On main roads the Golf is very pleasant to drive, nicely stable and needing only gentle movements of the wheel to change its course.'

The magazine noted to its great surprise that the cross-ply tyres (made by Metzeler to VW specifications) handled as well as a good set of radials but that the ride was no better than average and could become bouncy, as it had 'almost sports car' firm damping. The pleasure of hustling the car along (performance a 'good class average') was, however, marred by a surprising amount of pressure being required for braking, even though UK Golfs had front discs there was no servo (only on the S and LS). The feel of the brakes was not helped by the brake master cylinder and servo (where fitted) staying on the left-hand side of the car during the conversion to right-hand drive, so required an extra linkage across the car. For this test in windy conditions the fuel consumption was lower than expected at 30.1mpg and it took 15.5 seconds to reach 60mph from rest, one second more than a Mini 1275GT.

Refinement was marred by the 'quite objectionable' amount of road noise generated by the standard cross-ply tyres, which was picked up by others, even the naturally loyal *Volkswagen Safer Motoring*. 'There is some vertical bounce over undulating roads, and the bumps and clonks of the suspension at work can be heard quite loudly at times. This was worse in the case of the basic model, fitted with cross-ply tyres, which I subsequently drove, but even the LS on radials compared rather poorly with the Beetle in this respect.'

As in Germany, British writers continued to compare it directly to the Beetle, searching for Beetle-like features in a car that only resembled it in having the same length wheelbase. One theme was the sealing of the doors. The door sealing on Beetles had such a good reputation for airtightness that it could be difficult to close a door without some effort.

As to the 1.5-litre road testers discovered to their surprise that the combination of the willing engine in the lightweight Golf made for semi-sportscar performance. *Autocar*'s 0–60mph figure of 12.5 seconds and near-100mph top speed put it very close to an 85bhp Scirocco TS on acceleration and in the same category as more overtly sporting cars such as the 1600 Ford Escort Sport or the 1800 MGB plus the 'sports' versions of the Alfa Romeo Alfasud and larger-engined Austin Allegro. 'Why Volkswagen have chosen to play down the performance aspect of the 1500 in their advertising and promotional material I cannot imagine' wrote Chris Goffey of *Autocar*'s long-term test car.

The Golf 1500 had a confusing career, becoming a 1600 in 1975 going from 1,471cc to 1,588cc (also seen in the Audi 80 GT and the future Golf GTI) but for only

← Chris Goffey of *Autocar* enjoying his long-term 1500 LS in 1975. As the sporting nature of the Golf became apparent, the ground for the GTI was being laid. (LAT)

↓ The five-door Golf shared the same wheelbase as the three-door but with shorter front doors. The edges of the tailgate wrapped around to form part of the side of the car, adding solidity and simplifying the production process.

↑ ← One dial means you are sitting in a basic Golf (left), two means it's an L or LS. Radio optional in both instances. (Volkswagen Classic)

← The rear seats tumbled forwards for a useful load bay, but a high loading sill remained a bugbear for several generations of Golf. (LAT)

a 5bhp increase over the original, only to go to 1,457cc in 1977. The change, said *Autocar*, was carried out for a mixture of mainland European marketing and taxation reasons and to allow the use of low-lead fuel as a prelude to unleaded. The unit was not in fact exactly the original 1.5 but a slimmed-down version of the 1,588cc unit, retaining its larger 79.5mm cylinder bore but shortening the stroke to 73.4mm. The new 1.5 was found to be slightly faster and more flexible than the old one.

The Volkswagen buyer was changing. In 1974/5 devoted British Beetle owners mostly vowed to go nowhere near the Golf at all and bought another used Beetle, but UK dealers reported most Golf customers were new to the marque and on the whole younger drivers who regarded the newcomer as sporty yet practical. In the first five months of 1975 8,255 Golfs were sold in Britain compared to 3,134 Beetles to late June. By late 1975 Volkswagen UK was only selling the 1200L Beetle and said it could sell 30% more Golfs if only enough production could be squeezed out.

Whilst sales were strong the very first Golfs were not without quality problems, the chief of which was corrosion. According to Ernst Fiala, a testing step had been missed while getting the Golf ready for production and cars had to be put back into an eight-week programme of driving round and round a salt bath until things started to fall off.

Owners found other small faults such as rattling tailgates, throttle and clutch cables which moved off their mounts in right-hand drive cars and German-built Golfs exported to the US as Rabbits were the subject of a complete recall programme in 1976.

Volkswagen quickly responded to quality and specification grumbles and by 1976 all UK Golfs had radial-ply tyres, more comfortable foam-filled seats, a modified pedal linkage for lighter braking, an improved heater and revised exhaust system. The success of the diesel and the Golf GTI re-established credibility although sales had not dipped. After 27 months in production the one millionth Golf left the assembly line on 27 October 1976.

The Rabbit – a Golf for America

When the Golf reached America in 1975 it had become the Volkswagen Rabbit, and its story was one of a success that rapidly turned sour.

In common with its competitors, Volkswagen would change model names to the tastes of different markets, especially the US. Each of the new generation gained a frisky animal name as it crossed the Atlantic: the 1972 Audi 80 became the Fox and the 1973 Volkswagen Passat became the Dasher. So the Golf became the Rabbit.

Perhaps something animal-related was on the cards given that Ford called its 1970 subcompact the Pinto, after a small horse. The author was not able to pin down the exact origins of Rabbit, but it had been market researched along with Pampero for Europe as Board papers in the archive from 1973 note that 'The rabbit is not a racy, elegant animal, but lively and one to love and stroke'. The Scirocco escaped an animal name and being called the Blizzard.

Coming after the 'Bug' the Rabbit was going for the cute vote. German buyers thought the name amusing enough that in 1976 a Hannover Volkswagen dealer reported a rush on Rabbit badges, selling several hundred at five DM each.

Whatever the name, Volkswagen of America was desperate to have a US-specified Golf, as in the wake of the 1973 oil crisis Toyota was rapidly forging ahead with its economical small cars. Before the Rabbit went on sale in America in January 1975 it had already gained top honours in the US Environmental Protection Agency fuel-consumption tests, bettering the Beetle in city and highway driving – 24 against 22 miles per US gallon (city) and 38 against 33 (highway) or in imperial, 26 and 39mpg respectively. US president Gerald Ford called for domestic manufacturers to improve fuel consumption by 40% or face legislation.

Rabbits were marked out from Golfs by larger bumpers mounted on struts, which with body reinforcement added about 70kg to the weight of the car. The indicators were within the grille alongside rectangular headlamps (as Giugiaro had originally designed), and oblong reflective side markers were fitted to the front and rear sides. There were head restraints on all models and interior trim changed to reflect domestic tastes with dashboards matching seats, door panels and the steering wheel. This was later realised to be a mistake.

All Rabbits sold in America, like the Scirocco, were initially fitted with the 70bhp 1,471cc engine coupled to a catalytic converter. The more powerful versions of the Scirocco engine apparently could not be certified for US emission rules.
Both were available with optional auto and dealer-fitted air conditioning.

They also came equipped with an elaborate seatbelt system, which most Europeans found baffling (although seatbelt use was not widespread). The 1975 model year Rabbit was the first car in the US market with an optional $30 fully passive system where the seatbelt was part anchored to the front door so to enter the

↓ German enthusiasts thought this badge amusing enough to buy one for themselves. There was a ruder non-VW version. (Volkswagen of America)

↓ The Golf became the Rabbit when it arrived in America in 1978. A hatchback was an unusual (and economy car) feature. (Volkswagen of America)

car you were obliged to 'step into' the belt which then tightened around you as you sat down. Magazine *Road and Track* said this came as something of a 'cultural shock'.

But the rising value of the Deutsche Mark against the dollar looked set to handicap the Rabbit even before it had gone on sale. All Volkswagen's US prices increased substantially for 1975. The price of the basic Beetle rose $270 to $2,900 before delivery charges, $100 more than the base prices for the Ford Pinto and Chevrolet Vega. A basic Rabbit was around $3,100 – about the same price as a small domestic six-cylinder and already fuel economy worries were waning in buyer's minds.

Nonetheless at first the critics loved the Rabbit: 'Best car in the world for under $3,500,' said *Road & Track*, 'the Rabbit, like the Beetle, represents something special in an economy sedan.' But an extended test found VW's service image 'tarnished', the car suffering engine-mount problems, needing carburettor and driveline modifications to cure starting and stalling problems.

Volkswagen of America led an extensive recall programme in 1976 to upgrade 1975 models and for the 1976 Rabbit, Dasher and Scirocco went to the 1,588cc engine and it was judged to be finally sorted out. 1977 was the last year for the Beetle saloon in the US and all Rabbits and Sciroccos became fuel injected. The Rabbit convertible arrived in 1980, a year after Europe, and more closely resembled the Golf, remaining German-built and retaining round headlamps.

Appearing even more novel to American than European buyers, the Rabbit diesel became an unexpected hit. A major attraction for Volkswagen was that it could sail through 1976 US emissions regulations by some margin without having any extra anti-pollution equipment. At first it carried only a $170 price premium.

The performance figures were virtually the same as the European diesel Golfs and its 0–60mph figure was in the same league as a number of sporty imported petrol cars (albeit tuned to meet US emissions) including the Fiat X1/9. But it demanded a resourcefulness said *Car and Driver*: 'The biggest problem of course will be buying fuel for the diesel, a routine that requires as much discipline as anything. Still, with a theoretical 550 miles per tank it isn't something you would have to do every other day.' The bugbears of the 'bargain bunny' became the escalating cost of diesel, the messy nature of fill-ups with a restrictive fuel-filler opening, a fragile oil line (soon fixed in service) and the lack of supply in anything other than truck stops.

↑ There was no avoiding the passive safety belt, it wrapped around you as you got in. Note the padded lower dashboard shelf, which acted to protect the legs in place of a lap belt. (Volkswagen of America)

Home-grown Golf

As far back as 1957 Volkswagen had considered building cars in the USA and bought a plant in New Jersey for Beetle assembly, but it was sold when a study showed little difference between producing cars there and in Germany.

The idea was revived in the early 1970s by Rudolph Leiding as the boom years turned to a wobble. Between 1973 and 1976 Volkswagen of America's sales dropped from 540,364 to 238,167, and in 1975 Toyota overtook Volkswagen for the first time ever in the US (283,000 to 268,000).

The alternative to American manufacture would have been to make Rabbits in Mexico and import them into the USA, (from '77 they were made for the Mexican market as the Caribe) but it was felt this would harm the company's image. Volkswagen boss Rudolf Leiding (see Chapter 1) started work on a plan for US manufacture. Late in 1973 Volkswagen confirmed that a small study group was to head over to the US to look at possible plant

The Rabbit – a Golf for America (continued)

sites, but determined opposition from the unions and Board drove Leiding out of office at the end of 1974.

As feared, in 1975, its first full year of US sale, the Rabbit was being out-priced due to the strength of the Deutsche Mark, and it was reported Volkswagen of America was losing money on every one. The official reason for a tailing off in sales was a supply problem, down to 7,000 cars a month from 13,000 that spring. The starting price of $3,300 was seen as a real handicap.

New boss Toni Schmücker was making severe cuts at home but US production was back on the table. By September 1975 a team was in place looking over idle assembly plants, and the feasibility of using an existing workforce and management team, or even having another carmaker assemble the cars.

Three Chrysler plants were said to be in prospect and one from Ford. Initially Volkswagen had wanted to co-operate with a domestic manufacturer (AMC was rumoured) but opted to go it alone and selected a plant in New Stanton, south of Pittsburgh, Pennsylvania, which Chrysler had built in 1969 but never occupied as its sales dropped. Volkswagen named it the Westmoreland assembly plant. The ground space was about the size of 35 football pitches.

Engines and transmissions were to be shipped from Germany for 1978 production and Volkswagen sourced most other materials from US and Canadian suppliers. It was envisaged to have 2,500

↓ Blue vinyl and plastic was thought to be to American tastes but not, as it turned out, in a German car. (Volkswagen of America)

workers at start-up with 5,000 on full production in the early 1980s turning out 200,000 vehicles a year. The HQ was being set up in Warren, Michigan, and the connection to rabbits was not lost.

The first Rabbit rolled off the Westmoreland line in April 1978. There was great optimism, and of course it had to work. In September 1978 Schmücker told Edouard Siedler: 'All of our research proves that it will be very important [building cars locally] psychologically. When we have demonstrated that the Golf-Rabbit, a symbol of craftsmanship can be manufactured in the US as well as in Germany the public will have a feeling of pride and consequently of added identification with our cars. We will benefit from a nationalistic reaction on the part of buyers who do not like to buy foreign products. The Rabbit will be considered an American car in a relatively short period. Of course we must maintain our VW identity.'

Rabbit sales rose from 149,170 in 1978 to 214,835 in 1979, but the Westmoreland scheme was no lasting solution to what followed. Faced with intense competition from Japanese carmakers, and having prospered in the 1979–81 period when US manufacturers themselves were struggling, Volkswagen of America's production was halved and overall sales including Porsche and Audi were down by one third to 230,000 vehicles. The plunge in Rabbit sales was even more dramatic in 1982, down to 91,166 units. The interest in the diesel had proven to be short-lived and it had accounted for 70% of production. Car plants across America were closing down and a planned second Volkswagen factory in Sterling Heights near Detroit was sold to Chrysler before it was used. The Jetta saloon maintained more stable sales, running at about 20,000 cars a year at the start of the 1980s.

Aside from diesel motoring going suddenly out of fashion, the blame was put squarely at the 'Americanisation' of the Rabbit in looks and handling. The signals had been clear from the enthusiast magazines, which had been carping about the 'flabby' seats and poor finish compared to German Golfs. Head of Volkswagen since 1982 when Schmücker retired due to ill health, Carl Hahn was candid in a 1983 interview with *Autocar*: 'A European driver used to the Golf could fly off the road in the first turn with a Rabbit ... There was a lack of insight on the part of our American management who had a lot of freedom in their decisions at the time. They thought that what was good for America would be good for VW there. They were obviously wrong. We discovered that Americans now want a car with European qualities when they buy a European car.'

↑ The 1984 US Rabbit GTI seats were made in the USA and described as 'functional duplicates' of those in the Golf GTI. (Volkswagen of America)

→ With the Volkswagen Rabbit GTI, America had a performance Volkswagen just as Europe moved to the second-generation Golf. (Volkswagen of America)

Rabbit GTI – better late than never

Jim Fuller was moved from being vice president of Porsche and Audi in America to troubleshoot Volkswagen's problems in 1981. An internal corporate campaign called 'Roots' was initiated to 'Germanise' the cars with firmer suspension, better seats and more understated trim: 'We're through Malibuing these cars around!' he notably said in a reference to a conservative Chevrolet of the day.

However, the real hope for a Rabbit image revival lay with the introduction of an American GTI, hitherto ignored. In November 1981 *Motor Trend* had written an open letter to VW of America moaning that it had only ever been interested in selling economy cars. For the keen driver the Westmoreland-built Rabbit S was not enough. A new engine needed to be certified for a cost of $250,000 which could be recouped if it only sold 20,000 cars.

Ditching the idea of just adding GTI suspension to the Rabbit S, Fuller took up the challenge. The Rabbit engine was bored out from the stock 1,715cc to 1,781cc – matching the European Golf – with a compression ratio raised from 8.21:1 to 8.5:1. Larger valves were fitted with a lower-restriction exhaust system allied to a re-engineered catalytic converter to reduce back pressure. The five-speed gearbox was imported from Germany with the European GTI's sporting ratios. Thus the Rabbit GTI produced 90hp at 5,500rpm.

By 1982 this was of course 22bhp down on the Golf GTI, but the change was found to increase flexibility and refinement, with a top speed of 104mph and 0–60mph in 9.7 seconds. The car was also 63kg heavier and the suspension was made 22% stiffer than the standard Rabbit, with anti-roll bars front and rear. It sat on 14in alloy wheels newly introduced for the Volkswagen Quantum (a booted Passat/Dasher).

The Rabbit GTI was previewed in November 1982 for the 1983 model year whilst in Germany the Golf was about to be replaced. *Car & Driver* called it 'the most exciting automotive news of the year'. It was a much needed boost for the Rabbit's patchy image, but sales slipped to 68,362 in 1984 awaiting the second-generation Golf. This discarded the Rabbit name the following year only for it to stage a brief revival with the 2006–09 US-only Golf 5.

↑ A basic Golf at the October 1974 London Motor Show. Its price was considered relatively high. (LAT)

The first diesel revolution

In the early 1970s, despite the durability and fuel economy offered by the diesel engine it was largely confined to industrial and commercial-vehicle use. The diesel is also known as the compression-ignition engine, which operates by igniting injected diesel fuel at the end of a high compression piston stroke rather than a spark plug. The process created a great deal of noise and demanded heavyweight engine construction. In 1970 about 57,000 diesel cars were registered in Germany, but they were noisy and underpowered machines reserved only for the most serious high-mileage business user. However, development started to pick up notably by Mercedes and Peugeot, which extended its diesel engine range down to the smaller 204 in 1974, with Opel and Fiat both starting to invest.

The 1973 oil crisis and increasingly tough exhaust emission regulations brought the diesel back into focus and Volkswagen had already made the decision to move into the 1½-ton diesel and petrol truck market with the front-engined, water-cooled LT van – a larger companion to the Type 2 Transporter. The idea of putting a diesel into a Golf was not, however, on the agenda. 'On a hot summer day in 1973 I proposed it to Fiala, but he was already on this trip,' Peter Hofbauer recalls. 'At that time we had a monthly meeting with Mr Leiding, and he was very excited about a rotary engine (KA4/5) which I developed in the early 70s because it would have been cheap to manufacture. I proposed stopping his beloved rotary engine programme and starting a diesel programme.'

'We thought that the diesel would fit well with the philosophy of Volkswagen,' Fiala said. 'VW has a name for economy and reliability and the diesel car goes well with that.' A passenger car application was envisaged, with the Passat the prime candidate.

Hofbauer's team bought a Peugeot diesel and turbocharged it in ten days. The first prototype Leiding saw was on the test rig after three months. It was based on the established Audi EA827 petrol engine, which although not designed with any thought of a diesel conversion had a block strong enough to withstand the greater internal pressures associated with the diesel combustion process. As a result the diesel version was only 18kg (40lb) heavier than the 102kg (225lb) standard 1,471cc engine. It used the same block, crankshaft, connecting rods and bearings, and it was assembled on the same production line, but the injection system, cylinder head and other heavy-duty parts added cost.

The cylinder head used the Ricardo Comet Mk V swirl-chamber design (as did Peugeot and Opel), allowing a compression ratio of 23.5:1 (the petrol was 8.2:1) and gave maximum cylinder-head surface for optimum valve-head diameter. By paying great attention to head-gasket sealing, Volkswagen could retain the four-cylinder head bolts of the petrol engine's block (Mercedes used six) meaning it could be built on the same line with only a small diversion. One of the main reasons for the production engine's relative quietness was the use of a Bosch distributor-type injection pump, which had no noisy camshaft and plunger arrangement but worked with pure rotary motion. It was mounted on the front side of the block, inboard of the alternator, with a belt-driven horizontal shaft that carried the high-pressure pump and a distribution head. Fuel lines to the individual injector nozzles branched off from outlets, radially disposed around the central shaft, in a pattern similar to an ignition distributor.

However, Hofbauer recounts that when Toni Schmücker became CEO in early 1975, he stopped the diesel programme for the Golf immediately. 'But Fiala, [Ferdinand] Piëch and I tricked the PSK by claiming it should be developed for the Type 2. This was approved and after three months we put it back in the Golf.'

The diesels were tested on public roads in Germany and the VW test grounds at Ehra-Lessien, modified step by step to the production-ready version. Development cars were sent to other markets such as Brazil and the US, and 200 Golfs and Passats were built for a worldwide large-scale test in 1976 in places such as Scandinavia and Africa, loaded with extras such as automatic gearboxes and air conditioning. Volume production started at the former K70 and now Volkswagen engine plant in Salzgitter in August 1976 with initial daily output a conservative 100 engines.

'I managed, for the first time in history, to produce a gasoline and a diesel engine on the same transfer line,' said Hofbauer. 'We could switch during any regular break – about 20 minutes – from gasoline to diesel, according to demand. It was also the first time that a diesel was delivered to the car assembly lines without calibrating it on test benches, due to handling the tolerances in a

↓ Outwardly similar to a petrol-engined Golf, the 'D' badge marked the start of an automotive revolution.

↑ **Quite a bit of plumbing is apparent for the diesel injection system.**

↓ **A warning sticker on the windscreen of a 1976 launch Golf diesel warns the driver to 'preheat' the engine by ignition key position. The fuel-enrichment knob is to the left of the steering column.**

modern way. To calibrate 2,000 diesels a day we would have needed an additional factory.'

Apart from ease of manufacture, the new engine was revolutionary compared to the competition, which had larger and heavier engines producing far less power. The Golf's 50bhp 1.5-litre unit may have been down 20bhp on its petrol equivalent, but Peugeot took 2.3 litres to extract 60bhp and the 2.0-litre Mercedes diesel produced only 61bhp. It was easy to grasp that a 1.5-litre Golf diesel gave the same power as a 1.1-litre petrol but much greater fuel economy.

The motoring press was treated to a visit to Stockholm in September 1976. Like most journals *Autocar* approached the drive with huge scepticism of how nasty it would be with noise and sluggish performance. The starting procedure of competitor diesels from cold was a laborious process of warming up the combustion chamber by turning on glow plugs and waiting for them to go out. The Golf D could be started from cold without pre-heating if the ambient temperature was above 24 degrees C, but otherwise you turned the ignition key to its first position and waited for a light to go out after 15–45 seconds. 'Obviously the first thing to be done was to try and start the engine without a glow-plug warm-up period,' *Autocar* quipped. 'Surprise, with just two or three turns of the crankshaft the engine burst into life, and despite the cold, it settled to a regular tickover that would not be more annoying than a petrol engine whose choke was adjusted to give a little too much increase in idling speed.' The driver was asked to use a cold start knob next to the steering wheel from cold to avoid a puff of blue smoke and this could be pushed in after about 200 metres.

Once warmed up, the magazine found little difference in interior noise or throttle response – especially considering diesels at the time had a sudden bout of engine braking if the throttle was released quickly – and concluded that it was a remarkable device: 'After half an hour of driving, one had completely forgotten that there was anything "funny" about the car.' The best consumption figure on the test route was 59mpg, the worst 33.5 and in more controlled test conditions *Autocar* achieved a 46mpg average compared to the 1.1 petrol's 33 in 1978. It considered a figure of 40.1mpg on a fast motorway run to be 'amazing'.

As a 'dress rehearsal' prior to the Golf diesel going on sale, 300 diesel Volkswagens had been tested by employees and dealers. Salespeople were equipped with simple explanations of how a diesel worked and why this one was the best for urban fuel consumption, reduced air pollution, simpler servicing and long life.

However, no matter how good the diesel Golf was, its case was always an economic one, as Volkswagen admitted. There was always a premium to pay for the engine – although a £300 premium when introduced in Germany was a reflection of the controlled manufacturing cost, but, as was to be the case for decades to come, the amount of duty governments

The Volkswagen Caddy

Looking for another model to add to its US-manufactured Rabbit line, Volkswagen of America developed a pick-up as its own project with the help of engineers from Chevrolet. Identical to the saloon until the back of the front doors, the rear bodywork was replaced by a ladder-type chassis with simple leaf-and-coil springs to cope with a higher payload of 625kg. Its load bay made it half a metre longer and the wheelbase was stretched to 2.62 metres.

Built between 1979 and 1983 in the US, it found more favour in export markets, especially in South Africa, which loved small pick-ups or 'bakkies', and then Europe where it was introduced as the Caddy, with the standard Golf grille, in 1982. Production moved to Volkswagen's Sarajevo Tvornica Automobila (TAS) in the former Yugoslavia until 1992 and the outbreak of war (Golf production started there again in 2002). In South Africa the Caddy continued alongside the Citi Golf until 2007.

European Caddys could be ordered open or closed with a fibreglass hardtop and were fitted with many specialist adaptions from garbage trucks to caravans. The 1.6-litre 54bhp diesel engine was a natural choice for business users, but 1.6-litre 75bhp and 1.8-litre 95bhp petrol engines were also offered (the latter with a catalyst).

↑ Also built in Sarajevo, a TAS Golf. The TAS badge usually sat to the right of the VW symbol missing here. (Stiftung AutoMuseum)

↓ Once a project of Volkswagen of America, the Caddy migrated to Volkswagen in the former Yugoslavia and proved a versatile vehicle in Europe.

↑ **The diesel Golf was so novel that *Autocar* conducted a petrol vs diesel test in August 1976. The red diesel nearest recorded a 'phenomenal' 65.2mpg. (LAT)**

↓ **For a landmark car the first Golf GTI made a discreet appearance at the 1975 Frankfurt show, here nearest left amidst regular Golfs. (LAT)**

levied on diesel fuel made them uneconomic unless you covered vast mileages. When the Golf diesel arrived in the UK in 1978, 4% of cars in Germany were diesels and 6% in France where the price difference over petrol was a considerable 46p a gallon compared to 4p in Britain. Praiseworthy though it was, the first Golf diesel remained a minority taste in Britain while on the other side of the Atlantic demand unexpectedly boomed for a while. The Volkswagen Golf was to see a long association with the diesel engine and usher in many further innovations.

Sport Golf to GTI

The other big news of 1976 was, in hindsight, an innovation just as smart as the high-revving Golf diesel: the high performance petrol-engined GTI. It was even more of an unplanned derivative (see panel on page 72), but while there had been performance-orientated saloon cars before like the Mini Cooper – and it could be said that the Simca 1300 TI of 1974 was approaching a 'hot hatch' – the Golf's usable performance and the cachet of fuel injection was the magic combination.

As Volkswagen had no new product to show, the GTI prototype had been pushed in as a prototype for the September 1975 Frankfurt Motor Show to an incredulous reaction from press and public. Production had been cautiously sanctioned on the basis of a minimum of 5,000 sales – enough to spread around the dealer network and also to homologate the car for Group 1 Production Touring Car motor sport. It was not even two days' overall production of standard Golfs.

Volkswagen hadn't dressed up the respectably fast Golf 1.5 in sporting guise and there was no obvious market for the GTI. If you wanted a sporty car with a dose of practicality there were numerous four-seat coupes on the market, including Volkswagen's very own Scirocco. Hatchbacks were not sporting. Who might need to move a fridge that quickly?

But to enthusiasts the specification of this three-door-only Golf was mouth-watering, above all the use of fuel injection, hitherto reserved for elite and very expensive cars. The system's name, Bosch K-Jetronic, was to have an enduring ring to enthusiasts' ears. With a 9.5:1 compression ratio (a standard Golf 1600 was 8.2:1) the new 1,588cc fuel-injected Audi 80 GTE unit produced 110bhp at 6,100rpm – 57% more power than the Golf

↑ The 1976 Golf GTI in all its simplicity with small plain bumpers, steel wheels, a blacked-out VW badge and red piping around the grille. The black plastic wheel arch extensions fitted neatly.

↓ The larger EA827-series engine was inclined to the rear. The fuel injection system sat on top and an oil cooler was mounted alongside the radiator. (LAT)

↑ **This launch publicity shot aims to position the GTI as a businessman's express in the mould of the small BMWs of the early 1970s.**

↓ **Tartan sports seats, a golf ball gear lever, extra instruments and a sports wheel marked the GTI out from a basic Golf. (LAT)**

1500. Its kerb weight of 780kg (dry, no fuel) was only 30kg more than a 1974 1100 three-door.

With a four-speed gearbox the claimed acceleration times were 0 to 100kph (62.5mph) in nine seconds, a top speed of 182kph (113mph) and a DIN fuel consumption of 36mpg. It was faster accelerating than larger cars with larger engines such as the Ford Escort RS1800, BMW 520i, the Alfa Romeo 2000 and the Triumph Dolomite Sprint.

At first some thought this was simply too much in a small car. 'The press was very negative,' Fiala recalls. 'They said it's very aggressive, such a light car; 800 kilos with 110bhp you will have millions of injuries and people killed, but after the press really drove the car they corrected their understanding. This was only for a few weeks and then the discussion was over.'

The suspension was lowered by 20mm from the standard Golf with shorter springs and stiffer damper settings and the track widened by 14mm thanks to its 175/70HR13 radial tyres on 5.5J 13in rims. The front brake discs were ventilated, matched to a larger servo and a rear-wheel pressure regulator valve.

Nearest in trim to a Golf S, the GTI was marked by a matt black radiator grille, black plastic wheel arch trims covering the standard Golf's flared wheel arches and a black stripe on the lower half of the door joining the wheel arches. A deep plastic front spoiler was there to counteract the nose lifting. At launch the only exterior colours were red or silver. The effect was enough to distinguish it from a regular Golf but also not so much that the driver of a lesser model could see their car as 'almost a GTI'. A rear wash/wipe was standard fitment, one which those drivers often wished they had.

Black was *de rigueur* for sporting cars in the 1970s but the GTI's interior was funereal, with black headlining, carpets, dashboard, door panels and even sun visors. As a limited edition squeezed out on a tight budget, most of this was taken from basic Golfs, meaning the dashboard lacked a cover for the glove compartment. Some parts were borrowed from the Scirocco TS such as the steering wheel and some braking components. However, it did get Recaro bucket seats with the now famous tartan pattern credited to Gunhild Liljequist, a Volkswagen trim and colour designer from 1965 to 1992. The famous golf-ball gear knob is also credited to her. An oil-pressure gauge, rev counter, quartz headlamps and a heated rear window with a rear wash/wipe completed the equipment. The person behind the signature red strip round the radiator grille is uncredited.

Having created a flurry of excitement at Frankfurt, would-be GTI buyers had to sit on their money until summer 1976. In the meantime, German tuner Oettinger jumped in with a conversion of the Golf LS which involved transplanting the 100bhp 1.6-litre carburettor engine from the Audi 80 GT plus extra sports equipment for almost DM 6,000 more at 16,258. Its appeal can't have lasted long, as after nine months of final development and extensive durability testing the Golf GTI was unveiled in June 1976 at DM 13,850, accompanied by the new Scirocco GTI with the same running gear.

In its July 1976 edition *Auto Motor und Sport* was completely won over by the 'conspicuously inconspicuous' GTI. The author declared that the best part of the interior was the sports seats in which he would happily have driven 800km down French country roads.

↓ The first Golf GTI was launched alongside a Scirocco with the same engine, but it was the Golf that would cause more of a sensation.

➔ MKT 512R was the first left-hand-drive UK-registered Golf GTI tested by the British press. It came with alloy wheels, optional on other Golfs. (LAT)

The measured figures were 0–100kph (0–62mph) in 9.4 seconds and a top speed of 185kph (115mph). 'Who would have thought a few years ago that a mass-produced Volkswagen would be capable of this?'

Yet progress seemed so unruffled in this new Golf. There was praise for the calm way in which the car handled its power from the flexibility of the engine (although the 75bhp 1.6 was found to better it in some in-gear times), improved fuel consumption from the fuel injection and only a slight loss in overall comfort from the standard car. 'One of the most delightful tasks a driver can have is to climb an Alpine pass in a GTI.'

Motorway comfort and stability were equally praiseworthy up until about 170kph (105mph) when the front end of the GTI started to become light, despite the presence of the spoiler – a minor point in the test, which concluded that the new Golf was the true successor to the small BMW sports saloons.

For English readers John Bolster, famed correspondent of *Autosport* wrote: 'The new GTI Volkswagens are such outstanding cars that for once I am at a loss to find anything serious to criticise. They combine performance with refinement, extremely quick cornering with side-wind stability, and speed with safety. I can't say fairer than that.'

It was hoped to achieve the 5,000 sales for homologation by October 1976 but the GTI soon exceeded sales expectations, former public relations director Anton Konrad told the author in 2013. He had been part of the original team behind the GTI. 'We pushed the price from DM 10,790 for the Golf LS up

➔ Richard Lloyd in action in what was said to have been the first Golf GTI imported in to the UK, 1977.

In 1978 the Golf GTI was given sturdier wraparound plastic-covered bumpers. The UK only ever knew three-door first-series GTIs but Germany, Belgium and South Africa offered the GTI 1.8 as a five-door.

to 13,850 for the GTI. It was high, but on a small production number it was reasonable. But when we started selling the car in '76 people asked for more cars, more cars, so we increased the production numbers from 50 a day up to 500. The price was very high but they didn't reduce it when the sales register went up.'

The question of British sale was raised as soon as the prototype appeared at Frankfurt in 1975 and then 'negotiations' were said to be going on with Wolfsburg. For what was thought to be small-scale production a right-hand drive version hadn't been envisaged and the British June 1976 press release knocked the idea on the head while offering left-hand drive Golf and Scirocco GTIs to special order in September: 'For technical reasons it will not be possible to produce right-hand drive versions. Volkswagen (GB), who are investigating the motor sport potential for both cars, are importing them mainly for competition drivers.'

With booming sales in mainland Europe the special orders did not filter through until spring 1977. *Autocar* magazine of course pounced on MKT 512R, the first British press demonstrator in March 1977 with the caveat that left-hand drive would be unusual for many

continued on page 75

This 1978 GTI retains the original tail lamps, but for 1981 these were replaced by wider units shared with other Golfs and a new dashboard.

Who invented the GTI?

The trouble with a legend is the more it grows the more people want to be a part of it; none more so than the Golf GTI, the car that spawned dozens of imitators and gained instant cult status.

However, for a vast combine such as Volkswagen in the 1970s, the origins of the GTI can indeed be traced not to the product strategy committee but to a bunch of enthusiastic individuals working on their own unofficial project. The two names credited with the earliest involvement are the development engineer also responsible for the press fleet, Alfons Löwenberg, and PR director Anton Konrad, both of whom had strong motor sport backgrounds.

Löwenberg had been a member of Opel's experimental motor sport department from 1967 to 1970 and came to Volkswagen with ideas. 'I think in August 1972 Anton Konrad and I discussed the sense – or nonsense – of motor sport engagement for a passenger car production company,' he told the author in 2013. 'We agreed that it would be much more profitable to support private passenger car sports drivers than things like Formula Vee [Beetle-based engine racing]. Later on, the more I knew about VW products in design and development, the more I intended to introduce my knowledge in motor sport.'

However, while Ford and Opel increased their competition efforts, sporting derivatives were not on the agenda for Volkswagen, turning out four new models in three years (Passat, Scirocco, Golf and Polo). Especially so in the post-oil crisis 1974 as Konrad adds: 'When we launched the Scirocco the motorways were closed on Sundays so the situation was against cars and traffic. The engineers had to talk about fuel-consumption reduction and other things, not making sport cars. The official order was that nobody should have anything to do with creating sports cars.'

There had, however, been an indication of an appetite for a sports Volkswagen in 1973 with the unexpected enthusiasm for a limited-edition Beetle finished in yellow with black engine cover and bonnet, sports seats and wide wheels called the 1303S *Gelb-Schwarzer Renner* (GSR). With no more power than the standard 50bhp, owners were supplied with a list of tuning firms. A total of 3,500 were built between December 1972 and February 1973 and apparently caused political concern because Volkswagens were not supposed to be driven fast. There was later a Sports Bug for the US market.

Löwenberg was convinced that the Golf, not yet in production, had the ingredients to be a competitive rally car. On 18 March 1973 he wrote a memo to six senior managers, among them head of research and development Dr Fiala, head of car trials Dr Friedrich Goes, Anton Konrad and Hermann Hablitzel, manager of passenger car development. The memo noted which sporting models were no longer built that had a power-to-weight ratio similar to a Golf 1.5 like the NSU Prinz, BMW 2000 and Opel Kadett. Comparing them to the Golf he suggested it could also be used to encourage private motor sport entrants. Then he listed some essentials to introduce a sporty car, which he named the Sport Golf. According to FIA-Group 1 cars, these would be a 1,600cc 100bhp engine, 5-speed transmission, 6x15in wheels, ventilated disc brakes, oil cooling and bucket seats or similar.

'My memo was discussed at a meeting of engineers with Fiala,' he recalls. 'Hermann Hablitzel had really made the initiative his own and strongly pleaded for it. From Fiala, I got the impression that he had strong reservations against it from the start.'

With no official backing Hablitzel set up an unofficial working group led by Löwenberg, which included specialists who dealt in wheels, tyres and suspension, and bodywork. All the while Anton Konrad was a link between Horst-Dieter Schwittlinsky (marketing) and research and development. Special parts for the Sport Golf prototype were made in the test trials area. A number of discussions about the project were held away from the factory at Konrad's house. He and Schwittlinsky kept their board members positive for the project and were supported by the PR managers of the importers, especially Sweden, France and Italy. Konrad also started to arrange press events with a 'sports' theme, bringing along modified race or rally cars. In 1974 VW Motorsport at Hannover created a 1,500cc Group 1 Golf for Freddy Kottulinsky.

'After our first meeting we gave the order to Löwenberg to make a car in this direction; not a racing car, not a noisy car,' Konrad told the author. He recalls that he got hold of a pre-production Golf [official accounts have this as a Scirocco], a number of which were released for experimental engineering, and built the first Sport Golf with 6x13in wheels, lower springs, different shock absorbers, several parts via contacts at tuners Kamei and Bilstein, then an engine from 'friends' at engine testing. At the time Volkswagen itself was responsible for transverse installed engines and adapted the longitudinal Audi unit for transverse installation. The 1,588cc GT – on sale since 1973 – produced 100bhp with a twin-choke Solex carburettor. He had tried a twin-choke carburettor from a K70 on a 1.5-litre engine but this was discarded.

According to Volkswagen's own account this first Sport Golf was declared officially as a 'disguised chassis prototype', far more rally than road car with hard suspension and a sports exhaust and huge wheels and tyres (205/60HR13s when a Porsche 911 ran on 185/70 tyres). Löwenberg is said to have showed it to Fiala at the Ehra-Lessien test track in spring 1975 and he was sufficiently convinced. Encouraged by road-test reports, which suggested the Golf 1.5 was rather sportier than Volkswagen realised, and the need to have something new for Frankfurt in September, the Sport Golf project got official backing in May 1975.

Six prototypes were created in various states of civility, from a raw road-racer to a comfortable version. Herbert Schäfer, chief stylist since 1973, took control of the low-key and low-cost styling modifications, and Herbert Schuster, the new test manager arrived from Audi and later to be dubbed 'father of the GTI', developed the winning combination of wheel, tyre and suspension settings to give the best blend of sporting handling and comfort.

The ever growing Volkswagen-Audi parts bin came up with the final magic ingredient – fuel injection, which made the GTI fast yet utterly docile at low speeds. The Audi 80 GT and Passat were about to adopt fuel injection as a way of meeting US emission regulations and power was an important 10bhp more at 110. Anton Konrad recalls discussing the Sport Golf project at Ingolstadt with Ferdinand Piëch, by now heading Audi technical development. 'I came back with Dr Piëch having agreed to give us 5,000 engines before the Audi car became public.' Löwenberg might have preferred carburettors but Konrad admits these would have been impractical: 'To try and train customer service on how to service the Weber dual carburettor for just 5,000 cars was unthinkable!'

The Audi 80 GTE and Golf GTI duly appeared at the Frankfurt Motor Show on 11 September 1975. Herbert Schuster said the Volkswagen was labelled GTI merely to distinguish it from the Audi (the 'E' stood for Einspritzung, German for injection) the Golf's 'I' was never defined but much copied. For a car only predicted to be good for 5,000 sales a year the first Golf GTI sold more than 450,000 between 1976 and 1983, about 8% of first-generation Golf production.

➔ The press was let loose in Golf GTIs at the Hockenheim racing circuit in June 1976. The idea of a sports Golf was of great interest.

The Golf GTI 16S

As GTI competitors continued to appear in more powerful guises, Volkswagen France was especially concerned since by 1981 30% of petrol-engined Golf sales were GTIs.

The division looked to keep the GTI at the top of buyers' lists by offering a 136bhp version, named 16S (for 16 soupapes, French for valves) with a belt-driven cylinder head conversion by German tuner Oettinger or, to give it its full title, Oettinger Kraftfahrtechnische Spezial Anstalt, the company founded by Gerhard Oettinger in 1951, which had a long history of Volkswagen performance parts and had presented its 16-valve cylinder head in 1977.

The conversion entailed special pistons for the higher compression ratio (10.5:1 as opposed to 9.5:1), a balanced crankshaft and connecting rods, and modified oil sump and pump. The 16S took GTI power from 110 to 136bhp and a claimed maximum speed of 121mph. A front anti-roll bar was fitted and a BBS bodykit matching the colour of the car plus four headlamps and unique badging marked out the French super-GTI.

For the 16S to be sold with a full factory warranty through French Volkswagen dealers, the parent company demanded extensive tests. It was also homologated for Group 4 racing (400 examples needing to be produced) whereby Oettinger was sent standard GTIs from Wolfsburg to be fitted with the modified engines.

↑ The Oettinger cylinder-head conversion was a test bed for the company's own development for the Golf 2.

↓ The France-only Golf GTI 16S was the first 16-valve GTI and had its own badging and styling.

Produced between August 1981 and July 1983, the 16S conversion was viewed with interest in Wolfsburg. 'The Oettinger conversion wasn't suitable for large manufacturing runs,' Alfons Löwenberg told the author. 'It was too complicated and temperamental and in a small run there were a lot of rejects. That's why studies were done to see how Audi could develop its own 16-valve engine, which is what happened.'

At 75,000 Francs, France's Golf GTI 16S was 50% more than the standard car and equal to the price of a BMW 323i. There was talk in the press that the 16S would be sold in other markets – according to James Ruppert's 1996 Golf history it was recommended for UK sale but it remained confined to France. Only around 1,250 examples were produced and survivors are highly prized.

drivers. Riding on Continental 175/70HR13 tyres, at first the suspension seemed stiff: 'However, when the GTI is extended, one immediately begins to appreciate all the attention that has been given to the suspension … With so much power, the GTI tends to approach corners at a very high speed and it makes much greater demands on its driver than does the standard car.'

The inherent characteristic was for the nose to run wide at very high speeds and lift and spin the inside front wheel, but if the throttle was abruptly lifted, 'the car suddenly converts to oversteer which, if allowed to get out of hand, can result in the tail swinging a long way out of line … as one becomes more familiar with the GTI, one learns to exploit this trait to great advantage.'

The best maximum speed was 108mph and 0–60mph in 9.8 seconds, which it judged 'a most respectable rate for a 1.6-litre saloon car' at an average of 29mpg. Practicality was an added bonus: 'Even would-be Roger Clarks [famous British rally driver] have to carry dogs, children and the odd washing machine around sometime.'

At £3,372 it was of course expensive for a compact 1.6-litre car, especially only in left-hand drive, but it looked reasonable value against larger-engined competition such as the £3,729 Ford Escort RS2000 and the £3,833 16-valve Triumph Dolomite Sprint. Specialists such as GTi Engineering offered conversions, but official right-hand-drive cars did not arrive in the UK until July 1979. By then the bumpers were sturdier plastic-covered wraparound items and the gearbox five-speed (with sports rather than economy ratios).

Sales built relentlessly. Accounts will differ, but according to the 1984 British book *Volkswagen Golf, the Enthusiast's Companion* 10,366 Golf GTIs were produced in 1976 (not a full year on sale), comfortably twice the initial estimate, leaping to 31,746 in 1977 and by 1981 the figure was 72,394. Germany, France and Switzerland were bigger markets than the UK, which in 1978 posted just 22 GTI registrations but 1,573 in 1979. It was of course still a drop in the ocean of overall Golf production, which in September 1979 hit three million, including the newly on-stream US production of the Rabbit.

↑ Customisers set to work on the Golf early on. In 1978 Günter Artz, manager of Volkswagen dealer Norstadt, sandwiched the running gear of a V8 Porsche 928 between two halves of a widened Golf. (LAT)

➔ **The first Jetta was a saloon version of the Golf developed at a late stage. It was sold in two- and four-door versions, but only four in the UK.**

Jetta: added Golf

When the Golf was first conceived as a hatchback at the end of the 1960s, it had not been envisaged that there would be a conventional 'three box' (engine, passenger compartment and separate boot) version. However, there was, and remains a marked difference in preference for booted or hatchback cars depending on the country. Whilst in Europe Britain and France embraced the hatchback, Spanish buyers preferred saloons, perceiving them as more prestigious, and also Finland for some reason. At the time of the Golf's introduction Ford and Opel would oblige the booted saloon buyer with the Escort and the Kadett while Renault chased the Spanish buyer with a frumpy version of the 5, the 7. But it was America, above all, that preferred saloon cars.

With demand for the hatchback Golf outstripping supply, Volkswagen was in no rush to invest in another derivative, but with the engine and drivetrain all at one end of the car (just as the Beetle's had been at the opposite) the designers knew that you were free to graft pretty much what you wanted onto it. The idea was tested on the Polo, which at the start of 1977 was launched in a booted version called the Derby (originally styled by Audi as a 50 saloon). 'We made a Derby to prove whether the idea was correct and it turned out to be correct,' said Fiala. 'But the Scandinavian market is too small to make a decision and so I fought for four or five years for a Golf notchback. If you have a family and like to go to holiday you miss the room for baggage in a Golf.'

Thus when the Golf had shown itself to be a worthy Beetle successor there was time to develop a three-box saloon, first known as the Jetta (a wind-like name) at the 1979 Frankfurt Motor Show. At 40cm longer, the Jetta was endowed with a 630-litre boot – compared to a Golf's seat-raised 320 litres – grafted to the rear of the Golf behind the rear doors and the grille given rectangular headlamps to distinguish it from the front. A two-door version was available in some markets.

The Jetta was engineered with only a small weight penalty of about 30kg (dry) over a Golf 1100 five-door and test performance differed little, although an anti-roll bar added to the rear suspension was found to make the Jetta a little less sure-footed. Inside, the testers found the only complaint was that the boot space seemed to have been won at the expense of some rear passenger legroom.

Introduced late in the production run of the first-generation Golf, a booted saloon became a feature of each of the following generations but given different names according to the local markets. The attitude of the motoring press towards it also differed, the British especially keen to sound bored by the whole idea.

The five-year facelift

It was a testament to the inherent appeal of the Golf's design, and that customers couldn't get enough of them, that it remained visually unchanged for its first five years and three and a half million produced. A new Golf had been sanctioned in 1978 but was just starting its development, and by then the market was awash with numerous Golf-like cars. The most serious threat was the 1979 Opel Kadett (Vauxhall Astra for the UK), a squarely-styled hatchback, which General Motors made no secret of being based on a close examination of the Golf. By now a transverse engine with end-on transmission, MacPherson-strut front suspension and rear trailing-arm suspension linked by a twisting beam was the industry standard. The Kadett's fuel tank below the rear seat and negative offset steering geometry were also standard Golf. With the benefit of coming very late to the party, it offered among other features a loading bay unencumbered by a high sill and an estate version from launch. In 1981 Ford finally joined in with an all-new front-drive Escort.

The Golf facelift for the 1980 model year amounted to larger headlamps and wider tail-light clusters with wraparound plastic-covered bumpers. Inside, new seat and door trims were introduced with a revised dashboard including two extra central air vents. A new 60bhp 1.3-litre engine variant was added in October 1979, substituting the manual transmission 70bhp 1.5-litre to the disappointment of some British commentators, but buyers wanting more performance could now pay £440 for a lot more in a 1.6 GTI. This seemingly backward step was down to engine manufacturing demands; Volkswagen explained that as the 1.5-litre also formed the basis of the diesel engines for the Golf and Passat, they couldn't make enough of them.

Thus the new 1,272cc unit was a stretched version of the 1.1-litre Golf engine, which with its final drive ratio raised from 3.9 to 4.27:1 was judged to have rather low gearing by 1979 standards and a consequent drop off in the refinement for which the 1.5 was praised. In 1980 the Golf diesel grew from 1.5 to 1.6 litres, being based on the 1,558cc petrol unit, with a modest 4bhp increase to 54.

For 1980 the Golf GTI had a five-speed gearbox, which only added to its inherent flexibility while diluting nothing of its character. As *Car* magazine's October 1980 long-term test of 1,588cc five-speed GTI put it, 'Thus, for all the flexibility and manners of the engine, the Golf tends to

continued on page 80

↑ The competition of 1980 looked distinctly Golf-like, with the Giugiaro-styled Lancia Delta front, the Vauxhall/Opel Astra in white and Ford Escort in gold. The latter was replaced by a front-wheel drive version the following year. (LAT)

↓ Brazil was to get its own semi-Golf, the 1980 Gol, which had elements of the EA276 (see previous chapter) and started life with a Beetle engine at the front. (LAT)

Citi Golf – the longest survivor

The first-generation Golf proved so popular in South Africa that it lasted in production until 2009, some 26 years after production ceased in Germany.

Back in 1982 Volkswagen of South Africa (VWSA) was not entirely looking forward to the second-generation Golf, which it was due to receive two years later. It had been producing its own popular version of the original Golf since 1978 at its Uitenhage site near Port Elizabeth. After having made significant investment its Golf contained 57% local content and had a number of unique variants such as a five-door GTI.

The new car would be bigger, heavier and inevitably more expensive, so VWSA was faced with losing an entry-level model (Beetle production ended in 1979) and did not consider the Polo would suit its market, which demanded four doors.

The favoured option was the retention of the Golf 1 in another form and a study was prepared for an 'Econo Golf'. This was as dreary as it sounds, based on a 1978 Golf LS five-door bodyshell with an 1,100cc engine, beige paintwork, no carpets or interior handles. When presented to management and VWSA's advertising agency RS-TM it was agreed that the Econo Golf would hold no appeal to the younger age group who would buy such a car.

The agency came up with the idea of dressing it up with brighter colours and this developed into a two-tone treatment with the bottom of the doors and tailgate in white as well as front and rear bumpers. Somebody came up with the name Citi Golf and when consumer tested against competitor cars the Econo Golf hardly got a second glance even though it was the cheapest of the group; 89% chose the red Citi Golf outright. New Volkswagen AG chairman Carl Hahn backed the project and the Citi Golf was approved.

Launched in 1984, the specification was simple. It only came as a five-door model with no sunroof, the only engine available was a 65bhp 1.3, and there were no extras. Citi Golfs came in top-half colours of red, blue or yellow. It proved an immediate success and began to look like a long-term prospect.

For a market that always favoured sporty Golfs, performance increased steadily with the introduction of 1.4-, 1.6- and 1.8-litre engines. Carburettors gave way to K-Jetronic then multi-point fuel injection. Although the GTI didn't arrive in South Africa until the 1983 model year, it had produced a GT, a GTS and a GTX. The Citi took up this mantle again, with the 1990 Citi Golf CTI powered by a 110bhp 1.8-litre engine. It even built up its own domestic racing career.

Cooling and braking were improved, and, to cater for the long distances in South Africa, fuel tank capacity increased from 37 to 49 litres. In September 1988 the Citi was given its first facelift. The radiator grille was slightly angled along the lines of the Golf 2 and a unique hockey stick-shaped

← A simple two-tone colour scheme turned the Citi Golf from dreary economy car to fun entry-level model. (Volkswagen South Africa)

corrugation appeared on the trademark rear pillar, not for decoration but to strengthen the panel and eliminate creasing when it was pressed as by then the tooling was wearing.

Every year brought new special-edition Citis, which kept interest fresh, as did its low cost of ownership. The biggest interior change was an all-new dashboard in late 2003, based on the Škoda Fabia design.

In its last facelift of 2007, a circular brake-light inlay was added to the rear lights, and the front spoiler was given a makeover. The same year the 122bhp 1.8-litre Citi Golf R-Line was launched, the fastest Golf 1 produced by a Volkswagen factory.

There was no question of the Citi being imported to Europe as it would have failed crash test and emissions regulations. None received power steering or anti-lock brakes and the most major safety upgrade was a driver airbag in early 2009.

Deeply ingrained in the South African motoring scene, production ended in November 2009 with 377,484 Citi Golfs produced. It was succeeded by the Polo Vivo, a version of the fourth-generation Polo.

↑ Only 1,000 Citi Mk1 farewell editions were made, each with a unique number embossed on the passenger side dashboard and integrated into the Mk1 logo. (Volkswagen South Africa)

↓ It started with a 1974-vintage Golf dashboard and ended as a Škoda Fabia mixture but without airbags. (Volkswagen South Africa)

make its driver aggressive. It feels like a little tiger of a car and, without you necessarily being the type who'd set out to dash through traffic and storm into bends, you're liable to find yourself doing just that. If you like the GTI is a boy racer par excellence.'

But still the right-hand drive bugbear imposed by the extended brake linkage remained, five years after launch. 'The other disappointment about the GTI – as with all Golfs – is that the brakes are feeble. The pedal travels too far, its feel beneath the foot is mushy and the actual braking performance is out of tune with the car as a whole.' Luckily one of a burgeoning number of British specialists who would adjust your GTI for a fee, and one of the best known, GTi Engineering would change the brake pads for better-specification Mintex items and adjust the brake linkage.

Formel E

After the 1979 oil crisis, provoked by the Iranian revolution, energy efficiency was once more a priority for the US and European politicians. Car manufacturers needed to show marketable proof of economy and Volkswagen's proposition was surprising in its depth – perhaps a little too far ahead of its time. Hosting an Energy Symposium in Wolfsburg, it launched Formel E, a reconfiguration of gear ratios available on most models. On a four-speed gearbox third gear was designed to reach maximum speed, while the significantly reduced revs in fourth gear increased economy.

Formel E cars were seen as a half-way house between petrol and diesel cars, were cheaper than diesels but still attracted a price premium. In 1981 a UK Formel E Golf was £4,174 – £300 more than the standard Golf C but with five doors. The package was not offered on the Scirocco, Audi Coupe or Audi 200.

The instrument panel was fitted with an 'econometer' and lights that indicated the optimum point to change gear. The addition of plastic fairings on the pillars each side of the windscreen and a deeper front spoiler on the Golf were claimed to reduce its drag coefficient by 10% from 0.41 to 0.38, adding a claimed 4% improvement in fuel economy. A front spoiler similar to the GTI was added.

Volkswagen claimed the mechanical changes gave a 13–20% improvement in fuel economy. Formel E cars had a higher-compression engine allied to a manual gearbox where the ratios were arranged so the top gear was higher than normal as an economy (E) ratio and the car would achieve its best top speed in the gear below. The four-speed gearbox was termed a 3+E unit, the five-speed a 4+E and fitted to the Passat and Audi 100.

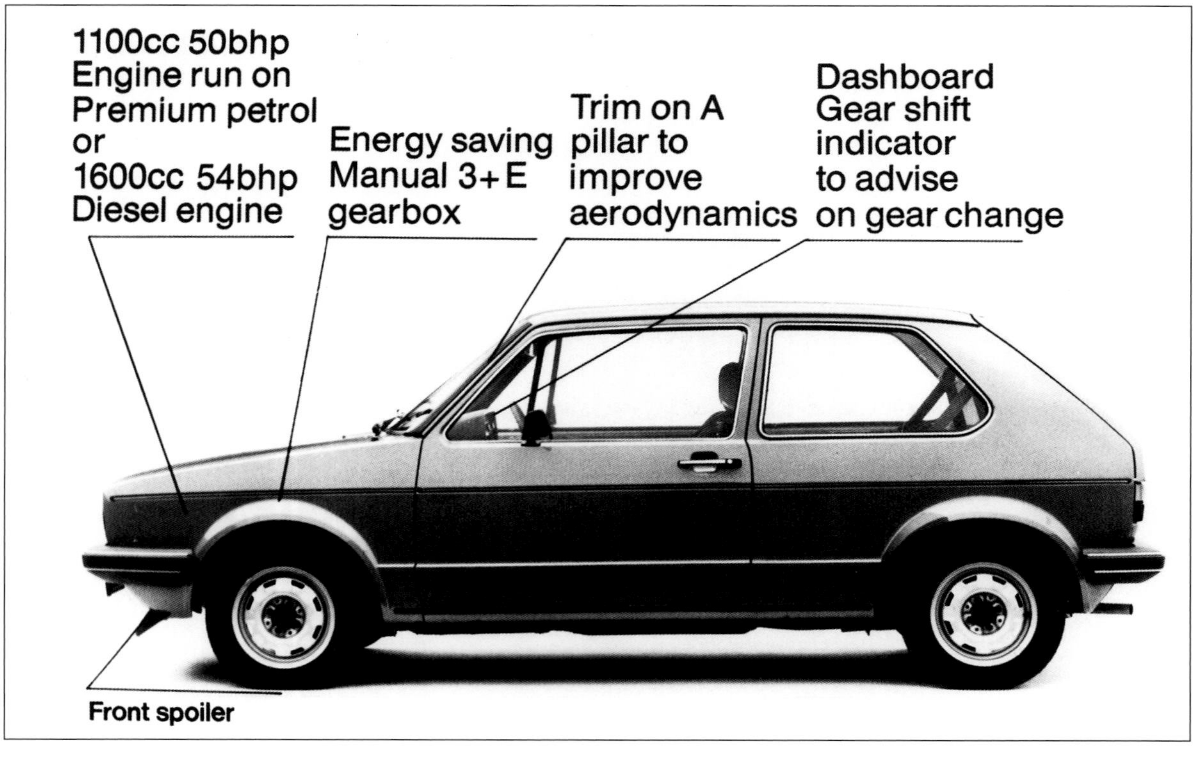

➔ **There was nothing complicated or costly about the Formel E modifications for the Golf. (LAT)**

The Golf and Jetta package was a specially developed version of the base 1,093cc engine running on a higher compression ratio of 9.7:1 (against 8.0:1) with a modified distributor and camshaft. Power was the same at 50bhp, but there was a significant increase in torque, or pulling power, between 1,500 and 4,000rpm. The cars would cruise happily in fourth gear as at 70mph engine revs dropped from 4,500 to 3,500rpm.

Volkswagen-Audi viewed Formel E as a groundbreaking development, the British importers hosting their own 'energy symposium' in 1981, and the economy claims from model to model were notable. A Formel E Golf was claimed to achieve 39.2mpg in urban driving compared to 30.4 for a standard Golf L. The diesel Golf claimed 47.1mpg to 41.5mpg. Formel E equipment continued to be offered through to the next generation Golf in 1983 and some features like the econometer with its gear change point indicators became mainstream.

The self-stopping Golf

The combination of Formel E features varied by model. The 4+E transmission could be had as an option on Golf diesels, but Formel E Passats and Audi 80s were fitted with a stop-start system whereby the driver could stop the engine in traffic by touching a button on the end of the wiper stalk. The engine would then restart if the driver depressed the accelerator pedal while at the same time dipping the clutch pedal. You would then have to accelerate again to move off, which some drivers found off-putting. The idea had been tested as early as 1973, when Volkswagen equipped 412 test models with stop-start systems in Wolfsburg.

However, behind the scenes Volkswagen had been testing a further development of the stop-start system for which the public was almost certainly not ready; the *Schwungnutzautomatik* (inertia flywheel automatic), also called the SNA or Glider automatic. Coupled to a diesel engine, a microprocessor would cut the engine once up to speed if you took your foot off the accelerator by a clutch disengaging drive until you put your foot back on and restarting. If you came to a stop the engine would also cut, and similar to Formel E, would restart once you selected first gear. There was no clutch pedal and drivers were warned not to rest their hands on the gear lever because it contained a sensor (the old NSU Ro80 had used a similar device).

Head of advanced propulsion systems research

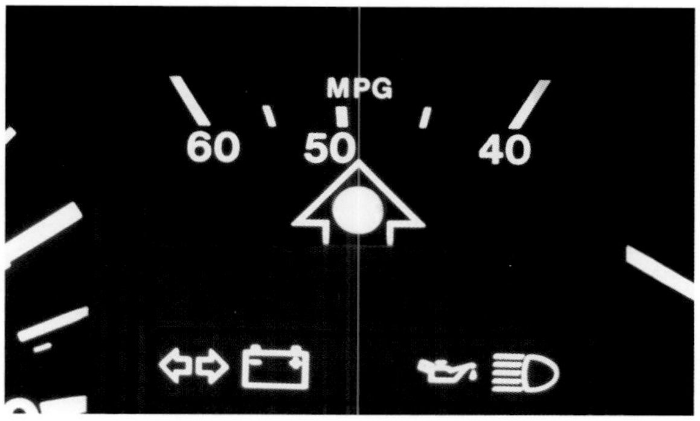

← The 'econometer' would swing around according to your driving style.

to 1978 then head of power-train development Peter Hofbauer had the idea when visiting British motor research company Ricardo in Shoreham, Sussex. Noticing the hilly roads (Wolfsburg is quite flat) he would dip the clutch when coasting and was interested to see the fuel savings. 'There is a lot of kinetic energy stored in the mass of the car so if you can de-clutch and stop the engine the car will move a long distance without really slowing down.'

He remembers an experiment in the late '70s where ten 'Glider' Golf automatics were given to the postal service at nearby Braunschweig and a further ten given to an environmental organisation in Berlin. Dr Fiala also recalls (and this may have been the same test) drivers at the large Dusseldorf postal centre being given Golfs with the US passive seatbelt system where you stepped into the seatbelt at the same time you stepped into the car as it was anchored to the door. These post Golfs also had the *Schwungnutzautomatik* system fitted. 'We told the postmen you step in in the morning and start the car. When you come to a post box you just stop, step out then step in, first gear, drive away,' Fiala said. 'At first everybody said it was so easy, you never have to start the engine again the whole day but after a few weeks they hated it. They said "just yesterday I was sitting at an intersection and my neighbour stepped out of his car and came to me and said, your engine isn't turning! You can't drive away!'

Intersection embarrassment was the main reason the Glider automatics were not liked (drivers used an override button to cancel the system so fuel savings couldn't be calculated) and a number were simply nervous of a car cutting out at speed. Volkswagen asked psychologists to contribute and they apparently concluded that older drivers felt impotent when the rev counter needle suddenly dropped...

'We invented a so-called "heartbeat" artificial noise to tell them that the engine was still alert,' Hofbauer told the author. 'It was to tell them "don't worry the engine is ready, if you push the gas pedal it will come."'

The *Schwungnutzautomatik* took a long time to find acceptance. The idea resurfaced at the end of the 1980s as the Eco-Golf and finally in production as the 1993 Golf Ecomatic (see Chapter 4) to a lukewarm reception. It then fell out of favour for nearly two decades until emissions requirements drove most carmakers to fit automatic stop-start systems and the rise of the hybrid petrol/electric car made fuller use of the technology.

The Golf cabriolet

Like the diesel and the Jetta, a convertible, or cabriolet, had not been part of the initial Golf programme. By the mid 1970s the industry believed that American safety legislation and lawsuits following rollover accidents would see off the four-seater convertible and two-seater soft-top sports cars began to fade away. But the Beetle convertible had continued in production at Karmann, an expensive anachronism but one with a loyal following. Its only four-seat convertible competition was the Rolls Royce Corniche and the Peugeot 504 cabriolet, but it was inevitably doomed as European production of the saloon was to draw to a close in 1978. It had made up a major part of Karmann's profits (aside from Scirocco assembly) and the impetus in the search for its replacement came from its own engineers not Volkswagen, which was amply occupied churning out Golf hatchbacks.

Karmann had tried developing a Scirocco convertible but abandoned it as too cramped. The popular view was that the shape of a hatchback simply didn't lend itself to a convertible, and indeed early drawings for a Golf soft-top were based on a 'three box' silhouette with a separate boot like the Jetta, and a prototype was built. However in 1976 Karmann engineers applied tape to the back half of a Golf three-door to resemble a closed convertible and invited Dr Fiala down from Wolfsburg. After some persuasion he agreed that a prototype could be built.

Thus in early 1977 the top was cut off a Golf hatch, robbing it of about 80% of its torsional rigidity and the engineers made extensive body modifications with a beam across the car and cross-beams between the front and rear wheel wells, but it was still a fully open car, with a hood that sat fairly flat on the rear deck as it was allowed to fold into the boot space. Its glass rear window zipped out and was hinged at the bottom.

The next step was decisive. 'Most people said the days of the cabriolet were over,' Ernst Fiala recalls. 'Most had disappeared from production because everybody said you will have a rollover accident and then you will be sued for making dangerous cars. We had to do something to show that we understood the problem.'

Although not required by law at the time, a rollover bar was added to the Golf convertible design and solved a multitude of problems. 'It wasn't a nuisance for the driver because he doesn't see it,' Fiala said. 'It's fine for locating the hood, the safety belts and for the window glass, plus we solved the problem of shaking.

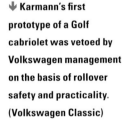

↓ Karmann's first prototype of a Golf cabriolet was vetoed by Volkswagen management on the basis of rollover safety and practicality. (Volkswagen Classic)

← **Hood up, the Golf cabriolet had a neat profile and the rear window was unusual in being glass and heated.**

↓ **Two latches secured the hood to the windscreen rail and it took about five seconds to lower.**

↑ **The production Golf cabriolet with its distinctive and useful rollover bar and a hood, which, like the Beetle, obscured much of the rear view when folded.**

↓ **This 1979 diagram shows areas of reinforcement in a darker shade. (LAT)**

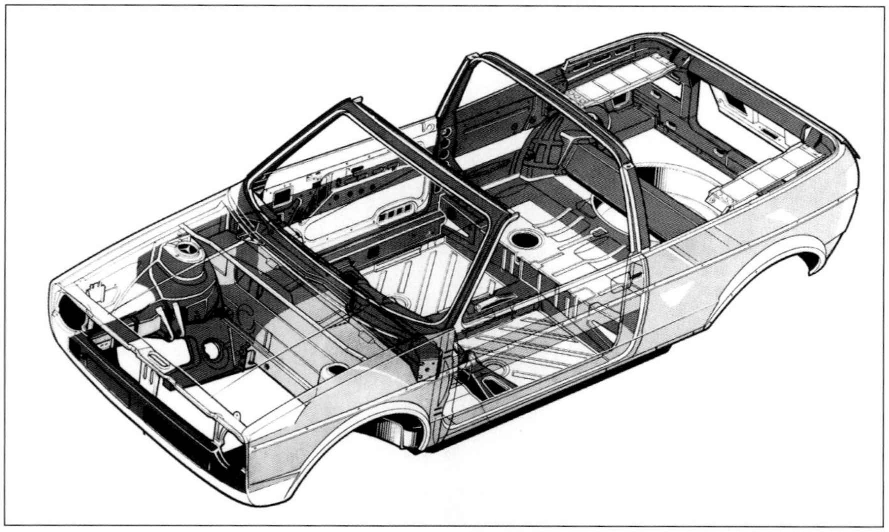

Then there was a riot from the Beetle cabriolet owners who said we were making a bad-looking cabriolet – like a coal scuttle.' However, the nickname that was to stick was *Erdbeerkörbchen*, or strawberry basket. At launch footage of rollover crash tests showed it could bear the weight of the car and it could also take a specially designed roof rack.

The Golf convertible was developed over more than two years and was far more than a three-door minus its roof. To restore structural rigidity the top extra inner wing, scuttle, sill door, floor and tail section reinforcement added up to some extra 90kg of extra metal pressings. Because Volkswagen insisted on reasonable boot space (apparently to take a crate of beer) the hood eventually sat on the deck. It was as thoroughly specified as the Beetle's hood and weighed 40kg more than the steel roof (a redesign for 1981 allowed it to sit 10cm flatter).

To achieve nearly the same level of interior noise the scissor frame carried five layers of an inner headlining and outer weatherproof layer with a 20mm-thick gauze-faced rubberised filling in between. A glass rear window with heated element was an essential part of the design and wind tunnel work helped Karmann pitch it at an angle to keep it clean and reduce drag (although the top speed of all versions was lower). Two latches secured the hood to the windscreen frame and the whole assembly took around five seconds to lower. At first its weight and bulk were said to have ruled out power operation.

The Golf cabriolet was launched at the Geneva Motor Show in March 1979 in two versions, GLS and GLI. Given the extra weight it was carrying, the 1.1-litre engine was only reserved for markets where it would have a tax advantage. Otherwise the GLS was equipped with the 70bhp 1.5-litre engine and the GLI the injected 110bhp 1.6 of the Golf GTI. Factory-claimed performance for the GLI was still 0–60mph in under ten seconds.

➔ **If a standard Golf cabriolet was not enough, in 1982 Artz Automobile of Hannover would expensively chop it down to create the Speedster, with a new interior and a host of Kamei styling parts. (LAT)**

➔ **Another take on an open-air Golf was the gull-winged Rinspeed conversion, which included a cocktail cabinet. (LAT)**

Road testers found the new Golf soft-top to ride with an acceptable amount of shaking over poor surfaces and almost as lively, with the GLS riding slightly better on softer suspension settings. The predictable complaint was lack of rear visibility, hood up or down, and drivers learnt to make increasing use of their wing mirrors.

The prospect of the Beetle convertible, with over 18,000 having been made in 1978, being replaced by a Golf filled devotees with horror and there were honking protests in Wolfsburg. However, PR manager Anton Konrad invited all Beetle cabriolet owners to the factory, gave them beer and sausages, thanked them for their devotion and asked them to give the new product a chance. Of course some new Golf cabriolets were to hand and after test drives some Beetle owners even signed on the dotted line to buy one. Like the GTI the Golf cabriolet started a trend. Fiat commissioned Bertone to design and produce the Strada convertible and Ford returned to Karmann itself for the 1984 Escort convertible, very similar to the Golf design with a glass heated rear window, hood sat on the boot lid and prominent rollover bar. Production of the Golf cabriolet settled to 2,000 a year, all that Karmann at Osnabrück could manage. It was to be an exceptional production run, lasting until 1993.

➔ **Karmann proposed a soft-top Jetta which would have had more luggage space than the Golf, but it went no further. (Stiftung AutoMuseum)**

➔ Not seen in the UK, the first Golf GTD had much of the GTI's trim and started the idea of a 'sports' diesel.

➔ The Golf GTD was the first factory-fitted application of a turbocharger to a Golf.

The second diesel revolution

Before the European production run ended, there was one more significant Golf variant: the turbo diesel. Launched for the 1982 model year but in development since 1978, adding a turbocharger to the 1.6-litre diesel produced petrol-engined levels of performance – 70bhp to match the 1.5-litre petrol. Hofbauer had wanted to turbocharge the diesel all along but had struggled to gain approval for the normally aspirated unit. 'There was enormous resistance from sales and finance during the PSK meetings against this step because the 2,000-a-day naturally-aspirated diesel sold so easily,' he recalls. 'At last PSK approved the turbo programme with the comment: "Let Hofbauer make his Turbo Diesel. The sales numbers will be so low so the losses which we will make are not significant." Prof. Tomee [Board member Finance] said to me: "Let them talk; with the diesel you saved VW."'

Through the 1970s Volkswagen engineers had publicly eschewed the turbocharger for boosting performance of petrol engines, citing an increased likelihood of engine wear, and turbo lag (the delay on early turbocharged cars between pressing the accelerator pedal and the turbo becoming effective) later turning to 16-valve engines and superchargers for performance Golfs. However, with the lower temperatures and stresses of a diesel engine, adding a turbocharger was the obvious way to boost power whilst retaining an economy advantage.

Still based on the 1.6-litre diesel, the turbo diesel necessitated over 30 changes including a larger oil circuit and oil cooler, a more powerful oil pump and reinforcement in all the areas subjected to the higher exhaust gas temperatures. A Garrett or KKK turbocharger was used and maximum torque was developed at 2,000rpm compared to 2,500rpm in the 1.5 petrol. Quoted performance figures were a top speed of 96mph, 0–62mph in 13.5 seconds and an urban fuel consumption of 42.5mpg. To accentuate the first 'sports' diesel, Volkswagen branded its new creation a GTD and dressed it in some of the GTI's details such as wider wheels with wheel-arch extensions and interior trim. The GTD wasn't offered in the UK where it didn't make economic sense.

↑ By the time of the GTD there was a new dashboard with central air vents (although quite low) and a larger glovebox.

↓ By 1983 this was the 1.8-litre Golf GTI's competition (front to back): Astra GTE, Alfa Romeo Alfasud TiX, Ford Escort XR3i.

Bigger-engined GTI

The real GTI was still the critics' choice, despite a growing number of high performance hatchbacks such as the Renault 5 Alpine/Gordini Turbo and Ford Escort XR3. In late 1982, just before the Ford was due on sale with fuel injection, Volkswagen introduced a bigger-engined GTI, increasing the bore and stroke of the 1,588cc engine to 1,781cc. Added refinements included improved balancing and a torsional vibration damper. There was a revised (lighter) camshaft, new combustion-chamber pattern and a 10:1 compression ratio (up from 9.5:1).

While this brought an increase of only two brake horsepower to 112bhp, the engine was, as intended, much more flexible and efficient coupled with new taller ratios in the five-speed gearbox allowing 19.7mph per 1,000rpm compared to 18.4 of the 1.6. The official British government fuel figure of 36.7mpg at 75mph compared to 32.5 in the old car.

New equipment included a multi-function trip computer, considered a great novelty in the early 1980s. Controlled by a button on the end of the wiper stalk, this could tell the driver journey distance, average speed and fuel consumption, oil temperature and inside/outside temperatures. The interior was unchanged with black trim, painted metal door tops and Recaro seats. 'Bigger-engined Golf GTI is still the hottest of the hot hatchbacks, and on balance, still the best,' concluded *Motor* magazine.

↑ A 1982 British-specification Golf with the facelift bumpers; an all-new Golf was a year away.

Towards Golf 2

For 1982 a tidying up of the Golf range saw new model designations of Golf C (for Complete, apparently) CL, GL and GTI and CD for diesels. The Golf C was only available as a three-door in the UK but still benefited from full carpets and cloth seat trim. Formel E options were available on top of these (bar the GTI). A small but very useful change in anti-corrosion measures was plastic front wheel arch liners, which shielded the door pillar, front floorpan and suspension-strut towers.

During 1983 various run-out models loaded with extras helped to clear the way for the next Golf's introduction in September, with special editions of the GTI especially popular. In Germany the Pirelli Special Edition was marked out by a double headlight grille and made available in three special colours: Helios Blue Metallic, Mars red and metallic Lhasa green. It rode on distinctive alloy wheels with holes cut in the shape of P for Pirelli and 185/60HR14 tyres of the same name. Planned production of 10,500 sold out in six months. Similar models were the Trophy for Switzerland, the Plus for France and 1,000 'Campaigns' for the UK, although there has been quite a debate among enthusiasts as to what constitutes a genuine GTI Campaign.

European production of the first-generation Golf ended in October 1983, three months after its successor started rolling off the line. Including variants such as the Jetta and Caddy 6.72 million units had been built in nine years. The concept was deeply embedded in European motoring, with common use of the phrase 'Golf-class car' and the initials GTI.

→ In the UK the 1979 Golf Driver special edition had most of the GTI's trim but a 1.3-litre engine, and so a consequently lower insurance premium. It proved very popular.

↑ One of the very last first-generation Golf GTI Pirelli editions from 1983 (the silver roundel is non-original) with the distinctive Pirelli 'P' cut-outs in the alloy wheels.

← By the end of the first-generation GTI's run the tartan seats had gone but the golf-ball gear knob was still there.

D
WOB GO 502
Volkswagen Classic

Golf 2 1983-1991

Golf grows up

Replacing a ground-breaking car was never going to be easy. Although the second-generation Golf was to benefit from major innovations in Volkswagen's engine and drive systems during the 1980s, at first all people could focus on was its looks.

In summer 1983 there was feverish speculation as to how Volkswagen was going to follow the first Golf's record nine years. Spy shots of disguised prototypes flew around the German press for months before its August premiere, all denied as false. Many thought that the Auto 2000 concept car, a high-technology showcase revealed in 1981 (see panel on page 94) and based on a Golf chassis, was a clue as to how the new Golf would look. It was said that Opel took it seriously enough to influence the styling of the 1984 Astra.

The reality was a conservative reworking of the previous Golf, with some of the aerodynamic lessons learnt from the Auto 2000. Having established a new market sector, Volkswagen had very carefully considered which way to go, and serious work on the second Golf started in March 1977. The decision to go ahead with a new model was made in 1978, when the original was still selling strongly but pressure to reduce production costs was growing from Japanese carmakers with more efficient manufacturing capabilities. The main consumer improvements needed were in rear head, leg and shoulder room, to make the Golf a full five-seater, and more boot space. Development costs were stated to have been £250 million.

To arrive at the final look ten designs were considered, two of them from outside suppliers including Giugiaro, and these were then said to have been viewed by 500 people in customer clinics. Two were selected in November 1978 and at the final showing of May 1979 Volkswagen chose one of its own in-house designs by Herbert Schäfer, who created similar evolutionary designs for the next Scirocco and Passat. The marketing department was reported to have requested that elements of the previous car be visible in the new one, so as not to alienate loyal buyers.

'It turned out to be a very good decision because the car sold well,' Patrick Le Quément told the author in 2013. Le Quément was director of corporate design at

← ↓ 1983 launch material for the new Golf had selected shots of styling clays being created. One, however, (left) appears to show more radical rear-end styling than eventually appeared.

Auto 2000

Volkswagen's Auto 2000 concept car of 1981 came from a project funded by the German Government and Federal Ministry of Research and Technology for domestic manufacturers to produce a car to meet the needs of the motoring public in the year 2000. Audi's entry, the BMFT saloon with its flush fitting glass was a forerunner of the Audi 100 the following year and Ford's Probe 3 also turned into the Sierra, so industry observers (notably Opel, which let it influence the next Astra) could hardly be blamed for thinking the Auto 2000 was a pointer to the shape of the next Golf. It wasn't, although the frontal styling appeared on the 1988 Passat.

However, with hindsight Auto 2000 turned out to have been fitted or tested with just about every feature that would appear on Volkswagens over the following thirty years. Masterminded by engineers Ulrich Seiffert and Hans Wilhelm Grove, it had a drag coefficient of 0.25, two different engine concepts, two transmission options and unique energy management systems.

For safety its body structure was designed to feed impact forces through to the transmission tunnel and the 'B' pillars and it was made up of steel, plastic and aluminium parts to reduce weight. With no production-cost constraints the rear axle was made of plastic and fibreglass. There was an anti-skid braking system developed with Teves and the US-market passive seatbelt restraint system from the Rabbit.

The driver was treated to a digital display of information such as fuel consumption, speed, amount of fuel in the tank, remote control of the radio and a plethora of warning systems such as low tyre pressure.

Auto 2000 was tested with both petrol and diesel engines. The latter was a three-cylinder 1,191cc version of the Rabbit/Golf 1.6-litre diesel with direct injection and a very high compression ratio of 20. Foreshadowing the arrival of the *G-Lader*, it was tested with two types of 'supercharger', one a turbocharger on exhaust gases and one a comprex 'pressure wave' supercharger. Although not fully developed, tests found the engine with the latter system resulted in higher torque and higher power output.

There was an automatic stop-start system by means of a flywheel, which disengaged, stopping the engine, but ran on for some time because it was designed with very low friction. If its speed dropped below 800rpm, an electric starter kicked in. When engine power was needed 'clutch C2' was closed and the flywheel started the engine.

Another 1,060cc four-cylinder petrol engine was fitted with a Roots-type supercharger and multipoint fuel injection, and a three- or four-speed automatic with a freewheeling function.

Professor Fiala, head of development at the time, told the author that there was a thought that rather than inspiring a new Golf, the Auto 2000 could be put into production as a new, high-technology brand sitting between Volkswagen and Audi, perhaps with a revival of the Wanderer name. 'In the end we decided not to do it but to stay with the old Golf image. In those days in the late 70s we were shocked about our disaster in the United States. This was perhaps the reason that they didn't do both the Golf and the Wanderer – or a new company – with the Auto 2000 bringing in a new class for VW, a middle-class Audi with a higher price, and extra technical car.'

Once mistaken for the look of the Golf 2, the Auto 2000 concept car did donate its bluff front end to the 1988 Passat.

Volkswagen between 1985 and 1987, when he left to head design at Renault. 'I think one of the qualities that Schäfer and VW added was the fact that the car looked more robust than what Giugiaro was doing at the time, with hard edged, relatively flat surfaces.'

Nonetheless, there was much grumbling from the domestic and international press that this approach had no 'wow' factor after Ford had launched the Sierra and Audi the super-aerodynamic 100. The jurors for the 1984 European Car of the Year contest (made up of around 50 journalists including seven from each major European manufacturing country) put the Fiat Uno and Peugeot 205 shot in the top two places above the Golf.

Jürgen Lewandowski of the *Süddeutsche Zeitung* voted the new Volkswagen fourth with the similarly cautious BMW 3 series: 'VW Golf: like BMW – a good car. The best Golf there has ever been, however: are there no aesthetes at VW?'

Hans Werner from *Stern* ranked the Uno first and the Golf second with damning praise: 'I would rank the VW Golf higher if its creators had not punished it with the most boring design of the year. Commendable are however many improvements.'

But for Volkswagen there was a lot at stake and this was not the time for revolution. The Golf now made up 40% of its sales and the market was awash with similar cars from manufacturers trying to emulate its success with an identical mechanical layout. The Opel Kadett was well established, the Ford Escort had been an all-new design in 1981, Fiat offered the Ritmo and also the Giugiaro-styled Lancia Delta. Japanese manufacturers were increasingly making the switch to front-wheel drive with cars such as the Nissan Cherry and Mitsubishi Mirage. The great hope for the UK carmaker Austin Rover was the Austin Maestro, which, as an aside, used a Golf gearbox in certain versions.

In common with other carmakers Volkswagen was also suffering financial difficulties, especially in the American market and in 1982, *Der Spiegel* reported the Group slipped 300 million dollars into the red, with shareholders denied a dividend for the first time in ten years.

'I considered it a very big step forward,' Carl Hahn recalls. He had arrived back at Wolfsburg from Continental as chairman a year before the new Golf was launched. 'It was much larger, but it had a serious

In August 1983 Christian Hildebrandt, project engineer for the Golf 2, invites comparison with its predecessor. (LAT)

Der neue Golf. Oder wie man
einen Bestseller noch besser macht.
WOB-AW 477

↑ The new Golf. How to make a best-seller even better, explains this early German publicity. (Author's collection)

➔ Chairman Carl Hahn, pictured in 1987, drove forwards Volkswagen's expansion into other brands.

design drawback. I considered there was too little glass in the space between the B column and the C so we changed the body. But apart from this I still remember appearing in the dealer shows and making jokes about the new small Mercedes at the time [the 190] which was bigger than the Golf and had less space inside.'

Shaped for space

At 3.98m long the new Golf was 27mm longer than the first, with an extra 75mm added to the wheelbase at 2,475mm. The new rounded body shape was 55mm wider but at 1,415mm high only 5mm taller. The front track (distance between the wheels) on a standard Golf was 23mm wider, the rear 50mm wider.

At a time when Audi was making aerodynamics a marketing tool with its flush-fitted-glass 100, the new Golf shape had also had great attention paid to it in the wind tunnel, reducing its total air drag by a claimed 17%. Although it had been built in 1965, the Volkswagen wind tunnel was not intensively used until 1978 when fuel crises and rising prices concentrated minds on the effects of drag.

The Golf 2 was wider in the passenger compartment but narrowed at the front to expose around the same frontal area as before. The smaller rear window was more steeply inclined (also for extra boot height) and particular attention had been paid to the joints between the glass, roof and sides of the car. The absence of protruding rain gutters along the roof was claimed to control both rain and wind flow along the roof and the front three-quarter windows were flush with the front of the door pillar. Volkswagen engineers claimed this alone was almost as effective as (and much cheaper than) the fully flush glass of the Audi 100. The underside was fitted with an air deflector and the sealing between the bonnet and radiator was designed to help airflow through the engine bay and keep turbulence to a minimum. The total effect was to reduce the new Golf's drag co-efficient from 0.42 to 0.34.

By using moulded inner door panels the designers had liberated 92mm of front elbow room and the increased wheelbase allowed the rear seat to be moved backwards (a split-folding rear backrest was available from GL upwards) and boot space was claimed to have been increased by 30% when a space-saving spare wheel was fitted. This item was mistrusted and optional in the UK, leaving the car with a lumpy floor when a full-sized wheel was in place.

↑ Some losses and some gains: the tailgate glass area was smaller but the boot was larger, still with a high sill needed for body rigidity. (LAT)

← It may have been bigger and heavier but the second Golf reaped the full benefits of Volkswagen's wind tunnel. (LAT)

↑ Sectioned Golfs at the launch were used to illustrate gains in interior space.

↓ The new plastic petrol tank and its complex shape to wrap around the rear suspension was considered a work of art worthy of a picture. (Author's collection)

The engineers were particularly proud of a new plastic fuel tank design, moulded in a complex shape to slot around the rear suspension and the spare-wheel recess. Allowing drivers to add fuel up to the filler neck, its capacity increased from 40 litres to 55 (8.8 to 12 gallons), giving a potential range of 650 miles for a Golf diesel. Extra space was factored into the engine compartment for air conditioners, and turbochargers for the diesel engines, and easier servicing. The heating and ventilation system was boasted to be a significant improvement as it was based on an air-blending principle. Hot coolant flowed through a heat exchanger all the time, so there was very little delay in obtaining warming air. The system was developed in America to cope with its extremes of temperature and an integral air-conditioning system was claimed to cool the interior far faster.

Turning to the inevitable weight gain, a 1974 three-door Golf 1100 came in at 750kg with no fuel on board and the new 1300 three-door was 845kg. Some of that weight was accounted for by an increased glass area and the fuel tank alone added an extra 15kg, but the

↑ The Volkswagen Jetta continued into its second generation with most of the Golf's engine options. The Jetta GTI 16-valve was considered a subtly effective car.

improved aerodynamics were claimed to largely take care of the extra mass in terms of fuel consumption and performance.

The one model missing from the line-up was a new cabriolet. The previous one had been launched only four years previously and was still selling profitably, so a decision was made to keep it running alongside the new car with a series of upgrades (see panel on page 100). A new Jetta arrived quickly in February 1984, having been designed alongside the Golf hatch.

Up-engined

Whilst only the door handles and gear lever were claimed to have been transplanted to the new Golf, the previous generation's engines were logically carried over, albeit heavily revised. As far as the 1983 launch material and brochures were concerned the basic engine was now a 55bhp 1.3-litre unit. However, apparently after pressure from the Italian market, which preferred smaller-engined cars under its tax regime, a standard Golf (below the Golf C) soon appeared in the price lists with a 45bhp 1,043cc unit from the Polo. With 5bhp less than the previous – lighter – standard Golf 1100 it not surprisingly posted an official top speed of 86mph and took 20.9 seconds from rest to 60mph. The UK market took it at the start of 1984 as it allowed it to start the Golf range at a lower price but dropped it that summer. Redesigned for 1985, power went up to 50bhp, but by mid 1985 it had been dropped in favour of the 1300 in most markets.

This had a higher compression ratio of 9.5:1 and fuel economy was claimed to be 17% better than the previous 1,093cc Golf. It was also available with a 3+E or 4+E Formel E gearbox and an automatic stop-start system with no need to press a button to turn the engine off, as it cut out two seconds after the speed fell below 5kph (3.1mph) – an unpopular idea well ahead of its time.

The 1.6- and 1.8-litre petrol engines also had an electrically controlled fuel cut-off at engine overrun speeds above 1,200rpm, claimed to fully shut off the supply at town speeds. (Fiat was offering a similar cut-off system on the Ritmo.) Lighter connecting rods and

continued on page 102

The durable cabriolet

With the launch of the Golf 2, a new cabriolet was eagerly anticipated but not to arrive. In 1982, with Volkswagen's finances in a perilous state, Carl Hahn looked at the likely development costs of a cabriolet and realised they would raise the sale price to an unacceptable level. He argued hard for the Golf 1 cabriolet to be retained, even though the new car was better for technology and comfort.

The Golf 1 cabriolet was still only four years old (on sale for even less time on the US market) and selling a healthy 2,000 units a year. It was a pragmatic decision not to spend resources developing a new one. By 1984 it had some serious competition in the shape of the Escort cabriolet – also developed and built by Karmann – and the Kadett/Astra. *Motor* magazine tested an £8,980 Golf GTI convertible in March 1984 and concluded that 'despite threatened obsolescence and a near £9,000 price tag, we have no hesitation in choosing the Golf.'

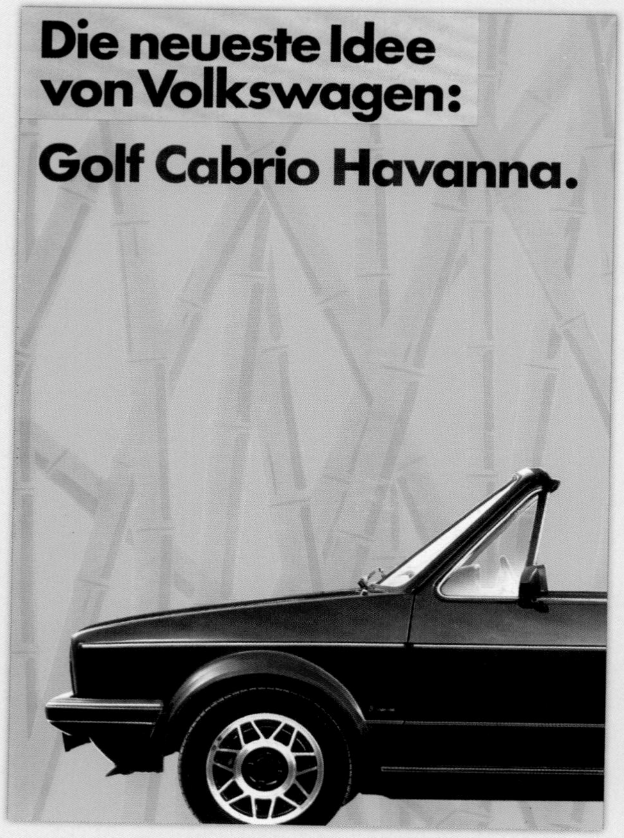
Die neueste Idee
von Volkswagen:
Golf Cabrio Havanna.

➔ The first-generation Golf cabriolet thrived in a myriad of special editions. (Author's collection)

↓ In 1983 the cabriolet gained body-coloured bumpers and plastic cladding in 1987 (here) made it look longer. The hood was revised in 1981 to make it sit slightly flatter.

For 1983 the Golf cabriolet was face-lifted with body-coloured bumpers and given a larger fuel tank. Engine options varied between different power outputs of the 1.6- and 1.8-litre petrol units – never a diesel. There was a single Golf 2 soft-top styling study, built in 1985 with the extended rear of the Jetta 2, but this was scrapped on the grounds it would not have been profitable with the original still selling like hot cakes.

The major cabriolet facelift came in 1987 for the 1988 model year when bigger bumpers and plastic cladding around the lower half of the bodywork contrived to make the car look bigger than it was and accommodate ever-widening wheels and tyres. For the 1990 model year buyers could at last opt for an electric roof mechanism.

It was no longer about price or practicality; the Golf cabriolet was a fashion accessory, with ever-changing colours and special editions giving buyers a reason to want one. Volkswagen UK dropped the GTI badge in May 1991 and replaced it with two limited editions, the Rivage five-speed and the Rivage 'leather', hopelessly out of date but commanding premium prices. In the summer months it would introduce lower-priced 90bhp Clipper editions.

↑ On a 'J' registration for 1991 this UK Golf cabriolet is in typical expensive specification with leather interior and alloy wheels.

Road testers complained of a ride that crashed and banged over poor surfaces and not even the option of power steering ('it's so heavy at slow speeds that we're amazed city users put up with it' said *What Car?*) but build quality and cachet seemed still to win out. A driver's airbag arrived in 1992, but the following year was the last of production, with the Golf 3 cabriolet Karmann's next project. With 331,848 examples sold, the Golf 1 cabriolet had became the world's best seller.

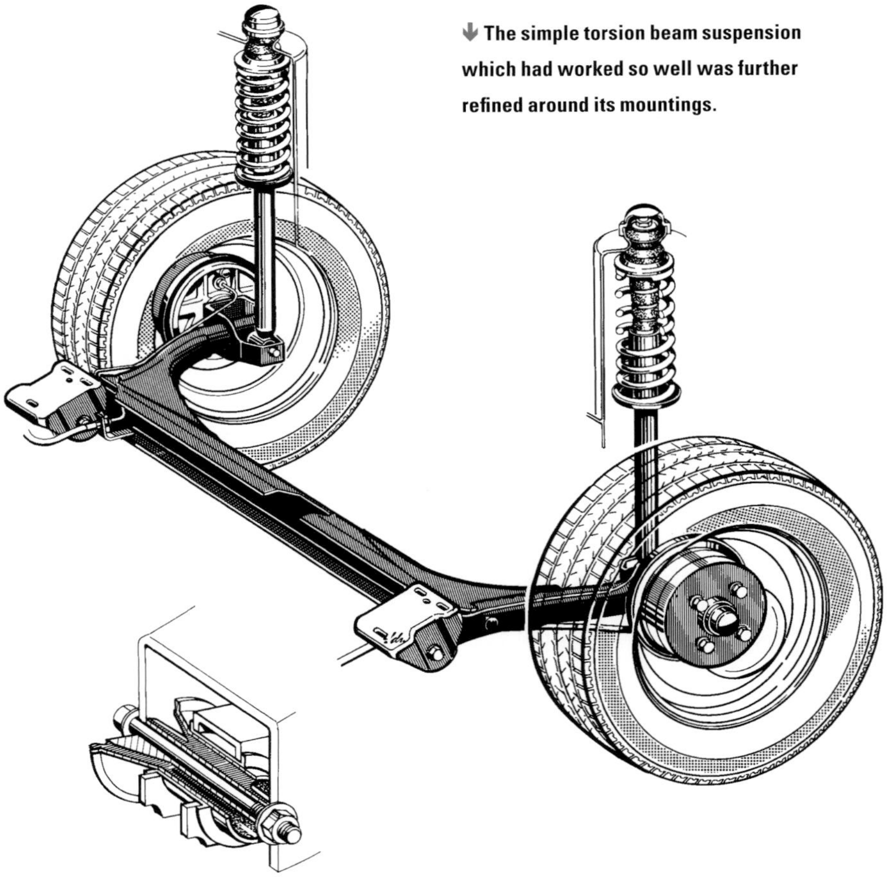

↓ **The simple torsion beam suspension which had worked so well was further refined around its mountings.**

pistons were also claimed to increase engine efficiency as was an electric warm-up in the inlet manifold.

The next petrol engine was the 75bhp 1.6-litre, later joined by a carburetted 90bhp 1.8-litre available for the first time in a standard Golf rather than the GTI. The five-speed (4 + Formel E) gearbox made for relaxed cruising with maximum power developed at 5,200rpm and peak torque at 3,300rpm. Although not immediately in the showrooms, the GTI's specification was previewed in August 1983 and it carried over the 112bhp 1.8-litre unit of the last car, with a 130bhp 16-valve promised later. The 1.6-litre diesel choice continued to be a normally aspirated 54bhp or 70bhp turbo diesel, the latter available (although not for all markets) in all trim levels plus the 'sporty' GTD.

The previous three-speed automatic continued as an option on the 1.6 and 1.8, and the engine/gearbox unit on all the new Golfs was mounted on a subframe to reduce noise transfer to the passenger compartment, one of a number of such changes in mountings.

Trim designations were the same as before, but the new range-topping 1.8 GLX featured such luxuries as central locking, electric front windows and power steering plus the trip computer from the GTI. Importantly, Golfs from the C upwards now had a rear wash-wipe system. Seats on all models were trimmed in cloth, ranging from a hard-wearing tweed to a more luxurious fabric on other models. For workaday Golfs simulated leather was an option.

The successful philosophy of MacPherson-strut front suspension and twist-beam rear continued but with a number of changes aimed at improving ride and handling. At the front the mounting of the lower wishbone (pivoting on a new rubber-mounted subframe) was more flexible and there was a little more spring travel. Still a simple-looking design, the rear suspension remained a pressed steel cross-member but now V-shaped in cross-section rather than T-shaped similar to the latest Passat, aimed at easier mounting of a rear anti-roll bar and a reduction in road noise. New bushing in the trailing arms was said to better control the rear tyres if they were deflected during cornering, so reducing any rear wheel steering effect.

Rack-and-pinion steering was fitted as before, with a new unit designed with bushings to resist lateral movement of the steering rack. Although power steering had been an uncommon option on the last of the American Volkswagen Rabbits, it was now standard on the Golf GL and would be increasingly offered in future. All Golfs now had front disc brakes and British writers especially noted that the braking system was designed so that in both left- and right-hand-drive versions the brake pedal acted directly on the servo rather than by a rod.

Easier to build and own

So while it might not have looked very much different, the new Golf continued the Beetle's philosophy of earnest rather than startling improvements. The prices inevitably rose but Fiala's team produced a calculation that buyers of the new 1.3-litre Golf would still make savings through reduced fuel consumption and improved technology, such as an exhaust system with double the lifespan of the old 1.1-litre Golf, amounting to DM 1,665 after four years. German prices started at DM 13,950 (about £6,000 at the time).

It looked a better long-term investment too. Anxious not to repeat the rustproofing mistakes on early Golfs, Volkswagen flooded hot wax into the bodyshell cavities leaving a thin film and carried over plastic wheel-arch liners to stop mud lodging at the join between the windscreen and front wing. This seemed to work; in 2002, almost 20 years later, 450,000 second-generation Golfs were still registered in Germany and in 2014 it was not uncommon to see one parked on the street in a European city. Its contemporaries had vanished.

Production techniques also had to make a step change for the new Golf. In response to the efficiency of Japanese manufacture and aggressive imports, Western car manufacturers were turning to increased automation, much to the displeasure of the unions. Fiat promoted the 1978 Ritmo as having been made entirely by robots.

The new Golf not only had to be a better-built car but also quicker and easier to build. Volkswagen began a programme of production rationalisation in 1979 and programmable machines were introduced into the body shop in 1981. New control systems meant each vehicle could be treated as a single order to individual customer requirements.

This culminated in June 1983 with Hall 54 in Wolfsburg achieving a 25% level of automation by the use of some 80 robots. Performing actions such as fitting the battery, fan belt, wheels and engine, they were claimed to assemble and tighten over 300 screws. On the first floor 53,000 square metres were devoted to the fully automated assembly of parts modules while the bodies were mounted on five lines and then transported to the ground floor for final assembly.

The new Golf's fastening bolts were moved to be accessible to robotic hands; the positioning of fuel and brake lines and the shape of the petrol tank were also changed to enable automatic assembly. The biggest change, however, involved the front end, which was redesigned so that the power unit could be installed in one process and the front panels were bolted rather than welded into place. It was also easier for the assembly line workers who could access the cars from more comfortable positions.

Respectable progress

New Golf deliveries began on 10 September to apparently eager buyers as waiting lists arose. As UK right-hand drive deliveries were not due to start until December 1984, *Autocar* magazine based its first November road test on a German-registered 1.6 GL three-door, a fairly unrepresentative specification for a market that favoured five doors. There was general disappointment over the looks of the new car, but it acknowledged that 'It is generally more refined than its predecessor in all the major dynamic areas bar road noise, and the engineers have done a good job of maintaining the virtues of which the Golf has always been known – excellent ride and handling, light, responsive controls and good cargo capacity.'

Compared with its 1978 test of a 1,475cc Golf GLS the magazine surmised that due to the new car's increased weight, the 5bhp increase in power of the 1,595cc engine and increased torque, only gave a marginal improvement in overall performance, with a top speed only 3mph better at 102mph and a 0–60mph time of 10.9 seconds, 0.5 seconds better than the 1.5 GLS. As was characteristic with the Formel E gear ratios, top

↑ An 'iron slave' in Wolfsburg inserts a thinner space-saver wheel into a Golf's floor. The recess was shaped for it to increase boot capacity.

↑ **During development a video camera films the movement of the drivetrain under different load conditions. Volkswagen was proud of the massive development efforts.**

speed was achieved in fourth gear, with fifth more suited to motorways.

The engine was recognised as being as smooth as before, but this pleasure was marred by the operation of the low-speed fuel cut-off feature which 'seemed to endow the accelerator pedal with a mind of its own. Especially in traffic, cutting back in and making the car creep forward slightly as an automatic gearbox would'. Nor did this seem to result in fuel savings, with a 'mediocre' 29.9mpg recorded over 1,000 miles, leading the magazine to wonder if its test car was maladjusted.

Comfort and interior space were marked as improvements but rearward visibility was not. Singling out the broad rear 'C' pillars: 'Spokesmen for Volkswagen claim that the thick rear pillar is partially required for rollover protection, but it seems clear that marketing people consider this feature of the car an important distinguishing mark.'

The verdict on this pre-British-sale example was ambivalent, praising the previous Golf as having been good up until the end. 'The new Golf is equally good and just a little bit more. But is that enough?' the magazine asked in the face of an anticipated new Vauxhall/Opel Astra and gave it equal ranking with the current Astra.

Sales proved the Golf 2 clearly was good enough. It topped European production tables for 1984 with 577,062 built, making it Europe's best-selling car for the second year in succession. The Fiat Uno and Ford Escort came second and third. Thanks to increased profits from Audi and improved performance from VW South America the group made a post-tax profit of DM 228m (around £60m at the time) for 1984.

Rabbit becomes Golf

The new Golf reached the American market at the start of 1985 badged as a Golf rather than a Rabbit. This had been announced as the last Rabbit left the Westmoreland line in June 1984. The *New York Times* reported that production of two- and four-door versions of the new Golf would begin in August after about

↑ The cabin of a middle-specification Golf in 1983. No painted door metal visible and the trim panels were shaped for extra elbow room. The dashboard brought a major improvement in ventilation. (LAT)

← A view of the rear seats in a three-door shows standard-fit rear seatbelts and two-thirds along the seat is where it can split-fold, a novel feature then. (LAT)

$200 million in retooling. Rabbit was gone, although for a while Austria and Belgium had late-model Golf 1 Rabbit special editions.

'I thought it didn't fit,' said Carl Hahn in 2013. 'We have such world cars and I see no reason that we badge them differently. With the mobility of our customers, enormous numbers of Americans travelling all over I think it would be a mistake to give America a different name.'

The Westmoreland Golf was once more easily distinguishable by its rectangular headlamps and under the skin the suspension setting changes were minimal, to account for the extra weight of emissions equipment. Having been engineered for air conditioning and power steering it was much more suitable to confront tough opposition from the Mitsubishi Mirage and Toyota Corolla.

Road & Track was underwhelmed by the conservative new styling: 'The Golf doesn't look exciting. It doesn't look different.' Nonetheless, the extra space and utility were much appreciated as was the new base American engine, the 1.8-litre four-cylinder with Bosch fuel injection and a three-way catalytic converter giving 85bhp as opposed to the European 90. This performance was almost equal to the previous Rabbit GTI. 'What the Golf engine has is flexibility. Volkswagen's chief power-train engineer says that's what American motorists want.'

The new US Golfs could also be had with a 1.6-litre non-turbo diesel and the Jetta, which appeared later in 1985, mirrored this choice with the addition of a turbo diesel. As in Europe, there was no second-generation Golf

↑ Seat fabrics were variations on a hard-wearing tweed-like material. Top to bottom; Golf C, CL and GL. The dashboard was black or brown. (Author's collection)

➔ For a small business there was now a Polo or Golf van with a flat floor and panel to stop goods sliding forwards. For larger work there was the Golf 1-based Caddy from 1983. (Author's collection)

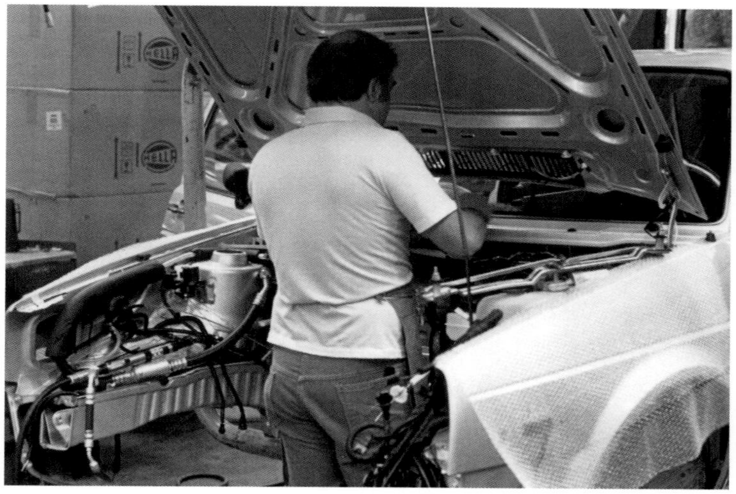

↑ **US Golf 2 assembly in Westmoreland didn't enjoy the same degree of automation but the workers seem happy enough. (VWoA)**

cabriolet for America, but it was up-engined to 1.8 litres and available in limited edition Wolfsburg trim with power steering, leather interior and alloy wheels as standard. It was known simply as the Volkswagen Cabriolet while the GTI became a name on its own, with no Golf badge, a practice that would continue.

However, these were the last days of the North American-built Golf. While the new Golf and GTI started well in its first year of US sales in the face of a slump suffered across the US industry in the face of Japanese competition, numbers dwindled towards the end of the 1980s, the Jetta saloon proving the better seller at around 60,000 cars a year. In 1988 Carl Hahn took the decision to close the Westmoreland factory. 'It wasn't profitable. We were expanding in other places automatically and we had to build a new factory in Saxony and other places so I thought it wouldn't be a mistake to close this factory. Had this happened in Germany this would have been seen as a catastrophe, but the Governor of Pennsylvania sent me a cable saying he fully understood my decision. We had a fair closing. At Christmas I had a card from our workers thanking us for having worked for us for ten years at a fair rate.'

With the once hard-fought-for factory gone, production of Golfs and Jettas for the US market would move to the modernised plant in Puebla, Mexico after all. After further turbulent years, Volkswagen only returned to US manufacture in 2009 with the construction of a new plant in Chattanooga, Tennessee, chasing a target to boost group sales in the United States to more than a million vehicles per year by 2018. It launched a version of the Passat specifically designed for the US market (with 85% local content) in 2011. This hit the market very successfully with annual sales for 2012 of 117,023,

continued on page 110

A Yuppie or a Sloane's car?

Britain in the 1980s was a country of 'tribes', at least as the media saw it. Once owning a Volkswagen marked you out as an eccentric, now it marked you out as clever, go-getting or posh. If you were a 'Yuppie' or a 'Sloane Ranger' you simply had to have a Golf.

Motor magazine mused on the GTI's solid appeal in June 1985: 'It's the Yuppie's car – the Young Urban Professional seen buzzing down the outside lane of the M4, slicing through Hyde Park Corner or fending off a traffic warden outside a Covent Garden advertising agency.'

Volkswagen Audi Group's market analysis supported the stereotype. The typical Golf GTI buyer was a young professional man but also just an intelligent person who thought carefully about which car to buy. 'Brilliant UK advertising in the 1980s helped,' says automotive analyst Jay Nagley. 'The 1980s seemed to be Dire Straits, Princess Di and Golf GTIs. Talking of Princess Di, "Girls love Golfs". It might sound sexist, but females who hardly know an Alfa from an Aston will coo over a Golf. Stylish without being ostentatious, reliable and easy to drive, it is the ultimate safe choice. No one will ever laugh at a Golf buyer – if you are not that fussed about cars, there is a lot to be said for the safe choice. After all that is how lots of men buy their clothes.'

A GTI was never cheap and even when the competition caught up and undercut it, that only seemed to boost its appeal. Canny buyers knew it held its value better. On introduction to the UK in 1984, a three-door Golf 2 GTI was £7,867 tax paid, nearly £1,000 more than some very capable rivals such as the Astra GTE. But success wasn't measured in numbers. In 1984 19,772 Ford XR3is were sold in the UK and 3,885 Golf 2 GTIs. It mattered not all at all that it was expensive – in fact it helped. This was the decade where a whole new class

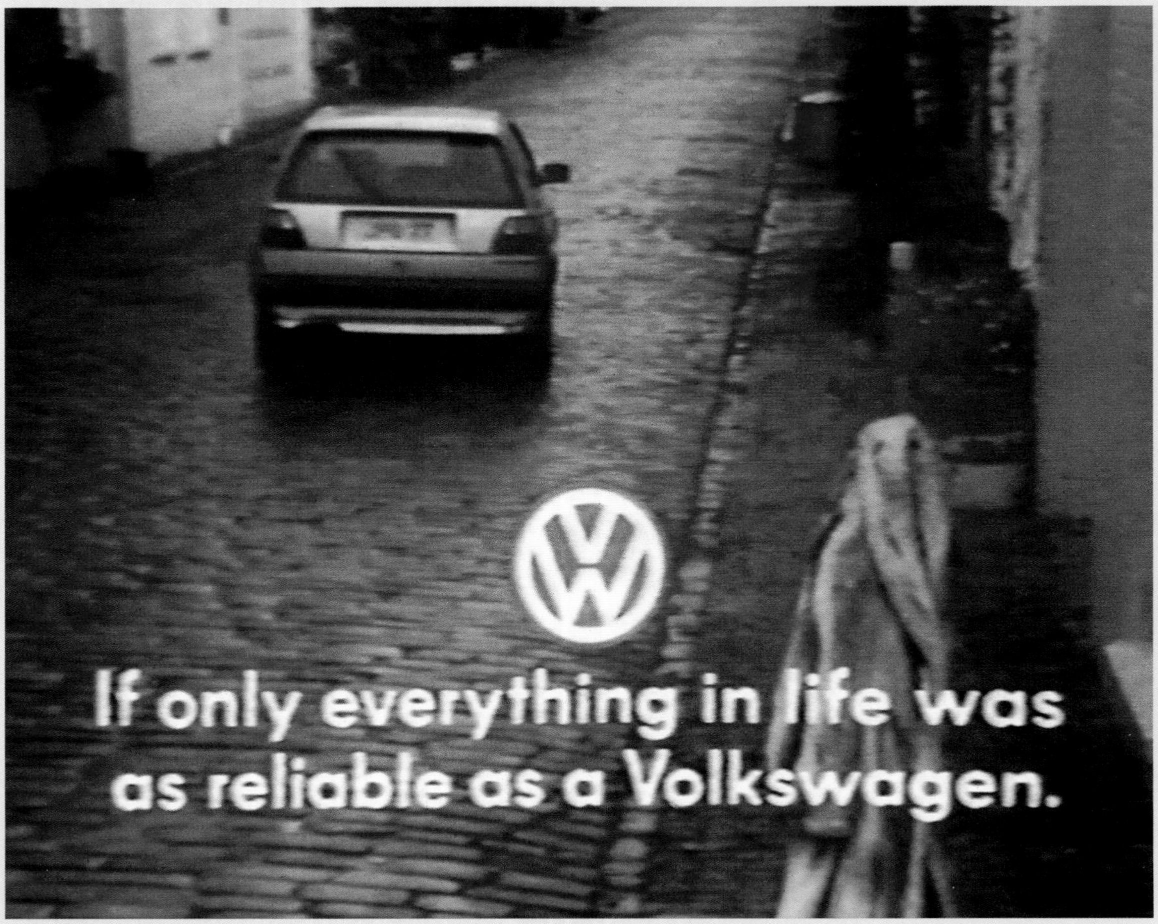

If only everything in life was
as reliable as a Volkswagen.

This late 1980s Volkswagen advert and its slogan were still recalled decades later. (LAT/DDB)

of people were making money and wanted to show it. German brands were the thing to have.

'Later Golfs, especially GTIs, became a fetish of the design decade,' says design critic Stephen Bayley. 'Owning a Golf was a form of social-promotion by design. They say the Mini was the first small car to be classless. Well, the Golf was the second. To the apex predators of the eighties, the not yet wholly discredited City boys, a Golf was an acceptable Porsche alternative. It did not make you feel poor.'

Author James Ruppert was part of all this, selling BMWs from London's Park Lane in the 1980s. 'From my perspective, behind a plate glass window of a BMW showroom, the Golf GTI looked really good. "But Sir/Madam, that's just a shopping car like an Escort, it doesn't have the prestige of a 3 Series. Sign here." Off duty though the GTI was the car I told friends to buy instead of a rather overpriced, under-equipped 3 Series.'

On the other hand, the Golf GTI also apparently belonged to the 'Sloane Ranger', an even more well-defined 1980s stereotype of an upper-class very English person (he Henry, she Caroline) whose life and habits were mapped out in the best-selling *Official Sloane Ranger Handbook* by Ann Barr and Peter York.

Sloanes did not care much about their cars but always had the right kind of car for their time in life. The Golf GTI was in the handbook's 'Young Ranger's nippy town car' class, which could mean a Mini Metro, jaunty foreign car like a Renault 4 or 'Faster, especially army men's cars: Volkswagen Golf GTI (black).'

In 1989 the 75,000th Golf GTI was sold in the UK. But there was a downside to this desirability. As the decade closed, values of GTIs fluctuated in proportion to their position in the top ten of stolen cars. Insurance premiums became punitive and in the early 1990s the once rock-solid used car prices started to fall.

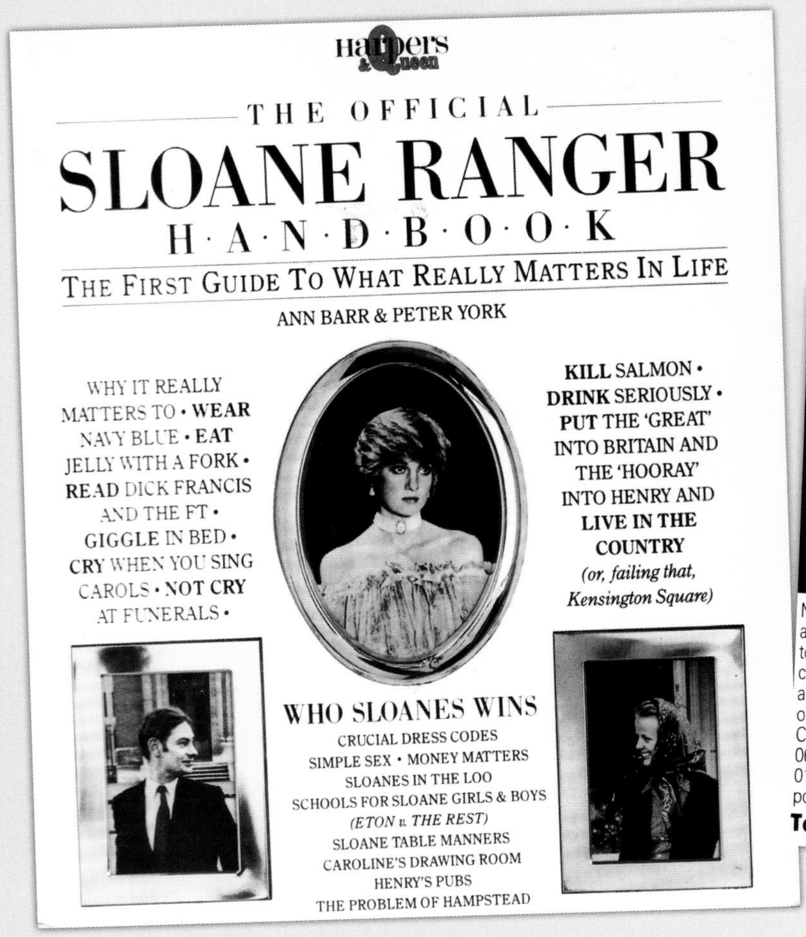

Harpers & Queen
THE OFFICIAL
SLOANE RANGER
H·A·N·D·B·O·O·K
THE FIRST GUIDE TO WHAT REALLY MATTERS IN LIFE
ANN BARR & PETER YORK
WHY IT REALLY MATTERS TO • WEAR NAVY BLUE • EAT JELLY WITH A FORK • READ DICK FRANCIS AND THE FT • GIGGLE IN BED • CRY WHEN YOU SING CAROLS • NOT CRY AT FUNERALS •
KILL SALMON • DRINK SERIOUSLY • PUT THE 'GREAT' INTO BRITAIN AND THE 'HOORAY' INTO HENRY AND LIVE IN THE COUNTRY (or, failing that, Kensington Square)
WHO SLOANES WINS
CRUCIAL DRESS CODES
SIMPLE SEX • MONEY MATTERS
SLOANES IN THE LOO
SCHOOLS FOR SLOANE GIRLS & BOYS (ETON v. THE REST)
SLOANE TABLE MANNERS
CAROLINE'S DRAWING ROOM
HENRY'S PUBS
THE PROBLEM OF HAMPSTEAD

← 1980s Britain was one of 'tribes' and the cheeky *Sloane Ranger Handbook* described how certain upper-class people might live. One of the proscribed cars was a black GTI. (Author's collection)

↓ The cachet of the GTI brought its own problems, as this 1990 ad illustrates. (Author's collection)

Does GTi stand for
GIGANTIC
TOP-LOADED
INSURANCE?
Not necessarily. We have very special arrangements to suit all circumstances and all kinds of cars.
Call us now on 0638 661861 or 01-631 3961 or post the coupon to:
GTI
Taylor Price & Co., 105 High Street, Newmarket, Suffolk CB8 8JH

↑ Another day, another big number in Wolfsburg. On 25 June 1985 the millionth Golf 2 rolled off the line after selling at a faster rate than its predecessor. It is flanked by the millionth Golf 1 and Beetle.

contributing to an overall figure of 483,133, the likes of which Volkswagen of America had not seen since the early 1970s. However, America continued to prove a hard market to maintain, and by the end of 2013 it had taken a dip once more.

The understated GTI

Back to Europe in the 1980s. Whilst previewed in 1983, a GTI in the new body shape didn't go into production until January 1984. At first the specification seemed to be little more than the previous 1,781cc 112bhp engine and gearbox decanted into the new body. However, it delivered that power in an even more flexible way than previously, achieving maximum power at 5,000 instead of 5,800rpm, torque was increased by 5% and developed at a lower engine speed of 3,100rpm. The final drive and the fifth gear ratios were altered to increase the spacing between fifth and the intermediate gear ratios.

The GTI's suspension was set 10mm lower than standard Golfs and had stiffer springs and shock absorbers with front and rear anti-roll bars. The wheels were now 14 rather than 13in items, steel in standard specification with an option of the Pirelli P pattern alloys and fitted with 185/60R14 P6 tyres. Disc brakes were fitted front and rear for the first time, 9.4in ventilated at the front.

However, it was the way the new GTI first looked that attracted – or failed to attract – most comment. The interior was as black as ever and had lost the tartan pattern on the sports seats in favour of two blocks of orange and red striping on the base and backrest. But the real problem was that it was now hard to distinguish a GTI from a GTD or a GLX because it had single headlamps and plain black bumpers. Perhaps customers had got used to four-lamped Golf GTIs in bright colours with the highly successful run-out special editions of the last model, but the proportion of GTI to total Golf sales fell from 30 to 13% with big GTI markets France and Italy distinctly underwhelmed.

Towards the end of 1984, less than a year after its German launch and less than six months after it had gone on sale in the UK it received a premature facelift for the 1985 model year. According to *Car* magazine, Volkswagen asked their dealers to suggest what could be done to improve things with a £250 limit per car. Changes were

made to the 1985 model year Golf GTIs to add a twin headlamp grille, additional red lines to the bumpers and side trim, black door sills, twin exhaust tailpipes, new sports seat upholstery and door trims plus new steel sports wheels in addition to optional alloys.

The car tested by *Motor* in early May 1984 was already sporting the four-headlamp grille as specified by the importer (British Volkswagens often had slightly higher specification) and all the improvements were duly noted. This time though it had to work hard to justify a price that was undercut by most direct rivals such as the Astra GTE and Ford Escort XR3i.

On paper, performance results were not startling, given the extra weight. The measured top speed was 114mph compared to 112 and the 0–60mph time 8.3 seconds to 8.1. This put it in the same ballpark as its competitors, but as ever it was the flexible nature of the engine that impressed *Motor*: 'Despite the eagerness with which it revs to the red line, it is equally content to slog away at the other end of the scale. Indeed, it will pull cleanly and uncomplainingly from below its 600rpm idle speed.'

↑ Granted it was wearing optional alloy wheels, but this summer 1983 launch photo of the new Golf GTI shows a single-lamped look, which potential buyers found too boring.

↓ Quick facelift: this January 1985 British-market brochure shows a more sporting GTI with red piping along the bumpers and twin headlamps. A five-door GTI was newly available. (Author's collection)

The Ultimate hatchback.

The Golf GTi has been described by motoring writers as the "ultimate hatchback". It is powered by the renowned 1800 cc fuel injection engine producing 112 bhp.

Combine this with a 5 speed close ratio sports gearbox, more aerodynamic body, improved suspension, disc brakes all round, low profile tyres and the new Golf GTi is all set for supremacy on the road. Top speed is 119 mph and 0—60 is reached in a rapid 8.3 seconds.

The GTi, now available with 3 and 5 doors, is immediately recognised by its red trimmed, twin headlamp grille, large wheel arches and black surround to the rear window — all features that have become synonymous with fast living.

New for 1985 is the addition of twin exhaust pipes, red trim strips for the bumpers, a wide side moulding, steel sliding sunroof and sporty striped upholstery. An attractive 6 J x 14 steel wheel is now offered as standard on the 3 door model with the option of specifying the Pirelli-styled alloy road wheels. The alloy wheels are standard on the 5 door model.

Interior of a 1986 GTI. The small sign below the air vent reminds the driver to use unleaded fuel only so as not to damage the catalyst.

To drive, the steering was felt to be heavier (no power assistance available yet) and with the wider tyres there came an increase in torque steer (where powerful front-drive cars pull at the steering wheel from a standing start) but it remained direct and precise. The new GTI had entirely predictable handling when it reached its cornering limits but not at the expense of suspension suppleness, which was also found to have improved. The all-disc brakes were judged to give powerful and fade-free stopping power. The conclusion of that spring 1984 road test rated it a winner but with a caveat: 'There is little doubt that the new GTI's virtues extend its appeal – as a family express it is certainly an improved car. Equally as a driver's car it still feels the same – it has lost none of its magic. But in seeking a wider audience, VW have taken no more than a sideways step.'

Back in America, enthusiasts were delighted that the Volkswagen GTI followed the Golf the same year, 1985. It was closer to European specification but with options such as power steering and cruise control. With a full closed three-way catalytic converter, power was down at 110bhp. However, if money was no object then famous tuner Reeves Callaway of Connecticut would heavily rework the engine, adding a turbocharger good for about 150bhp.

Golf GTI 16-valve

At launch a faster factory-built Golf GTI had been mentioned and with more and more manufacturers wanting some GTI cachet a performance race was already in progress. In early 1984 the regular competition offered 105 to 115bhp, but Fiat introduced the twin-carburettor Ritmo Abarth 130TC in June 1983 with a 2-litre engine and Ford added a turbocharger to the 1.6-litre XR3i to create the 132bhp RS Turbo in 1984.

Volkswagen's answer was not to turbocharge its 1.8. Company engineers had long eschewed the turbocharger for petrol engines, equating it with poor low-speed torque and fuel consumption. Turbos were considered for all the GTIs and tests began in

1981 with the 1.6-litre engine, according to James Ruppert's history, then again in 1983 with an American specification 1.7-litre, but heat and fuel consumption were both excessive. 'If we were ever to use forced induction,' one VW engineer said, 'it would be with mechanical supercharging, not turbocharging.' And this later turned out to be true.

Ernst Fiala recalls: 'We made a turbocharged Scirocco with a 150bhp engine. It was ready for production and we made the first cars, but there was an accident where a flywheel exploded. It had nothing to do with the turbocharger but that was the end of that experiment. We came back to it in the Audi 200 [200 5T, 1979].'

The next engine development was true to racing-engine practice, extracting more power and better efficiency by having four overhead valves per cylinder (two intake and two exhaust) driven by twin overhead camshafts. With a four-cylinder engine that equalled 16 valves – an alternative to turbocharging that was just as marketable. While European manufacturers had been slow (the Triumph Dolomite Sprint being a somewhat unusual exception) by the mid 1980s most of the Japanese manufacturers were building sporty 16-valve units and it was to become the norm on mainstream European cars eventually.

Volkswagen started development of a 16-valve cylinder head for the 1.8 in 1981 alongside the 1.8-litre version of the GTI. Initially the new unit was to power versions of the Golf and the Scirocco but later other models. Informed by its experience of the Oettinger 16S (see Chapter 2), and reportedly with pressure from Volkswagen's French sales organisation, an official 16-valve programme was developed by Audi on the basis of the trusty EA827 unit. A prototype unit was shown to the press in September 1983 but delayed into production as Audi engineers were reportedly not happy with its refinement. Two versions were engineered: one for premium grade leaded petrol and another for the unleaded fuel demanded by a catalytic converter.

Keeping the standard GTI's Bosch K-Jetronic fuel injection and 10:1 compression ratio, the fuel and air mixture was fed into a bigger plenum chamber above the new cylinder head. To cater for the higher temperatures the exhaust valves were filled with sodium while the undersides of the piston crowns were cooled by jets of oil from the crankcase when pressure exceeded 28psi, and the engine was fitted with the larger capacity oil pump from the Golf diesel. Because the new 16-valve cylinder head had to bolt onto a block designed for a narrower unit, the valve layout was not symmetrical, with the exhaust valves placed vertically and the inlet valves inclined by 25 degrees to save space. To aid refinement and reduce maintenance, the valves were activated by hydraulic tappets, a feature that soon found its way onto lesser Golf engines.

It was usual practice for a chain or toothed belt to drive both overhead camshafts, but to save space in this transverse installation Volkswagen followed Porsche and designed the exhaust cam to be belt-driven in the conventional way with drive to the other cam by a small chain taken off the drive at the opposite end of the cylinder head. In pre-production the drive was by gearwheels, but this was changed to chain drive for quieter running. The bottom half of the 1,781cc engine block was largely unchanged, but the crankshaft was reshaped to cope with the extra stresses and both it and the pistons were lightened. It gained a reputation as a very tough engine.

↓ Long and thorough development of the first Volkswagen 16-valve engine paid off in service.

↑ **With its discreet 16V badges the 1985 GTI 16-valve restored lost sparkle to what was now an integral part of the Golf line-up.**

In its final form peak power compared to the eight-valve was up from 112bhp to 139bhp, developed at 6,100rpm. In development it had been safe at speeds in excess of 7,000rpm but when released a rev limiter was set at 6,200rpm. The performance improvements over the standard GTI were decisive, with power up by 24% and torque up by 9%. There was a debate though among 1980s GTI fans as to whether the eight-valve was preferable day to day because of its better low-down torque.

The Scirocco GTX 16V went on sale in Germany in August 1985 to allow time for engine production to ramp up. The following year some were officially imported into the UK in left-hand drive, but redesigning the brake pedal linkage for right-hand-drive production was judged too difficult because it was still based on the first Golf floorpan. The Golf GTI 16V went on German sale in November 1985, reaching the UK in late 1986. A catalysed version for other markets was introduced with a 10bhp loss of power, considered low at the time. Tested by *Motor* it was the fastest Golf to date with a 124.6mph top speed (VW had claimed 130mph was possible) and 0–60 in 7.5 seconds with an overall fuel consumption of 28.1mpg. This put it comfortably back in contention with its direct turbocharged rivals.

Outside, it resembled the eight-valve GTI apart from discreet badging, slightly bigger front and rear spoilers and a ride height further lowered by 10mm. There were uprated springs, shock absorbers and anti-roll bars and the disc brakes had larger pistons and extra venting for the front pair. Helping to soften a £1,900 price premium, UK 16Vs came with alloy wheels, electric front windows and central locking. Power steering was an option. However, over the following years the UK specification jumped around with some of these items travelling to and from the options list.

Other markets took different approaches to positioning the 16V. America downgraded the eight-valve GTI to GT status, resorting to rear drum brakes and plainer seats but did get a 134bhp 2.0-litre 16v in 1991. From 1987 South Africa sold a five-door version with power steering, leather seats and air conditioning called the Executive, which kept the suspension settings of the regular GTI.

↑ With the arrival of the 16V in 1987, Volkswagen of America rebadged its eight-valve GTI as a GT, still with an American-built 102bhp (US) engine. (VWoA)

Greener Golfs

By late 1985 all Volkswagen petrol engines had become easier to maintain with hydraulic adjustment-free tappets, electronic ignition, long-life spark plugs and self-adjusting clutches. Main service intervals on petrol Audis and Volkswagens went from 10,000 to 20,000 miles. The base engine was now the 1.3, which gave the Golf C an advantage over the equivalent Ford Escort and Opel Kadett/Vauxhall Astra, which had 1.1s. 'In its basic version it's a car with many positives and few negatives,' said *Auto Motor und Sport* in July 1985. 'In its cheapest form it offers exceptionally high value.' All the same, this model only represented 13% of German Golf sales.

While one side of the Golf range was all about efficient high performance, the other was increasingly catering for environmental concerns voiced by customers and changes forced on carmakers by legislators. Germany saw a growing awareness of environmental concerns and the Green Party, formed in 1980, was to become highly influential. The use of cars, fuel and pollution became issues for domestic buyers and European legislation would eventually make catalytic converters for petrol engines obligatory in an effort to reduce the smog cause by unburned hydrocarbons reacting with carbon monoxide. By the late 1980s some German cities were banning the use of private cars on days when smog levels were high, encouraging Audi and Volkswagen's experiments with hybrid cars (see Appendix 1).

Of course, three-way catalysts with fuel injection had been fitted to American-market Audis and Volkswagens since the 1970s but usually sapped a noticeable amount of power. In 1983 Audi made catalysts an option across its range and the following year Volkswagen offered one for European buyers designed for smaller capacity engines. The motoring press hotly debated the worth and durability of catalysts and to this end two catalysed Group A racing specification Golfs lapped the Nürburgring circuit for 24 hours in summer 1985, suffering no more than wheel bearing problems.

By November 1987 Volkswagen had completed the changeover of its production to catalytic converter technology – although Opel was the first to fit them as

continued on page 118

GTi Engineering and the Golf 2

By the mid-1980s the Golf GTI's image was sky high in most of Europe, not least in Britain. Lots of people were spending lots of money on their GTIs and as Volkswagen's approach to increasing its power was thorough and cautious, the market for aftermarket engine tuning thrived.

Select a British car magazine or a Golf history produced in the 1980s and time and time again the name GTi (small 'i') Engineering comes up. It was founded by racing driver Richard Lloyd, credited with buying what was said to be the first left-hand-drive GTI imported into the UK and racing it with great success from 1977 to '79, also running Volkswagen UK's racing activities. Together with Brian Ricketts, formerly of Broadspeed, Lloyd set up GTi Engineering in 1978 initially to convert left-hand-drive first GTIs to right-hand drive until the first official car arrived. It was based at Silverstone racing circuit in Northamptonshire, not far from Volkswagen's Milton Keynes headquarters.

The company developed performance Volkswagen and Audi engine conversions, which stayed one step ahead of what VAG was doing. The ever-burgeoning catalogue offered performance, ride and handling, and styling accessories. There was always a GTi conversion demonstrator available for the car magazines and Lloyd was equally available for a quote.

'We'll make your GTI everything you want it to be' ran the advertising slogan. In 1986 the 'Plus Pac' power conversion would raise power from 112bhp to 135bhp, then there was a 2-litre, 8-valve 152bhp conversion and a 2-litre, 16-valve 170bhp Oettinger conversion, which cost over £4,000 (a regular GTI was about £8,000 then).

Once the official GTI 16-valve was in prospect, Lloyd produced the 1900RE which kept the 8-valve engine but enlarged the valves and cylinder capacity to 1,870cc rather than 1,781cc. Power was a claimed 142bhp and the price for engine conversion considered reasonable at £1,475 if you didn't have the 'Aero Tech' bodykit.

While other companies such as Janspeed made a name out of turbocharging, GTi Engineering avoided it, preferring to go through engines in great detail and enlarge their capacities for a reliable conversion. It did, however, venture into supercharging ahead of Volkswagen, in 1985 plumbing an American Magnacharger supercharger onto the development 1.8-litre conversion and touting the car around the car magazines. With quoted power of 165bhp, in-gear acceleration was described as 'truly astonishing'. The conversion, though, was more of an exercise to keep publicity going before the factory 16-valve arrived and the company was not keen to offer kits. Brian Ricketts was notably quoted in one article saying: 'It's a bit like giving an 18-year-old a 12-bore isn't it?'

By September 1987 GTi engineering had produced its 1,000th conversion. Into the 1990s Lloyd was more involved in racing and the company was eventually sold off.

↑ A704 XNH was one of GTi Engineering's well-used development cars, here tested by *Motor* in March 1985 with a supercharger. It started life as a standard GTI but acquired the latest Hella DE styling kit, colour keyed to match its paintwork. (LAT)

← GTi Engineering lines up its extensive range of styling and performance options from Polo to Audi Quattro in May 1981. (LAT)

→ Adding the supercharger required a good deal of rearranging in the engine bay, virtually obscuring the actual engine. The fuel injection unit is relocated top left in the corner of the engine bay atop the supercharger. (LAT)

standard in 1989 – and it became mandatory for the German market in 1989 (for cars over two litres), but it was not a legal requirement for British-registered cars to have catalysts until 1992. In 1988, when Volkswagen offered a two-way catalyst option on the 1.3 and 1.6 Golf for £200 extra and only 3bhp less power it was considered enough of a marginal novelty for *Autocar* to give it a road test. The only issue then was the availability of unleaded petrol, lead being harmful not only for human health but to the precious metals inside a catalyst. More efficient closed-loop catalysts arrived in 1990.

More than a million diesel Golfs had left the productions lines since 1976 and the fuel was seen as more environmentally friendly than petrol because the engine consumed less of it, although attention was turning towards the content of diesel exhaust gases. Diesel engines were now offered in most Golf-class cars and for buyers in mainland Europe the Golf turbo diesel became increasingly popular, especially as a GTI-lookalike GTD. The Golf GTD, fitted with a Garret T3 turbocharger, developed 70bhp compared to 54 of the standard 1,588cc diesel and knocked over four seconds from its 0–60mph time to 13.5secs. Its official urban fuel consumption figure was still 47.1mpg. It was slow coming to the UK with diesel sales only taking up 2.5% of the total market in 1985. *Motor* magazine noted sagely that 'many engineers believe the turbo diesel will be the power unit of the future, though the engine's inherent complexity makes it expensive.' Thus although the GTD was praised for its flexibility, refinement and overall fuel consumption of 40.1mpg at £7,445 it was nearly £1,000 more than the popular Citroen BX diesel.

Overall Volkswagen diesel sales faltered after 1986 when every fourth Golf/Jetta was a diesel and by late 1989 the share had dropped to 15%. Nonetheless, the same year Volkswagen premiered the first diesel engine with a two-way catalytic converter, an oxidisation catalyst that was able to cut down on carbon monoxide and hydrocarbon emissions but not the nitrogen oxide and soot particles. To tackle this Volkswagen used a small turbocharger not to increase performance but to optimise combustion, reducing soot emissions. The Umwelt diesel (for environment) produced 10bhp less than the regular turbo diesel at 60bhp and had no sporting pretensions. It did, however, undercut all emissions limits at the time. In Britain it replaced the standard diesel, slotting in below the regular (non-catalysed) turbo diesel. The latter was fitted with an intercooler in 1989, boosting power to 80bhp.

↓ A 1984 GTD diesel gets close to the GTI look but not its performance. Still at this point not for the UK.

Syncro, the four-wheel-drive Golf

When Audi launched its four-wheel-drive Quattro coupe in 1980 to great acclaim it was only a matter of time before Volkswagen started to produce cars with drive to all four wheels. At the time, four-wheel drive in regular cars was still highly unusual. Japanese maker Subaru had carved out its own niche of cars with selectable four-wheel drive and some European companies such as Sinpar in France would convert front-driven Renaults. However, there was no obvious market for a production family car. The Quattro's image and sporting success changed all that and in 1983 Audi applied the same transmission to the more mainstream Audi 80. Fiat launched a four-wheel drive Panda in 1984, Ford launched the Sierra 4x4 in 1985 and 4x4 became an '80s buzzword along with 'Turbo'.

For Audi's quattro transmission (with a lower-case 'q'), a differential was placed between the gearbox of the front-driven longitudinal engine and a propshaft taking drive to a specially designed rear axle and transmission. It had permanent four-wheel drive split 50:50, and the central and rear differentials were lockable to help traction in icy or slippery conditions. As it shared the same mechanical layout, Volkswagen first applied this to the Passat in 1984 and coined the name syncro.

In March 1985 the Caravelle/Transporter became the second Volkswagen available with a syncro option. Developed since 1978 by VW and Austria's Steyr Puch, drive was taken forwards from the rear engine to a viscous coupling mounted behind the new driven front axle. A viscous coupling is a sealed unit with two sets of plates inside filled with a thick fluid, which becomes more viscous as its temperature increases. One set of plates is connected to the drive from the engine. Normally both sets spin at the same speed (the liquid remaining cool), but if the driven plate spins faster, as it would when slipping, the fluid between the plates warms (due to shearing forces), becoming more viscous and eventually locking up, dragging the second plate with it and thus connecting drive to the other set of wheels. Unlike the quattro system, syncro was not permanent four-wheel drive, only driving the rear wheels when conditions got tough.

↑ The four-wheel-drive Golf Syncro was hauled up an incline at the 1985 Frankfurt show. As its driven wheels span on a loose surface drive would be sent from front to rear and back. (LAT)

Volkswagen and SEAT

Looking to create a domestic car industry and mass transportation, the Sociedad Española de Automóviles de Turismo, S.A. (SEAT) was founded in 1950. The Spanish government signed with Fiat for assembly of a Spanish version of the Fiat 1400, which started in 1953. Volkswagen Beetle assembly had been contemplated but judged too politically sensitive.

A string of rebadged Fiats followed, with the occasional unique model. However, in the late 1960s and early 1970s a number of tie-ups with other European manufacturers were discussed and in 1979 a merger was agreed with Fiat, only for the Italian giant to pull out a year later, with SEAT reliant on huge loans.

SEAT's problems at the start of the 1980s drew the attention of Volkswagen's Toni Schmücker and a series of informal meetings and visits took place. While it was secure elsewhere in Europe, Volkswagen had little sales presence in Spain. Schmücker signed a letter of intent with the Spanish Government in 1981, but was succeeded by Carl Hahn after his death from a heart attack.

Hahn wanted Volkswagen to be seen as an international company. Up until that point it had been German-American and the latter was in real trouble. Now the focus turned back to Europe. In 1982 Volkswagen was fifth in Europe. By adding SEAT it could be second or first. Southern European sales were excessively dependent on the Golf, Jetta and Scirocco taking 45% of sales while the Polo took only 12%. In Spain, VW took only 0.6% of the market and SEAT could provide a whole new dealer network and lower build costs.

Industrial and commercial cooperation agreements were signed with Volkswagen in September 1982. SEAT plants started Spanish production of the Passat and Santana, then the Polo. Once quality was acceptable these were exported back to Germany.

Just as when US manufacture had been mooted ten years before, the idea that Volkswagen might be 'exporting jobs' to Spain was highly sensitive at home. In the end it created 2,000 new jobs and a new factory at Martorell near Barcelona opened in 1993.

Needing its own range of cars for a European sales offensive, SEAT had developed the 1984 Ibiza supermini with styling by Giugiaro, an interior and engine contracted to Porsche and body design by Karmann. The SEAT/Fiat Ritmo was restyled as the Ronda. In 1985 Volkswagen took full ownership of SEAT, giving Fiat a vast cheque for future design royalties.

Toledo – Spanish for Golf

The first all-Volkswagen SEAT was the Toledo five-door hatchback, designed and developed in a rapid three years to 1991. A European cocktail of inputs, styling and early development work went to Turin's Italdesign, which assembled over 20 initial running prototypes, modifying them to meet

In March 1985 Volkswagen engineering chief Wolfgang Linke revealed that the major task of adding a new axle and drive to the rear of the Golf 2 had been allowed for in its development, taking up the space where the large new fuel tank had been set. He confirmed to the press that syncro would be offered as an option on both low- and high-powered versions of the Golf.

As predicted, the Golf Syncro was launched just ahead of the Frankfurt Motor Show in September 1985. Volkswagen billed it as a new four-wheel-drive system with 'slip sensitive power distribution'. The design was one that could be fitted to any Volkswagen with a transverse engine and an end-on transmission. A new housing was bolted to the gear/differential casing and a short driveshaft took the drive to an angled bevel gear set mounted in line with the centre of the car. The drive was then taken to an all-new rear axle via a three-piece propshaft and the viscous coupling – Volkswagen's own design developed over four years – mounted ahead of the rear-driven axle. The rear suspension of the Golf Syncro was radically altered from the front-drive car with struts and lower wishbone suspension rather than the standard trailing arms. While the changes to the floorpan were minor the new rear axle demanded a much higher boot floor, which lost one-third of its capacity.

Most of the time all but 5% of the Golf's drive went through the front wheels, but as the system kicked in when the wheels started to slip, up to 100% of power could be transferred to the rear. At the time it was realised that four-wheel drive had a tendency to

Wolfsburg's requirements. Some very fast ones were even built using the Golf Rallye engine and transmission.

According to the story of the Toledo's development, Volkswagen was sceptical that Giugiaro's design could be cheaply produced, but SEAT said it could be made at the same cost as a Jetta and it was signed off by Ferdinand Piëch.

The Toledo was based on the heavily modified floorpan of the second-generation Jetta as the platform of the 1988 Passat was judged too large and the third-generation Golf too near to launch. Initially using a mix of the 'System Porsche' Ibiza and Volkswagen engines, more Golf engines were used during its run and the engine bay was designed to accommodate the VR6. It was crash tested in Wolfsburg.

As was to become Volkswagen's standard practice, the Toledo exhibited little evidence of Volkswagen ancestry on the surface (barring its switchgear), but underneath the German parts bin was amply used. The instrument panel had in fact been designed for a future Audi and came from the advanced design studio in Dusseldorf.

SEAT's initial strategy was for 'in between' cars; the Ibiza sized between the Polo and Golf and the Toledo between the Golf and Passat, so that they would complement rather than compete with the German brand. So while the first Toledo was much longer than a Golf (with a vast boot) it wasn't any wider. This strategy, however, changed with the second-generation Ibiza and 1998 Toledo, adopting the same footprints as the Polo and Golf from which they were derived. Unlike Škoda, SEAT's fortunes under Volkswagen ownership would be more mixed. Said Carl Hahn: 'All we ask of them is that they retain their Spanish, Latin character while maintaining a level of quality equal to that of the rest of the group.'

↑ Although the Spanish market preferred saloons with a separate boot, the Toledo had to satisfy wider ambitions. What gave the impression of a boot was in fact a large tailgate.

lock the wheels under heavy braking and Volkswagen incorporated a freewheeling device into the rear axle, which decoupled the system under such conditions and would allow anti-lock braking to be fitted when it became available later. The springs and brakes were upgraded to cope with the likely demands of towing but otherwise it sat no higher.

'Twenty or thirty years ago we were laughed at for having 4WDs,' says Carl Hahn. 'But I can imagine all the excuses to the chairman of the board of all the chief engineers of Mercedes and BMW for not bringing four-wheel drive when you were invited uphill in St Moritz. The Mercedes owner walked to the house, the Audi owner drove up, and that impressed everybody!'

However, the Golf Syncro had its critics. The system was no heavier than Audi's, but it did add 90kg of extra weight to the regular Golf. And despite the promise of low- and high-performance versions there was grumbling that the latter did not at first materialise. VW claimed that, while the system could cope with the Golf GTI 16-valve's power, the 90bhp carburettor 1.8 was better suited because of its good torque and because the primary customer was the country dweller, not the fast driver – although the German market had a GT Syncro. In 1989 power was increased to 98bhp. Whichever market, there was a hefty price premium. The Golf and Jetta Syncro did not go on sale in the UK until October 1988 because right-hand drive was delayed to satisfy the demand from Germany and Italy. At £11,884 the single-spec Golf Syncro five-door was more than a GTI and a modest target of 1,000 was set for the next 12 months but only 678 were sold to 1991.

↑ The Golf Country was an-almost SUV before its time. Not really a serious off-roader, it did have a protective under tray. A gun rack was an option.

↓ This cabriolet-based oddity is a Biagini Passo, an Italian-built combination of Golf Country running gear and reworked styling reported to have been made between 1990 and '93. (Volkswagen Classic)

Almost an SUV

The Golf Syncro gave rise to an oddity of Volkswagen history, an idea ahead of its time. In the late 1980s the European interest in 'off roaders' or, to use the American term, sports utility vehicles (SUV) had yet to emerge, but at the 1989 Geneva Motor Show Volkswagen exhibited the 'Montana' concept, a kind of Golf Syncro on stilts with the embellishments of an SUV such as a 'bull bar' across the front and a boot-mounted spare wheel. It was a great favourite of Ernst Fiala: 'It was clear to me that most buyers like the idea of having a heavier car and sitting one step higher than the average looking above the roofs of the others. For Volkswagen the simplest idea was to raise the car by 50mm or so and this is very inexpensive.'

On sale in summer 1990 as the Golf Country there were hopes of 4,000 sales a year and Volkswagen invested £4m on conversion facilities at Steyr-Daimler-Puch in Austria. Regular 98bhp Golf Syncros would arrive and have 11.9cm spacers put between the bodywork and the suspension. Longer springs and struts increased ground clearance by 13cms and the total ride height rose by 18cms. Steyr then fitted a sump guard, front bull bars and a bracket for the exterior spare wheel, decals and alloys wheels. There were special seats and a sports steering wheel. This lofty Golf commanded a £1,900 premium over a standard Syncro, and with the extra weight was slower and heavier on petrol. Georg Kacher in *Car* called it 'Neither fish nor fowl. Off-road it can't compete with the serious mud-luggers; on-road it's among the slowest and least economical Golfs you can buy.' However, there was a 'Wolfsburg' edition of the Country just for people who worked for the factory with a 1.8-litre GTI engine but no GTI badging. In total 7,735 Countrys were made to December 1991 and the idea was not revisited for the next Golf.

Minor facelift

The decision to give the second Golf a conservative yet distinctive look paid off with a shape that needed only minor changes in an eight-year career. In 1987 there was a new grille with wider slats, wider side rubbing strips and a bigger VW logo. The front quarter-light windows – once touted for being flush-fitted – were removed to give larger opening front windows, and the wing mirrors moved further forwards, tardily countering criticism that they were fitted too far back for some.

A final facelift came in August 1989, with bulkier bumpers for the GL and GTI models bringing their looks more in line with other Volkswagens plus small changes to the interior.

The supercharged Golfs

Towards the end of the 1980s, as the third-generation Golf entered development, Volkswagen produced a wave of super-fast Golfs to both satisfy its motor-sport programme and keep on top of a feverish market for performance hatchbacks. Its methods intrigued commentators.

Although by the early 1980s top Audis such as the Quattro were turbocharged and there were a number of aftermarket Golf turbo conversions, Volkswagen still maintained the turbocharger was best for diesels. From 1978 it had been experimenting with the supercharger, a device used on high-performance cars in the 1920s and '30s. The most famous supercharger or 'blower' of that time was the Roots type, which introduced compressed air into the engine for better ignition, having squeezed it between two rotors. The Volkswagen version was based on a 1905 design, which squeezed the air through metal scrolls, although at that time the technology to machine the parts with sufficient accuracy had not been available. Over 400 variations were said to have been tried.

↓ This 1988 British-market base Golf shows that year's modest facelift: side rubbing strips, new grille and front windows with no quarter-lights.

Turbochargers and superchargers are both forced-induction devices, but while a turbocharger works from waste gases in the exhaust system, a supercharger is driven by a belt from the crankshaft. A supercharger spins all the time and boosts in proportion to engine speed, not load as a turbocharger does (early turbochargers suffered from 'lag', a gap under acceleration where nothing happened until they boosted in a surge).

Volkswagen considered the supercharger superior because it produced boost from much lower speeds and developed torque across a broader rev range. The supercharger also did not generate as much heat as a turbo, which demanded special materials for exhaust manifolds and pipes. It was potentially quieter and demanded no special lubrication. Before entering the engine, the compressed air was cooled by passing it through an intercooler to increase its density.

The first Volkswagen recipient was the second-generation Polo, which had needed an image boost when the market failed to take to its van-like styling and a 'coupe' version was added in 1982. It wasn't possible to fit larger engines into the Polo for more sporting variants, so Volkswagen turned to superchargers. In 1983 an experimental 1.3-litre supercharged Polo was shown to selected press and at the 1985 Frankfurt Motor Show the Polo coupe GT G40 arrived. With similar power to the standard Golf GTI, its 1.3-litre four-cylinder engine developed 115bhp thanks to what Volkswagen called a *G-Lader* (G-Charger) after the G-shaped spirals inside the supercharger unit. The '40' stood for the height of the spiral walls in millimetres.

The Volkswagen design had two fixed spirals with a twin spiral operating between them. One was fixed to the inner face of the drum-shaped casting, the other able to rotate within the fixed spiral creating air pockets that would be forced toward the centre of the fixed casing, becoming denser as they went. The air would then be intercooled and forced into the inlet manifold.

To launch the new technology three modified 129bhp Polos were sent out to break a 24-hour/8,000 mile speed record and they averaged 132mph. At first unsure of demand, only 500 Polo G40s were built for sale in 1986, but the first series of 1,500 ran between 1987 and 1988. A Golf application was clearly possible as a G60 for a 1.8-litre engine was already under development.

The first mainstream recipient of the G60 *G-Lader* was a GT version of the new transverse-engined 1988 Volkswagen Passat, then the Corrado, a sub-Porsche four-seat coupe priced above the Scirocco but based on the second-generation Golf. In both cars the G60 was allied to the group eight-valve 1,781cc four-cylinder engine, and the compression ratio was lowered from 10.0:1 to 8.0:1. Spinning at 1.7 times engine speed, it delivered a maximum boost of 0.65 bar (9.4psi), and the intercooled air temperature was reduced by up to 55 degrees. Volkswagen claimed its 160bhp performance and flexibility could be compared to a 2.6-litre V6 engine (which was known to be in development – see Chapter 4). The Corrado and subsequent Golf models with the G60 engine adopted the Passat's cable-operated MQ five-speed gearbox.

In June 1988 Volkswagen released pictures of what it called a 160bhp supercharged 'Super Golf', which combined the same engine with the syncro four-wheel-drive system. The photo was of a three-door Golf with slim rectangular headlamps, a wide grille covering an intercooler and bulging wheel arches covering wider tyres. It was ready for production, the company claimed, depending on reaction in a series of customer clinics, and could be built the following year.

One look at those flared arches told you the real intention was to produce a car for motor sport. Audi's triumphs with the Quattro and Quattro Sport earlier in the

↓ The concentric spirals of the *G-Lader* or G-shaped supercharger can be made out here. Supercharged Volkswagens took a break when the Polo G40 ended in 1994.

decade meant that Group B rallying became dominated by four-wheel-drive cars – above all Lancia Deltas – reaching 500–650bhp, until a series of tragic accidents in which spectators were killed called for the cars to be banned. Audi shocked the rally world by abruptly withdrawing its team in May 1986 to concentrate on a different image for the brand, and a move towards circuit racing.

Volkswagen Golf GTIs had been active in rallying throughout this time and in 1986 a 215bhp GTI 16V won the newly established non-turbo Group A World Rally Championship driven by Kenneth Eriksson and Peter Diekmann. Once the syncro system had been on the market, the way was open for Volkswagen to go four-wheel drive for the 1990 season and Group A homologation rules required at least 5,000 road cars be built in a year. The best way to ensure these would sell was to drum up excitement by testing the water with the 'Super Golf' and orders flooded in. In fact 5,600 were eventually built with 2,000 of the left-hand-drive-only model staying in Germany.

This highly specialised project was taken away from Wolfsburg (which built the ten millionth Golf in June 1988) to Volkswagen Brussels. Project manager was engineer Rolf Trump who had been with Volkswagen since 1973 and was to work on a number of generations of Golf. 'Brussels was better equipped to produce special cars,' he told the author in 2013. 'The plan was really to stay with that small production run. We had some tools fitted for that type of run and if it had gone beyond the 5,600 which we actually built we would have had to go for further investment.'

Thus the Rallye Golf G60 was essentially a cocktail of Golf GTI and Golf Syncro, with the Corrado's eight-valve G60 engine. The engine was downsized slightly to 1,763cc from 1,781cc so that when it was multiplied by the forced-induction conversion factor of 1.4 demanded for the World Rally Championship it came in under the equivalent 2.5-litre class limit. That the Rallye was fitted with the eight-valve engine was said to be because Volkswagen could not satisfy demand for the 16-valve

↑ The G60 featured the 'big bumpers' of late-model Golf 2s and the distinctive 'bee sting' small rear aerial of the Golf GTI, which transferred to all Golfs in time.

↑ **The 1989–90 Golf Rallye was the start of a performance race in the latter half of the Golf 2's career.**

cylinder head, now being used across Golf, Scirocco, Corrado and Passat ranges. The G60/eight-valve combination was readily available. Twin catalysts were fitted as standard to the Rallye.

The competition Rallye produced 280bhp, but although the road-going version was the most powerful factory-produced Golf to date, with the weight of the syncro system (230kg more than the GTI 16V), on paper it didn't produce performance figures very much different to its cheaper relative with a top speed of 130mph as opposed to 127 and a 0–100kph (62mph) time of 8.6 seconds. Of course it did gain by having superior torque and the ability to safely put all that power through four wheels.

Sold in Germany at DM 44,500, 80 left-hand drive Rallyes were said to have been allocated to the UK market to special order. In mid 1990 it listed at £17,261 compared to £14,449 for the 16V five-door. As well as the mechanical package and the unique styling, equipment was complete with leather seat trim, power steering and improved anti-lock brakes. *Car* magazine praised it for its refinement but said it was, 'As ugly as a Staffordshire bull terrier, but without the bite.'

The hoped-for rally success did not materialise with the only notable result a third place in the 1990 New Zealand Rally. Lancia and Toyota's faster cars, more advanced four-wheel-drive systems and greater World Rally experience all conspired against the Golf. Volkswagen withdrew from rallying after 1990 and did not re-enter until 2011 (a round-up of Golf in motor sport is in Appendix 2).

G60 Limited

If there was disappointment over the Rallye Golf G60's specification, in May 1989 Volkswagen's motor-sport department announced it had produced a 210bhp Golf G60 destined for full production with syncro four-wheel drive and the 16-valve engine.

It was reported that VW Motorsport would build two cars a week when it moved into its new factory that July and development of a 16-valve version of the G60 Corrado was already underway, with production planned for later that year. Over 100 orders had already been

↑ **The 1990 four-wheel-drive Golf G60 Limited was the ultimate understated hot hatchback, with no big bumpers and only a blue Motorsport badge at the back and blue front grille surround.**

taken before the announcement was made, so it was a car for Volkswagen insiders.

The reality turned out to be the most exclusive of all factory performance Golfs. The Golf G60 Limited took the regular five-door GTI bodyshell but with the inner wheel arches and suspension of the Rallye. It was only ever built as a five-door although one three-door was made and retained by Volkswagen. Not fitted with the larger bumpers of the 1989 facelift, the only quick way to distinguish it was by the VW Motorsport badges and a blue line around the front grille. Klaus-Peter Rosorius, head of motor sport at the time was quoted as saying, 'We wanted to have a nice elegant-looking production Golf without any external alterations, but lots of fascination under the bonnet.' British writers soon termed it a 'Q' car, used to describe an anonymous but very fast car.

The engine was more or less the same as the G60 eight-valve unit although it had special pistons and a camshaft profile giving increased lift. The compression ratio was reduced to 8.8:1 and again twin catalysts were used. Golfs were now running Digifant fuel injection, rather than the famous Bosch K-Jetronic system. This was developed in house by Volkswagen and used from 1987 onwards. Maximum power was produced at 6,500rpm. When *Autocar* tested Volkswagen UK's press demonstrator in March 1991, it recorded a top speed of 140mph and in-gear acceleration from 30 to 50mph in 6.5 seconds, drawing comparisons with the Ford Sierra Cosworth and the BMW M5.

All of this was delivered in a relentless but well-controlled surge of power. Although the G60 Limited had four-wheel drive, Volkswagen fitted what it called an Electronic Differential Lock (EDL) as standard, an early type of stability/traction control, which would attempt to apply brake restraint to the spinning wheel.

The Limited was hand-built at the rate of one a week from 1989 to 1991 at Volkswagen Motorsport in Hannover, although Rolf Trump remembers them being built in Wolfsburg's Hall 18, which is also known as the pilot hall for pre-production cars. Only 71 were built, already sold, even at DM 68,500, about £23,000 at the time.

↑ **The supercharged Golf GTI G60 was the final development of the second-generation GTI in 1990, needing traction control for its 160 supercharged engine but also with syncro for some markets. (LAT)**

GTI G60

The final and rather more attainable development of the second-generation Golf GTI was announced at the 1989 Frankfurt Motor Show. The Golf GTI G60 had the same eight-valve 1,781cc engine as the Corrado, developing 160bhp at 5,800rpm. It lasted less than two years.

The GTI G60 came onto the German market in March 1990 at 14% more than the regular GTI, but then it did have 24% more power. Volkswagen UK wasn't even sure it was going to import it and right-hand drive was not contemplated because apparently there wasn't room for the MQ gearbox in the engine compartment when it was converted.

'Volkswagen believes it has rejuvenated the GTI,' wrote Michael Scarlett in *Car*. There was optimistic talk of 40% of entire GTI production being turned over to the G60. The quoted performance figures were a 134mph top speed and a 0–62mph (100kph) time of 8.3 seconds.

It boasted the kind of flexibility that meant you could amble through a village with the engine barely ticking over and then pull away in fifth gear, likened to a V6 engine. There were, however, complaints that the MQ gearbox had the same widely spaced intermediate ratios as the Passat, with a big gap between second and third, and that the change quality was less precise. This standardisation was apparently to help gearbox production at the Kassel plant.

Golf G60 chassis changes included 15in wheels to accommodate Corrado-sized brakes with anti-lock fitted as standard, as was power steering, which gave only a little assistance. There were thicker anti-roll bars and 185/55R15 tyres as standard. The suspension was lowered by 10mm at the rear, 20mm at the front.

By now it was clearly asking too much to be putting 160bhp through the front wheels alone without furious wheelspin and torque steer, but the Electronic Differential Lock (EDL) of the Limited was only offered as an option. Without it, you faced a challenge. 'Driving this delightful Q-car fast needs a fair bit of concentration along a country road – it is trying to steer itself all the time under acceleration, while the squat Continentals walk about under braking and tramline along any longways ridge,' Scarlett observed.

The GTI G60 lasted until late 1991 and the third-generation Golf. A syncro version was added for the final year, but this also didn't come to the UK in right-hand drive. There was also a special edition, the Fire and Ice (named after a film) with special paint and badging. The G60 was regarded as the pinnacle of the second GTI's career.

As the second Golf headed into its final years different markets added special editions and more equipment. The GTI was finally getting some price competition, so from 1990 BBS alloy wheels became standard on the 16-valve for UK buyers, then the regular car. Smoked plastic lenses for the rear lights were also added. The UK importer also found the quickest way to sell basic Golfs was to give them a GTI-like four-headlamp grille and dynamic names such as the Driver and Ryder.

Reflecting the booming car market created by re-unification (see panel on page 130) the second-generation Golf continued in production after the autumn 1991 debut of its successor for a further year in the new factory in Mosel, near the old Trabant factory, to meet demand from the re-unified Eastern Europe.

↑ This 1989 British 16V has optional BBS alloy wheels, integrated front fog lamps and at the rear darkened tail-light lenses. It wasn't considered that well equipped by the press.

↓ While the second-generation Scirocco continued in production Volkswagen chased some of Porsche's customers with the Golf 2-based Corrado, here in its VR6 form.

Into the East

In the late 1980s political and economic factors combined to mark the end of the Soviet Union as countries once under communist control declared independent statehood and Russian president Mikhail Gorbachev started his *perestroika* (reconstruction) policy of political and economic liberalisation.

It was to end the Cold War, a fact of life since the end of World War Two, when swathes of Eastern Europe under Soviet communist control were cut off behind the infamous 'Iron Curtain' of border controls, the most famous of which was the zone dividing Berlin in half. Hungary opened its borders to Austria in May 1989 and the Berlin wall fell in November 1989.

There had been two Germanys, the prosperous West and the austere East, and now they met. The exchange of one East German Mark to one Deutsch Mark released a lot of pent-up demand for the latest consumer goods, not least cars. Some 450 million repressed car buyers were waiting and their nearest neighbouring car industry was ready and waiting.

While others looked to Poland and Hungary, Volkswagen set its sights on the other half of Germany – after all, Carl Hahn could see the church towers from the window of his office. 'We have discovered a new Asia,' said a Volkswagen manager to journalist Georg Kacher in 1990. 'Its border is only 60 miles from Wolfsburg and for a change the people over there even speak the same language.' Although their domestic cars were from another age and strangled by lack of development funds, a few East Germans had experienced Volkswagen Golfs since 1977, when a limited number were allowed to be imported.

There was also manufacturing to be had. Fiat, Volkswagen and General Motors (Opel) vied with each other to offer the most attractive deals to impoverished Eastern carmakers. Volkswagen was surprised to be outbid by Opel for the Automobilwerk Eisenach, makers of the Wartburg, but it already had a firm foothold in Eastern Germany as in 1984 it had signed with the IFA-Kombinat group of car producers to build an engine-assembly line for production of modern VW engines for Wartburgs and Trabants in Chemnitz (then Karl-Marx-Stadt in the German Democratic Republic) in return for an extra supply of engines for its own products. However, the German Democratic Republic (GDR) refused to let foreign partners hold more than 49% of stock at the time.

Post 1989, Volkswagen formed a planning company to prepare for the development and production of an internationally competitive vehicle, what Hahn called a 'new Trabant'. It turned out people really just wanted a new Volkswagen.

Chemnitz supplied Volkswagen engines while cylinder heads were manufactured in Eisenach. Decades later Chemnitz became the centre for advanced Volkswagen engine development and production.

In July 1990 the last Trabant 601 was built at the Zwickau factory, but a modernised version, the 1.1 with a Polo engine vainly sought buyers until April 1991.

Hahn elected to build a brand new factory, at Mosel, north of Zwickau, now named Mosel-Zwickau, with a capacity of 250,000 vehicles a year. It started Polo assembly in 1990 with a somewhat uneconomical arrangement where engines would be united

← The Bertone-styled front-wheel-drive Škoda Favorit came with Volkswagen's purchase of the company in 1991 and was a good place to start. (Škoda)

➔ The Škoda workforce assembles the Golf 4-based Octavia. There was no question of a lack of quality. (Škoda)

with painted bodyshells shipped across Germany from Audi in Ingolstadt. From 1991 former Trabant workers were also assembling the final run of second-generation Golfs before they began full production of the third-generation Golf.

Škoda

After having successfully adopted SEAT, Volkswagen under Hahn set its sights on Czech carmaker Škoda, a marque founded in 1895 whose headquarters were and remain in Mlada Bolesev, 50 miles north of Prague. After years with rear-engined cars mocked by Western enthusiasts, it was doing well manufacturing the front-wheel-drive Favorit hatchback, but development costs had been crippling and each car barely made a profit. Škoda's search for a partner included BMW and Renault, but Volkswagen, with its ready-made family of transverse four-cylinder engines was the ideal choice for expanding the Favorit line and developing a new larger saloon. VW management was impressed by the workforce's skills, relatively modern factory and, of course, low labour rate.

'When the iron curtain opened I learned what the value of Škoda was,' Hahn recalls. 'This was my main target. The Bratislava factory is today where we produce all complicated vehicles – all four-wheel-drive passenger cars for instance – due to high-quality labour. The Hungarian factory, which Audi started, is also very important as it permitted us to transfer all Audi engine production out of Germany.'

In December 1990 the Czech government awarded Volkswagen AG the rights to acquire 100% of Škoda Automobilová a.s and in April 1991 it joined the Volkswagen Group as its fourth independent brand. The Favorit was redesigned as the Felicia in 1994 when Golf engines joined the range. Thereafter, new Škodas were derived from Volkswagen models.

However, with Volkswagen seemingly supplying customers with increasing numbers of differently branded and cheaper hatchbacks, was there not a worry that the number one seller, the Golf, would gradually lose it place? 'There was some concern,' says Hahn, 'but you can never avoid a little substitution. As it turned out all these companies have gained and maintained their own identity and we were successful in making these cars so distinct from Golf that you have no problem – provided of course that you go through different dealerships.'

At the time this book was completed, it turned out to have been an excellent investment, its design centre feeding into Bentleys and supplying engines and transmissions for Audis. It was reported that there were worries within Volkswagen that Škodas were getting so good they were indeed starting to cannibalise sales of more expensive group brands.

D
WOB GO 503
Volkswagen Classic

Golf 3
1991–1997

Big, green, safe

↑ **An early sketch released at launch seems to emphasise something was lost in translation to the metal. (LAT)**

In July 1991, with total Golf production around 18 million, Volkswagen presented a new look to see its best-seller through the 1990s (Golf now accounted for 47% of sales). The styling had once more taken an evolutionary step but Golf technology advanced with a V6 engine, anti-lock brakes, traction control and ground-breaking diesel engine design.

Much of its detail had been accurately trailed. This was the Golf that would last Volkswagen a decade it was said, and chief engineer Ulrich Seiffert had a ten-year plan to keep interest going with more variants and engines than before. An all-new cabriolet and the first Golf estate were promised for 1993 production, as well as electric and four-wheel-drive versions. A saloon version (Jetta/Vento) came soon after the hatchback.

The new Golf was fully launched at September's Frankfurt Motor Show and for the first time there was a new Opel Astra to compare it to, also in its third generation with a name now standardised across Europe. At the time the Golf took 32% of the German market and 11% of the share for its class in France, Italy, Spain and the UK.

As well as its permanent home in Wolfsburg, the new Golf was built in Puebla in Mexico, Uitenhage in South Africa, Brussels and the new Mosel factory near the old Trabant plant at Zwickau in the newly-unified Germany. In 1994 Volkswagen Bratislava (Škoda) took over sole production of the Golf Syncro and was to become a centre for the group's four-wheel-drive cars.

Carl Hahn felt this expansion was fully justified by ever increasing demand. The German market for new cars had been expected to be 2.8 million in 1991 but with re-unification was looking at 3.5 million after some of the pent-up demand had been sated by used cars. Some East Germans had been importing used Golfs from Chicago.

Solid styling

The new Golf's exterior design was credited once more to Herbert Schäfer, chief designer from 1972 to 1993. His most recent design, the 1988 Passat had proved to be a radical break in styling, but the Golf followed a more evolutionary route. Some called it a boxy, upright style and the wide, windowless three-quarter rear pillar (even larger and regularly complained about) was a continued feature. However, the frontal styling broke with the Giugiaro round-headlamp look for almost oval lenses behind which were single or double headlamps. Where possible the window glass was flush fitting with the bodywork.

In the lead-up to the new look there had been changes at Volkswagen design, with a desire to attract a more international group of stylists, like other carmakers. Carl Hahn had recruited Frenchman Patrick Le Quément from Ford in 1985 as Volkswagen group director of corporate design, anticipating that Schäfer would be retiring. 'They felt they lacked creativity,' he told the author in 2013. 'Basically they had been exploring variations on what had been done on previous models – namely it all started with Giugiaro – but they thought that aside from changing packages the design language hadn't changed and that when they were entering into a project there was just not enough differentiation.'

Le Quément was given free rein in setting up an advanced design studio away from Wolfsburg, not least because he wanted to give his new team outside influences and be away from unannounced visits from senior management. Thus he settled on a studio in Dusseldorf, looked upon as the fashion city of Germany and recruited designers including Gert Hildebrand who would later oversee the development of the new Mini and Axel Breun who followed Le Quément to Renault.

The new designers were invited to pitch into the design competition for the third Golf, making their own proposals. According to Le Quément, Schäfer did some designs and Hildebrand, head of concept design to 1989, was asked to do one, Audi produced a further proposal and his studio produced two cars. 'One was clearly a little too advanced but we knew it,' says Le Quément. 'We did a car with a split backlight, which is what Audi did years later on the A2, and a classic design which picked up all the cues of the Golf. There was a presentation where all the models were put together and they liked the car that we produced, but thought that Gert Hildebrand's was not enough Volkswagen, too sporty, and they thought that Schäfer's car was too bland.'

Le Quément says the more conservative Dusseldorf car, which had rectangular headlights and the grille-less look of the Passat was reworked by Schäfer and presented again some months later to be approved in 1987. By this time the Frenchman had already decided to leave as he had an offer to head design at Renault, although Hahn was worried that the experience over the Golf 3 was the reason.

↓ The 1991 third Golf is seen as one of the most heavy-looking. This basic version is not flattered by unpainted black plastic bumpers.

WOB CP 704

← **Road testers questioned the omission of a rear anti-roll bar on regular Golfs. (LAT)**

The Golf proportions were familiar but expanded in the name of passenger comfort, luggage space and safety. It had the same 2,475mm wheelbase of the Golf 2, was only longer by 25mm but had a wider stance to convey the very real solidity it was carrying; about 100kg more on average per version. The front track was widened from 1,413 to 1,478mm and varying offset wheels meant they were always flush with the line of the bodywork no matter how narrow the tyre was. One welcome development was a boot aperture that opened to bumper level.

With substantial plastic bumpers front and rear being one example, there were fewer parts to this Golf, making it easier and cheaper to build, but *Der Spiegel* reported in summer 1991 that internal analysis showed many competitors were building for less. The company had about a 23% productivity disadvantage in Europe despite 80% of each car in Hall 54 being assembled by machines.

Passat into Golf

As well as the traditional filter-down of Audi features, other models in the Volkswagen range were contributing to the 1991 Golf, especially now the Passat was transverse-engined and could donate engine and suspension components.

The rear suspension was torsion beam as expected, wedge-shaped track correction mountings coming from the Corrado and Passat which Volkswagen said gave a degree of rear-wheel steering to keep the car in line. A rear anti-roll bar was fitted to the GTI and VR6 versions.

The MacPherson-strut front suspension set-up was carried over from the previous Golf, but there were two different types: the GTI and VR6 models used what was called 'Plus' front suspension to improve steering under power. The distance between the steering axis and the point of wheel contact with the road surface was shortened from 52 to 40mm to improve straight line running and was claimed to virtually eliminate torque steer. The power-assisted steering (standard on all bar the base 1.4) was now firmer on fast Golfs with matched springs and dampers, gas filled at the rear.

Although they had not featured on non-sporting versions of the previous Golf, commentators were perplexed as to why a rear anti-roll bar was not fitted to anything less than a GTI on the new car, which while praised for its ride and refinement was criticised as rolling too heavily around corners with its newly gained weight. It was perhaps a reflection of the impact the first Golf had made that family hatchbacks were now expected to have sporty handling characteristics.

A traction control system (called TCS) was standard on the Golf VR6 and an option on the GTI at launch. It required standard anti-lock brakes (optional for all but VR6 Golfs) with four electronic sensors monitoring the speed of each wheel. A computer compared the speed signals with pre-programmed values and could reduce or increase hydraulic pressure between four and ten times a second – as the driver felt the pedal vibrate beneath their foot. TCS would brake the individual wheel which was starting to spin.

Quality equipment

Keeping up with the competition, Golf equipment was slightly more generous than before, but the range retained a slight price premium over other brands and left plenty on the options list. The contents of this varied depending on which country you were in. The familiar CL, GL, GT, GTD and GTI designations remained

but Volkswagen's UK importers opted again to preserve the GTI brand by not importing sporty-looking GT or GTD models.

For example, while the 1991 French GL specification was representative of what most buyers expected to have, with standard power steering, central locking and electric windows, when the Golf went on UK sale in 1992 the electric windows were extra but metallic paint was included. The VR6 had the most complete equipment. As before, specifications became more generous the longer the Golf was in production.

← The second-generation Golf Syncro (here one for the country sports set) was introduced into the German market in February 1993 as a 1.8-litre petrol and 1.9 TDI and was given the Corrado's 2.9-litre VR6 the following year.

All Golfs had a rear screen wiper as standard and height adjustment for the driver's seat, which raised the entire seat rather than the front or back of the cushion. Occupant space had increased with more headroom and the already good driving position was boosted by the option of an adjustable steering column. The seats themselves were all fabric covered, varying from a hard-wearing black with a small flecked pattern to a velour-like material on the GL and above.

The substantial new dashboard unit was assembled and quality checked outside of the car. It ushered in rotary controls for heating and lighting, which would be carried over to subsequent generations. There were a number of features that were regarded as Mercedes-like such as one-touch electric windows, electrically heated wing mirrors and the rotary head and side-lamp control, which stopped the driver leaving the fog lamps on accidentally.

There was plenty of room for stowage (built-in cup holders for the USA) and top models had six small drawers for cassettes in the centre console. Where offered, the radio integrated neatly into the dashboard. Behind it, a pollen filter was claimed to remove 99% of pollen particles and where fitted the air conditioning featured automatic temperature control and a compressor that used less power.

Volkswagen highlighted attention to quality in small details such as the side pillar trims and headlining being held in place by clips not visible from the outside. There was a full complement of plastic trim, even in the far corners of the boot. BMW had not long launched an all-new 3-Series with surprising build quality problems and *Autocar* magazine said the Golf's quality feel of trim and minor controls could teach it a thing or two. As well as this, Volkswagen must have been delighted at a number of references to Mercedes.

Spacing between panels was uniform and narrow, Volkswagen boasted, and the electrical system had sealed, watertight and corrosion-resistant plugs. As robots (or 'iron slaves' as they were called in Wolfsburg) had freed up production-line workers, they had been deployed on assembling and checking modules before they were fitted to the car, so quality should have been up to the expected standard, if not improved.

The interior plastics used were said to prevent the 'fogging' of the windows which would happen when cars were new.

Safe, green and heavy

Volkswagen's market research declared safety was the prime factor for German buyers and an immediate publicity war began between Golf and Astra over which was the safer. They matched on many other aspects, for example the lowest Golf drag factor was the same as the Astra at 0.30, the highest 0.33.

Befitting its ten-year life cycle and the continued importance of the US market, the third Golf was designed to meet crash-test standards as far ahead as possible, especially those demanded in North America. Volkswagen's advertising would sometimes be based on one aspect of the new Golf's safety features, such as a picture of a crashed car in the standard yellow paint illustrating the new model was able to withstand a 35mph head-on crash test, 5mph more than required in Europe. Volkswagen was vocal in its frustration that this legislative disparity existed.

There was an extra imperative for Germany's best-selling car to go beyond what was required by law as – much to the consternation of carmakers – in the early 1990s the German magazine *Auto Motor und Sport* started to do its own crash tests with the Bavarian Technical Office (TUV), sharing the results with sister magazines in an attempt to push European lawmakers into adopting tougher tests than the existing head-on crash at 30mph into a concrete block.

Adopting a widely respected German standard, it would buy a new car and then hurl it at a solid barrier at 34.2mph (55kph) but expose only half the front of the car to the impact. Known as the offset test, it was agreed it was closer to real-life accidents where the driver is taking some sort of avoiding action. This was far harder on a car's structure as the load was concentrated only on one side. A poor showing in the AMS test sent some very big names back to the drawing board. The Ford Escort and the Fiat Tipo both underwent redesigns – the Ford to the tune of £75 million. After a 1992 crash test, Opel had to recall its Vectra for a seatbelt fault, the first Renault Twingo folded up and even though the Golf 3 performed well in the offset test its performance led Volkswagen to speed up the introduction of airbags.

With doors reinforced by side-impact beams (again, Golf and Astra advertising showed cutaway doors and striped beams) the Golf 3 was ready for the 1994 US 33.5mph side-impact law. Carl Hahn was now pleased to have the economy of scale of a single Golf safety specification engineered for both the European and US markets.

Elements of the bodyshell were designed to absorb impact energy in a controlled way. Golf launch material explained that a key design feature was the use of 'mash seam welded' side-members where layers of metal of different thicknesses were welded together before being pressed. Under impact they folded with a concertina effect.

With the reinforcement of the passenger safety cell Volkswagen claimed the new Golf was 30% more rigid than the last one – which wasn't known for being insubstantial. A rigid cross-member ran across the car and provided a mounting for the pre-assembled

➔ In summer 1992 Volkswagen put on an expensive show for journalists at Ehra-Lessien, propelling a Passat into a Golf at 50mph and discussing its safety research. (LAT)

dashboard with another under the front seats to stiffen the floorpan. The seat backs of the rear seats were improved so they remained in place when struck by luggage in a collision.

All of the Golf's seatbelts had variable height adjustment and on the driver's side a locking device inhibited movement in a crash. The Astra, however, went further with the use of seatbelt pre-tensioners, where a small explosive charge takes all the slack from the front belts in the early milliseconds of a crash.

Although the padded steering wheel looked like it already contained an airbag, these became Golf and Vento options in May 1992, for both driver and front seat passengers at a cost of DM 1,200 (£470) with the option to retro fit the driver bag before that date. Twin airbags were standard on the 1994 US models.

In addition to safety concerns, by 1991 environmental awareness was running at a much higher level in Germany than in other markets. The building, use and scrapping of cars was a big domestic issue. Even before the first customers got their Golfs Volkswagen was discussing how they could be recycled when they were finished with. About 60 plastic parts such as the bumpers and door pockets could be completely recycled (in April 1991 Volkswagen launched pan-European bumper collection) and the inner wheel-arch liners were already made out of recycled plastic.

Politicians had been pushing the industry to take

↑ The steering wheel was heavily padded until an airbag was introduced. Rotary headlight control (to the side of the wheel) was considered an improvement. The six slots in the centre console are drawers for cassettes.

→ For its insistence on a full-sized spare wheel the British market got a hump in the boot floor, but the aperture was at last down to bumper level. (LAT)

↑ **The Golf 3 was often a dark place to be seated. Eventually there was a lighter contrasting lower section to the dashboard.**

responsibility for 'end of life' cars and from the 1992 model year the Volkswagen Group was the first manufacturer in Germany to offer to take back old models in exchange and dismantle them. Opel had presented the new Astra only a few weeks before the Golf and, not to be outdone, it too offered to take back and scrap all old Astras a day after Volkswagen.

Opel had been the first European manufacturer to fit catalysts as standard in 1989 and all new petrol-engined Golfs were now thus equipped. Volkswagen invested nearly DM 1 billion in a new paint shop running to new environmental standards and the Golf 3 was coated with paint with greatly reduced solvent content.

Mixed performance

With its extra safety equipment, the lightest Golf now weighed 960kg against the Astra's 930kg and the lightest previous generation Golf had been 845kg. This dictated larger engines, which were developments from the last generation apart from the all-new VR6. The emphasis was on flexibility and refinement rather than outright power.

At launch there were four different-capacity petrol engines (all fuel injected) and two diesels from 1.4 to 2.8 litres and power outputs from 60 to 174bhp. All had cylinder heads with two valves per cylinder, similar to European rivals, but Japanese competitors such as the Nissan Sunny did not reserve 16-valves for just their sports models. The Umwelt diesel Golf was offered only at first in its small-turbocharger form, the cleanest diesel in its class.

The basic Golf petrol unit was now of 1,391cc (1,390cc from 1994 when it went into the new Polo) developing 60bhp over the previous 55. Although the Astra range then progressed to a 1.6-litre, new Golf engines initially jumped to 1,781cc. This was the familiar 1.8 four-cylinder from the previous GL but in two different states of tune via differing compression ratios, 75 and 90bhp, the latter power output confined to the GL or GT specification. In markets such as France this made a difference when you paid road tax on the basis of power output rather than engine size. A 1.6-litre appeared later in production.

The GTI Golfs were set to be available with a pair of 2.0-litre engines of 8 and 16 valves as before, and initially the 115bhp engine already fitted to the Passat was on sale while the 16-valve version suffered a lengthy delay. The diesel had increased in capacity from 1.6 to 1.9 litres (1,896cc) and was already doing service across the Volkswagen Group cars.

Apart from the 90bhp 1.8, every petrol engine had gained 5bhp and on paper Volkswagen claimed modest improvements in performance and fuel consumption. The press took immediate exception to this. Critical of the performance of the 1.4 from its debut, *Autocar & Motor* tested a 1.4CL fully in April 1992 and could only recommend buyers spend more for a 1.8-litre Golf. It recorded a maximum speed of 94mph and 0–60mph in 15.3 seconds: 'The 1.4-litre engine is simply too underpowered for the Golf,' it said. 'Its performance is so far off the pace of other five-door rivals such as the Citroen ZX 1.4 as to make comparison embarrassing.'

Testing a 1.8-litre 90bhp Golf GL, it didn't find a great deal more performance over the old 1.6 – in most respects quicker in all but top speed – but greatly increased flexibility in third and fourth gears and with little need to change out of fifth when cruising. Testing the 75bhp 1.9 Umwelt diesel, the same magazine was also happy to offset the modest performance (still better than the 1.4 petrol) with fine engine flexibility. In contrast, when French magazine *L'Auto Journal* tested the Golf diesel as the GTD (with sporting trim but no more power) it complained that with the heavier bodyshell the performance measures had reversed compared to the previous GTD. However, this was corrected in 1993 with the introduction of the TDI direct-injection diesel.

Four- or five-speed manual gearboxes were offered across the third-generation Golf, with no further use of the Formel E or 4+E descriptions. Good fuel economy was now expected, not an extra. A seven-speed automatic gearbox had been developed between Volkswagen and Renault but was reported to have foundered two years before launch so the Passat's new four-speed became available on the Golf from the 1.8-litre upwards, including the VR6. This was not quite the full story, though, as Peter Hofbauer, head of power train until 1987 told the author. Volkswagen and Renault had indeed teamed up to save development costs on a more economical seven-speed auto and the Volkswagen design was eventually chosen for manufacture at Kassel by Renault. But although a four-speed appeared, the seven-speed wasn't dead at all. 'In the end we couldn't use the seven speeds because it was too nervous and marketing didn't want it,' he said. 'We used the original design but the car only ran at four speeds, to go from second to fourth we used the third for microseconds to make the shift smoother. It was the same design, but controlled differently.'

The six-cylinder Golf

If the four-cylinder petrol engines of the new Golf underwhelmed the commentators, they were completely distracted by the all-new six-cylinder VR6 engine at the top of the range. Long in development and first launched in the Passat (see panel on page 146) it was unprecedented for a car in the Golf class to have a six-cylinder engine, let alone one compact enough to mount transversely.

In no small part the VR6 engine helped the Golf win its first Car of the Year title, up against the much-praised Citroen ZX (third place), the Jetta 2-based SEAT Toledo and the Volvo 850. Even if the judges were as lukewarm to the new car's looks as the last one, the VR6 was described as 'superb' and 'outstanding' by some. Georg Kacher (Germany) enthused: 'The new Golf isn't the milestone car it should have been, but it has few flaws and many virtues, and it sets new standards in terms of active and passive safety. The VR6 in particular is a gem with true cult car potential.' On the other hand, Britain's *Car* magazine's forthright writer L.J.K. Setright scored no points for the Golf at all and went for the ZX to his surprise, reserving stinging words for the Volkswagen: 'VW presented their Golf as mainly an exercise in political greenery – or marketing cynicism, which is nowadays the same thing.'

The arrival of the VR6 upset the expected hierarchy of Golf models. While examples of the 115bhp GTI were available for the summer 1991 launch, there was no sign of the expected 16-valve version but a jump to the 174bhp Golf VR6, much faster yet very different in character. It was technically fascinating because it combined the width of a four-cylinder engine but added two further cylinders by 'staggering' them within a cylinder block that had only one cylinder head rather than the normal two of a traditional V6 engine. In the latter the angle at which the two banks of three cylinders opposed each other would be 60 or 90

degrees but the angle of the VR6's cylinders was only 15 degrees. The initials were explained as being for *Vee Reihenmotor*, which translated to 'in-line vee', although it later became known simply as the Volkswagen V6 during its long life. Although it had been tested in various capacities, in its first Passat and Golf applications the VR6 was set at 2,792cc and gave 174bhp. A 2.9-litre 190bhp version was reserved for the Corrado.

This top of the range Golf featured bolstered sports seats, electric windows, sunroof and mirrors, with a leather-trimmed steering wheel, handbrake and gear-lever gaiter. It rode 20mm lower than the standard Golf and had a thicker front anti-roll bar. 205/50 Continental tyres were fitted to 6.5 x15in BBS cross-spoke alloy wheels. Anti-lock brakes with discs all round were coupled to standard traction control. Leather seat trim and air conditioning were optional.

The front indicators of a Golf VR6 were white and the rear light clusters had darkened covers but it was hard to tell apart from a four-cylinder Golf GTI, especially in a sombre colour, but then perhaps this subtlety added to its appeal.

As told by author Ian Wagstaff in his Golf GTI history, Philippe Defechereux, the company's head of marketing in 1991, said: 'I believe we have reached the sales ceiling for the GTI in numerical terms. The VR6 tends towards a similar direction, but what is more emphasised is that it is a more comfortable, deluxe kind of car with a high capacity engine, low level of interior noise, very flexible gearbox, good acceleration in the higher gears, and an engine which does not have to be shifted very often.'

What that really meant was that you didn't have to buy a 3-Series BMW. In the 1980s and '90s the typical ambitious Golf owner would have had a GTI in their early

continued on page 149

↑ The six-cylinder Volkswagen Golf VR6 was a surprising first in its class, promoted as a BMW rival.

The difficult development of the Volkswagen VR6

The development of the VR6 engine dates back to the 1970s. The idea of a six-cylinder engine compact enough to fit across the engine bay of a front-wheel-drive Golf-sized car was that of former head of Volkswagen advanced propulsion and then power train Peter Hofbauer. He told the author it was partially his concept and that of colleague Dr Kruger as they had been discussing various engine packages in the mid-1970s. It had the full support of head of research Dr Ernst Fiala.

It was originally called the RV6 *Reihenmotor* V6, because while it is a V6 it has features of an in-line engine, namely a single cylinder head and fairly compact width/length. Hofbauer though realised this name was not going to work: 'When Fiala and I were in America we saw signs for Recreational Vehicles – RVs, so we said we can't call it that! We'll have to change the name to VR.' So VR6 it was and then plain V6.

According to Eberhard Kittler of Volkswagen's AutoMuseum, a 2.0-litre engine producing 100bhp was built in 1978/9 and then a 2.2- and 2.4-litre were tested under the bonnets of first-generation Jettas and Golfs. 'We increased the displacement because we didn't get the right gas exchange,' Hofbauer recalls. 'We had to compete with a new architecture against a very well-known 80-year-old system [the V6]. I think they are much better now.'

The VR6 continued as a research project but there was little appetite for a V6 Volkswagen in the early 1980s – perhaps understandable with the company's emphasis on fuel economy. But the idea gained new ground with the arrival of Carl Hahn as chairman in 1981. In his autobiography *Meine Jahre Mit Volkswagen* he said: 'We needed a credible, competitive six-cylinder programme...our [Audi] five-cylinder engine

← Small enough to be developed in a first-generation Golf GTI, this early 2.0 VR6 developed 100bhp. (Volkswagen Classic)

→ Cross-section of a 2.2 (still branded RV) illustrates it occupied little more than the width of an in-line engine. It has four valves per cylinder whereas at launch only two were fitted. (Volkswagen Classic)

was too long and European and Japanese competitors already had six-cylinder engines from the Passat class upwards. For U.S. automobiles a four-cylinder engine from this class was as good as extinct.'

With the Passat due to leave its Audi roots and become a transverse-engined car for 1988 it became imperative that a compact six-cylinder engine that could be mounted transversely be developed to assure its place in the American market.

The two sixes

However, although Audi had made its use of five-cylinder longitudinally mounted engines a trademark, it too was looking to a V6 engine, which could form the basis of a V8 and its entry into a higher class of the luxury car market.

It would follow that the group should develop one engine for both brands but with the agreement of Ferdinand Piëch – head of Audi and the man who would succeed him at Volkswagen – and in the latter half of the 1980s Hahn allowed engineers in Wolfsburg and Ingolstadt to develop two different six-cylinder concepts with the view that one become a group engine for both brands. He says each design was so good he and the Board agreed to release both for development and production.

However, with the rivalry between Ingolstadt and Wolfsburg, meetings of the *Produkt Stragie Kommittee* (PSK) were not harmonious when discussing the engines. 'Piëch liked it from the beginning,' Hofbauer recalls. 'He wanted both and Fiala wanted both, but you can imagine the finance and the sales guys, they wanted to make a decision so this was a long fight. I think it's still not over.' A V6 design was a known quantity but the VR6 was potentially easier to build because it had one rather than two sets of valve gear. Versions were engineered with single and twin overhead camshafts, two and four valves per cylinder.

The first prototype of Audi's V6 ran in 1985 (as recorded by author Eric Dymock in *The Audi File*) and was more conventional than the narrow-angled vee of Volkswagen. It had first a 60-degree angle but then a 90-degree vee, enabling it to be made on the same production line as the new V8 launched in 1988 and use some components from the venerable EA827 four-cylinder engines.

It might have been compact when mounted longitudinally in an Audi but across the engine bay of a Volkswagen it would have been nearly twice as deep as a four-cylinder engine. A traditional V6 has air entering through the central V and the exhaust gases exiting either side. Put that across a car and you would have been unable to mount any components in front of the engine because it would have been too hot.

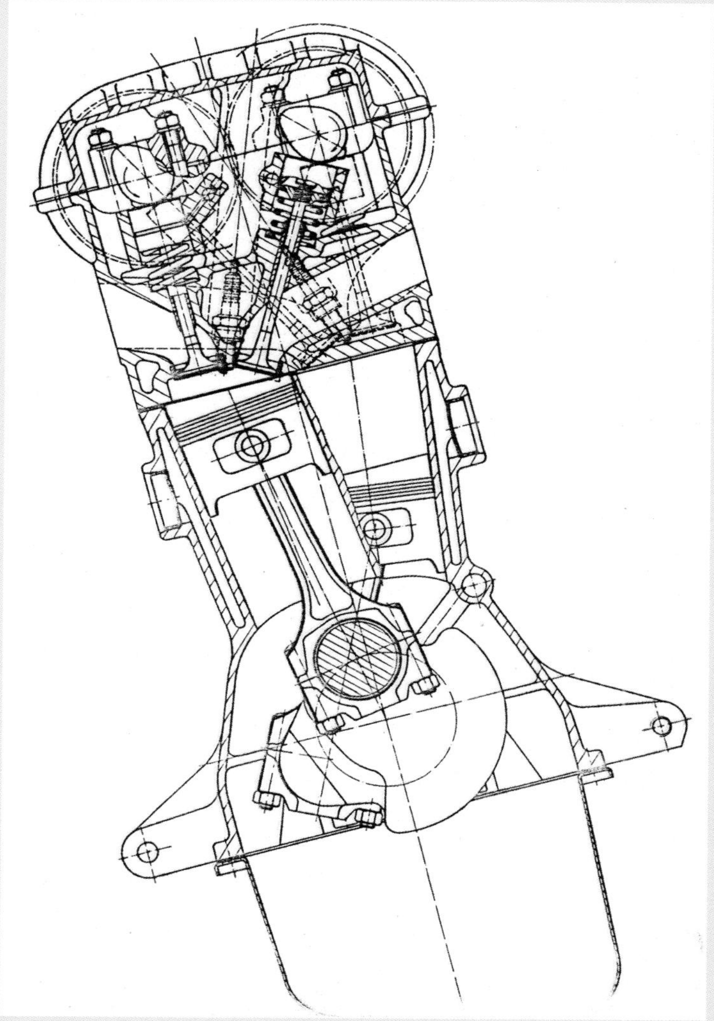

Even in a small vehicle, the VR engine left more room for a front crumple zone and, if there had been a market for it, Hahn even envisaged fitting it into a Polo. As an aside, an agreement was reached in 1993 for VW to supply VR6 engines and transmissions to Mercedes for its 1996 V-Class people carrier because the Mercedes V6 would not fit under its short bonnet.

The VR6's development was played out as on/off in industry gossip in the last few years running up to its 1990 unveiling. In an August 1988 interview with newly appointed Audi chairman Piëch *Car*'s Gavin Green reported: 'He won't talk about the

The difficult development of the Volkswagen VR6 (continued)

possibility of an Audi V6 although it's well known that he wants one. The problem is that VW is also working on its own V6 – the revolutionary narrow-angle VR6 – and Audi's masters are understandably reluctant to commission two, separate, in-house V6s. A senior VW executive recently told me that Piëch is arguing strongly for an Audi V6, on the basis that BMW and Mercedes have their own six-cylinder engines. It does Audi's up-market drive no good, argues Piëch, if it continues to use engines that also find their way into Volkswagens.'

Audi's V8 was introduced in 1988 and the V6 in 1994. The introduction of the Volkswagen Corrado with the G60 *G-Lader* supercharger and peak power of 160bhp only raised questions about the prospects for the VR6, and in October 1988 German magazine *Auto Zeitung* reported it had been dropped because of noise and vibration problems and that an Audi-developed V6 would be used instead. Dr Ulrich Seiffert refused to confirm at the Paris Motor Show that the VR6 project was going ahead and would say only: 'These cars will have a six-cylinder engine in the future.' Rumours about vibration and overheating problems persisted into the following year, although Hofbauer, who left Volkswagen in 1987, does not recall any real cooling problems as the spaces between the cylinder walls allowed a generous water jacket.

After the VR6 made such an impact in the Golf there remained no direct competition in its class, although power outputs of subsequent GTI models from other carmakers climbed relentlessly upwards. The now-forgotten little Mazda MX-3 coupe of 1991 had the world's smallest transverse-mounted V6 of only 1.8 litres but with 24 valves.

It was widely anticipated that there would be a host of V6 hatchbacks following the Golf's example but it was to remain on its own in its class, with highly developed VR6 Golfs until 2009. The Astra was said to have been engineered for a V6 but never got one.

← The final VR6 in a brochure shot. The first six-cylinder Golf was highly marketable. (Author's collection)

↑ **Partially covered here, the Volkswagen VR6 engine was compact enough to fit alongside items such as an air conditioner. (LAT)**

years on the career ladder then graduated to a BMW 3-Series with the extra prestige that implied, especially a six-cylinder version.

Although the comparison was between a rear-wheel-drive saloon and a front-driven hatchback, the first *Car* magazine road-test pairing was a Golf VR6 against a BMW 325i. The BMW engine was a twin-camshaft 24-valve design, compared to the single-cam 12-valve VR6, and gave 192bhp, but it was heavier and the 325i had a very similar power to weight ratio to the Golf. Both were nearly 140mph cars and both offered immense engine flexibility and refinement, the Golf with 147lb ft of torque available from 2,000 to 6,000rpm while being able to rev all the way up to a 6,200rpm red line. The fuel consumption wasn't all that daunting, in most tests averaging 25mpg. At around £19,000 in the UK in 1992, a VR6 five-door was at least a couple of thousand pounds cheaper than a 325i. A four-speed automatic was offered with a 'dynamic shift programme' which was claimed to learn the driver's progress and adjust the change points accordingly.

At the time, the Golf's chassis was judged capable of coping with the extra power and the power steering well set up for enthusiasts, although *Car* magazine termed its traction-control system, which was claimed to control wheelspin only under 25mph, as 'half hearted'. Nonetheless, it decided the Golf beat the BMW in a way worthy of its December 1991 front cover. Sadly, the next time it made the cover it was represented by a lemon, describing a catalogue of woes the magazine had had with a long-term test car.

Where now for the GTI?

If there was still a GTI in the Golf range it seemed that even its maker was bored with it, directing all the attention towards the VR6. The GTI was a mature car, too mature for enthusiasts. What GTI meant even differed as to where you lived. When the Golf was launched in the US in 1994 GTI was applied to the VR6 – the 115bhp European GTI engine was fitted to regular Golfs and Jettas with no sporting associations.

↑ **It was now very hard to tell a GTI from the front. Like all Golfs, door handles required only to be pulled – you no longer had to press a button at the same time.**

If the second-generation GTI's first appearance had been considered too close to the regular Golf, this applied even more so to the third. As all Golfs now had a single headlamp cover, a twin-lamped GTI couldn't readily be distinguished from any other from the front, apart from the badge and clear indicator lenses. The red piping was absent from the front grille, but it was body coloured and had a large GTI badge. Even at the 1991 Frankfurt show German tuner ABT was offering a Golf 'Sportline' package, which included a twin round lamp conversion. There were sports seats and lots of black trim, but the golf ball gear lever had gone.

By 1991 the European car market was awash with high-powered hatchbacks from the little 85bhp Citroen AX GT to the 227bhp Ford Escort RS Cosworth. Everybody was squeezing over-large engines into family cars. Below the GTIs there were now ranked slightly slower but sporty-looking XSIs and SXIs. British writers started to use the phrase 'warm hatch' to describe outputs with which the original Golf GTI had once made such an impact.

The eight-valve 2-litre GTI engine with an iron block and alloy head was derived from the well-proven 1.8 with an increase in stroke from 86.4mm to 92.8mm and an increase in bore from 81.0mm to 82.5mm. Digifant, Volkswagen's own version of Bosch's L-Jetronic engine-management system, controlled ignition and fuel injection for each cylinder. Its claimed top speed was 123mph and the 0–62mph figure had reduced only slightly from the Golf 2, from 10.3 to 10.1 seconds.

Sharing the 'Plus' front suspension with the VR6, the GTI was lowered by 10mm at the front and 20mm at the back, with 280mm internally vented discs at the front and 226mm discs at the rear, and six-inch alloy wheels with 195/50R15 tyres. As noted, power-assisted steering was standard, but at first anti-lock brakes and traction control were optional, and you needed to buy anti-lock to have the latter.

Unlike its competitors, the Golf GTI continued to be offered in three- and five-door forms. In March 1992 *Autocar & Motor* tested a five-door Golf GTI with the latest Ford XR3i, which seemed to present a real threat to it, possibly for the first time.

Its 1.8-litre Zetec 16-valve engine was a new design

↑ **No tartan or stripes for the third GTI, nor golf-ball gear lever.**

for Fords in the 1990s and in the XR3i produced 130bhp to the Golf GTI's 115 from 2.0 litres and eight valves and, of course, cost less than the Volkswagen. As before the Ford was only available as a three-door.

British buyers needed to pay Volkswagen for many extras to match the Ford's equipment down to an adjustable steering column, electric front windows and a split rear seat backrest. Anti-lock brakes were optional on both, £807 for the VW.

When a second or so made a real difference to enthusiasts, it was hard to argue that the new, heavier eight-valve GTI was a competitive hot hatch with a recorded 9.9 seconds to 60mph against the Ford's 8.6, and a top speed of 121mph against 125mph. Looking back at *Motor*'s 1984 test of the Golf GTI 1.8 it was clear that there was a trade-off for refinement and safety, even if the engine was bigger. Six years previously the three-door Golf had achieved 0–60mph in 8.3 seconds but, giving credit to the new car's better aerodynamics, had managed a 115mph top speed.

However, in this instance (other road tests were less kind) although it was faster the Ford was judged to have lost out to the flexibility, refinement and slick driving experience of the Volkswagen: 'The XR3i wobbles the new GTi with a set of performance figures that the VW, for the most part, can't get close to. Not that the Golf falls over. It's far too good for that; too accomplished technically, too well made, too steady on the feet. It's a car that knows how much performance equals a good time without making it a means to an end.'

If the 16-valve was to recover some of the excitement created by its predecessor, its late arrival allowed rivals and the VR6 to make a lot of headway. Meanwhile, the old-shape 16-valve Golf and Jetta GTI continued in production in Yugoslavia, Mexico and South Africa. The last-generation Golf was by no means over, with a projected 200,000 units for 1992.

At the GTI eight-valve's launch Dr Ing Ulrich Seiffert, who had succeeded Fiala as head of research and development, refused to specify a date for the 16-valve until they had released the pre-production engine, so he would only indicate production in the first quarter of 1992 – in the event it was at the end. As recounted by Ian Wagstaff, chief engineer Herbert Schuster – by

The A59 rally car

In 1992 rumours started to circulate that the Golf would once more spawn a super high performance variant with an eye to motor sport, and taking on the mighty Ford Escort Cosworth.

In its 18 March 1992 issue *Autocar & Motor* reported that the green light had been given to a 200bhp-plus super Golf. Two prototypes with different engine and four-wheel-drive combinations were said to be already under development and Volkswagen had started assembling a team to make the car a world beater on the road and in the World Rally Championship.

Mindful of the failure of the Golf G60 Rallye – best result third on the Rally of New Zealand in 1990 – the new car was billed to have the maximum permitted two-litre forced-induction arrangement used by Lancia, Toyota and other WRC regulars to produce well over 300bhp in rally trim.

'We haven't decided on the final specification of the engine yet,' said Klaus Rosorius, VW Motorsport's managing director. 'We're thinking about a two-litre 16- or even 20-valve four with either turbo or supercharging.'

The final specification would have needed to be signed off soon, the magazine reported and production of at least 2,500 road cars start in 1993 for the car to qualify for the 1994 World Rally Championship season. Karmann was said to be the likely assembler. *Autocar* continued that three key personnel had been hired for the project: Konrad Schmidt, Toyota's chief rally engineer Karl-Heinz Goldstein and Walter Röhrl, Audi world rally champion to help with development.

And a prototype did appear, powered by a two-litre turbocharged four-cylinder engine with 275bhp and four-wheel drive. It was made by tuner Schmidt near Nuremberg, which already made Audi rally cars. Dealers were calling for a small series and a run of 2,500 at a price of DM 80,000 (about £35,000) was discussed only for the project to come to a halt. Europe being in recession in 1993 cannot have helped any thoughts of Volkswagen returning to motor sport.

While the third-generation Golf was rallied, the A59 never reached the WRC. Two prototypes were built, and one is still in the Volkswagen museum in Wolfsburg. (Volkswagen Classic)

↑ **A US-spec Volkswagen Golf GTI featuring the VR6 engine. American specifications were part of the European design, so it looked much the same. (LAT)**

then known as 'Mr GTI' – told the press that the 2.0-litre 16-valve was going to be an all-new engine of 142 to 150bhp. He then somewhat dampened anticipation by saying that because the VR6 was expected to have such an impact, the 16-valve would 'not have the importance that it might have had'. Wagstaff noted that it was being suggested in August 1991 that the 16-valve had in fact been postponed due to lack of power and refinement. The then current 2.0-litre 16-valve fitted to the Audi 80 had been judged 'vociferous, undistinguished and coarse' by *Autocar & Motor*.

So why not use the G60 supercharged unit already proven in the Corrado? Even with two valves per cylinder, it produced 160bhp and a wide spread of torque. Schuster said that Volkswagen was considering using the G60 *G-Lader* with the new 16-valve engine in another bid for the World Rally Championship (see panel opposite) but it didn't appear in a road-going Golf. For road cars, Volkswagen had already discounted it in favour of the refined VR6 as *Autocar & Motor* recounted in its test: 'Believing the next generation of hot-hatch drivers will favour refinement above all, but with no loss in performance, VW realised the supercharged G60 engine would not do for the pinnacle Golf Mk III. Instead Wolfsburg has gone for two more cylinders and a 40 per cent increase in power.'

With hindsight one can see that towards the mid 1990s Volkswagen's interest was shifting away from the supercharger – with hindsight temporarily – and towards turbocharged petrol engines. The Corrado G60 was the last model of the 1990s to use the supercharger, and in 1994 Audi applied a turbocharger to its four-cylinder 1.8-litre A4 for an output of 150bhp. Engineer Rolf Trump told the author in 2012 that the *G-Lader* had not been without its challenges: 'The problem back then with the charger was that production had to be extremely precise in order to have these two coil-like discs running against each other. Back then it wasn't

← To distinguish a 16-valve Golf GTI you had to search for the badges or know which alloy wheels were fitted as standard.

↓ Alloy induction piping dominates the top of the engine of the second-generation Golf GTI 16V.

← Twin headlamp conversions were a popular replacement for the Golf 3's one-piece units to add some distinction to a GTI. These accessories are from Votex.

easy for large scale production and that was the reason why we discontinued this, because of the difficulty in precision production.'

In January 1993 the 16-valve GTI finally emerged as a new design offering 150bhp, a logical midway power and price point between the eight-valve and the VR6. Not the same engine as had been fitted to the Passat from 1988–93, at 1,984cc it had gained 200cc over the previous generation by a longer piston stroke and increased cylinder bore. The cast-iron cylinder block was 16.5mm taller with reinforcing ribs and an alloy oil sump. It was claimed to run more quietly than the old 1.8. The 16-valve cylinder head was developed by Audi in Ingolstadt and was in aluminium alloy, with a chain drive connecting the two camshafts as before.

The GTI 16V was as subtle as the eight-valve with a GTI 16V badge front and rear plus in the side strips, black wheel arches and sills, and 'Le Mans' or 'Monte Carlo' alloy wheels with optional black Recaro sport seats inside. TCS traction control was standard and at first the brake and suspension settings the same as the lower-powered car, although they were upgraded in 1996. In 1994 ABS brakes became standard on the GTI and on all models from September 1996.

In the UK it commanded a healthy premium over the regular GTI; in 1994 £2,000 more at a list price of £15,999 for the three-door, but the consensus was that it had restored honour to the GTI badge, with a 0–60 time of 7.7 seconds, almost two better than the eight-valve and a top speed of 134mph. 'The new 16V joins the VR6 as the MkIII Golf that knows the meaning of fun,' said *Autocar & Motor*. However, its reign at the top was not to last that long.

A new open-air Golf

By 1992 the long-lived first-generation Golf cabriolet had become the most successful convertible in the world. A Volkswagen market analysis of August noted that there was plenty of competition and the convertible segment in Germany had expanded by 44% the previous year, accelerated by products such as the Mazda MX-5. By 1995 the European soft-top segment was expected to be 170,000 cars. It noted that newer cars had better equipment levels but were more expensive than the old Golf. But it was the 'fashion leader' for colours and interior trim.

Time to face up: 'The now 13-year-old design is becoming more and more outmoded. In particular, since the appearance of the new A3 Golf, the old fashioned character of the convertible's exterior and interior design has become very obvious.'

So the Frankfurt Motor Show in September 1993

↑ Although prototypes were built without one, the new Golf cabriolet featured a rollover bar. Hood operation was electric.

→ Statistically rollover accidents were rare, but the Golf 3 cabriolet had to match the safety credentials of the hatchback. (LAT)

saw the second all-new Golf cabriolet. It had been painstakingly developed by Karmann, which carried out over 120 trials for bodywork rigidity for real as this was the last project before it went over to Computer Aided Design (CAD) technology.

Fully open prototypes without a roll bar had been built, but with a reputation for class-leading rigidity and having to meet the same safety standards as the hatchback plus US rollover safety standards, Herbert Schuster, by then board member for technology, insisted on a fixed rollover bar. Although Volkswagen itself was the first to admit that rollover accidents involving convertibles were extremely rare, in independent tests in 1994 the bar preserved space above the occupants' heads while in other cars – including the Audi 80 cabriolet – the windscreens collapsed. High-backed stronger seats came as an option on that car.

The rollover bar retained further benefits: good hood and window location, and the ability to accommodate a roof rack and go through a brush car wash without incident. The old nickname of *Erdbeerkörbchen*, or strawberry basket was safe, even if the basket was bigger and heavier than before.

To achieve the same claimed level of refinement as the regular Golf it boasted front and rear 'harmonic vibration dampers' consisting of a 10kg cast iron weight mounted on rubber blocks behind the left-hand rear wheel and the entire mass of the engine and transmission at the front used as a damper through a specially designed mounting system. Floorpan, front and rear structure and door sills were reinforced.

As before, the soft-top Golf was built by Karmann in Osnabrück and from April 1996 production started in Puebla, Mexico for the US market, although was reportedly delayed by quality problems.

There was a new, fully open, Astra convertible to contend with too, built in Italy by Bertone. Based not on the hatchback but the saloon, it offered what was claimed to be the biggest boot in the class while the Golf retained a boot lid larger than the previous car but still a little restrictive. Volkswagen opted once more not to recess the hood fully for better luggage capacity, which was 50 litres more than the old car.

In Germany the new Golf cabriolet featured anti-lock brakes and twin front airbags as standard. Power steering, central locking and heated back window were standard for all markets. There was an optional wind deflector for use when only driver and passenger were present, and this attached over the top of the rear seats.

↑ The Golf 3's rollover bar allowed it to meet US rollover laws, could have a mesh screen fitted to it, and meant it could go through a car wash and carry a roof box. Just mind your head getting out though.

The six-layer fully insulated fabric roof was up to the expected standards of insulation, and folded flatter than before for better rear visibility. In the UK Volkswagen opted to introduce it in a highly specified form in 1994 with a Mercedes-like trim name of Avantgarde with the 115bhp GTI engine, and 1.8- and 1.6-litre choices followed. An electric hood was standard on the top specification and cruise control and heated seats could be specified. While there was to be a diesel cabriolet, the third-generation was not offered with the VR6 engine or in GTI trim.

The first Golf estate

The arrival of the long-awaited Golf estate or kombi derivative came in 1993, and was promoted in Germany as the *Golf mit Happy End.* Since the first generation Volkswagen had maintained that the buyers would simply upgrade to the Passat, but that was now a bigger car and there had been Ford Escort and Opel Astra estates for years. The new Golf kombi retained the rear

The Vento

A Golf with a conventional boot followed the hatchback swiftly into production and was introduced in February 1992 with a new name: Vento, suggested by a Wolfsburg employee. The Jetta name was dropped in Europe but retained in North America. Production of the Vento began in Mexico and South Africa.

Most of the Golf's competitors now offered booted versions with alternative names, but these were far outsold by their hatchback brethren. The second-generation Jetta took only 10% of Golf sales and 11% in the UK. The Vento matched the Golf on safety equipment and engines and, being 36cms longer at 4.38m had a vast boot of 550 litres capacity with fold-down rear seats. A rear anti-roll bar was standard to cope with the extra luggage this might entail.

The Vento had its own frontal styling but was difficult to distance from the Golf hatchback as it used the same rear doors. Mindful of its extra weight, no engine was smaller than 1.6 litres and while there was a range-topping VR6 the Vento was not offered with syncro transmission.

Volkswagen argued to the motoring press in vain that this was not just a Golf with a boot but a new class of car, sitting between the Golf and the Passat and challenging models such as the Peugeot 405 and the Opel Vectra in the 4.4m class. The European car magazines were having none of this and especially resisted the idea that it was equivalent to a BMW (Audi was making much better progress on prestige). However, the Vento has been credited with having saved Volkswagen from pulling out of the US in the early 1990s. Overall sales went from 49,533 in 1993 to 97,043 the next year following the third Jetta's introduction and continued to climb.

➔ Entering a market dominated by the Ford Escort estate, the Golf variant/estate was long overdue.

Not sold in economy trim, the Vento was fitted with body-coloured bumpers from the outset. The huge boot still gave the appearance of being added on.

doors of the hatchback but was extended behind the rear wheels by an extra 32cms at 4.34m long, essentially a Vento saloon platform. The rear suspension differed from the hatchback by using redesigned suspension struts where the spring was at the lower end of the strut rather than the top, so reducing load space intrusion.

Barring the 1.4, it was available with the same range of engines as the hatchback including, in 1994, the Syncro four-wheel-drive option coupled to the 2.9-litre version of the VR6, which upped power from 174 to 190bhp to cope with the power losses in the system. In view of the lack of interest in the previous version, the third-generation Syncro wasn't imported into the UK. A popular choice, the first Golf estate outlasted the hatchback, with production moving to Karmann from 1997 to '99. It became an established part of the Golf range.

There was some revision of Golf petrol engines for 1994 with the trusty 75bhp 1.6-litre engine replacing the lower-powered 1.8 and a new 100bhp 1.6 from 1997 having been introduced in the Passat and the Audi A3.

Diesel becomes TDI

After the turbocharged and catalysed diesel engine the third Golf saw another development with a set of initials that would become very familiar to car buyers in the 1990s: TDI (also spelt TDi in Volkswagen advertising). It addressed the public perception that diesel-engined cars,

With redesigned rear suspension the Golf estate's load bay measured one metre between the wheel arches. With the rear seats folded it boasted 1,425 litres of space, only 75 less than the Passat estate.

The estate provided the basis of this unproduced pick-up to replace the Caddy. (Volkswagen Classic)

↑ **How far you could go on a tankful of diesel in a Golf TDI was a popular theme of 1990s Volkswagen adverts – up to 891 miles one claimed.**

even with turbochargers, simply could not match their petrol counterparts on performance. The 'T' was for Turbo and the 'I' stood for direct injection of the fuel straight into the cylinder at much higher pressure, rather than via a pre-combustion (or 'swirl') chamber.

Combined with a turbocharger fed with air from an intercooler, the benefits were greater torque at low engine speeds, lower emissions and 15 to 20% better fuel economy. The first Volkswagen Group TDI was the 2.5-litre five-cylinder engine introduced in the Audi 100 in 1989. Direct injection, with its higher pressures, had been used on commercial vehicles but had a reputation for harshness. To combat this Audi developed fuel injectors that pumped diesel in two stages to 'soften' the combustion process, and hydraulic engine mounts, which would change from soft to hard once the engine was above idle speed. The engine compartment was also soundproofed by flexible seals around the driveshaft openings.

The 1,896cc Golf diesel went TDI in 1993. Sitting above the standard turbo diesel Golf, the TDI offered 90bhp to its 75 with performance on a par with the 1.8-litre petrol but with a claimed European mixed fuel consumption of 56.9mpg. Road tests averaged figures in the mid 40s. They did, however, observe that the indirect injection diesels from Peugeot-Citroen were quieter and cheaper.

British Golf TDI advertising boasted of 891 miles between fill-ups and Volkswagen and Audi embarked on a series of record attempts for the longest distance on a tank of fuel, which became somewhat of a tradition.

Offered in addition to regular diesel engines, the TDI was soon used right across the Volkswagen brands and in all parts of the Golf (and Vento/Jetta) range. In 1995 it became available in the cabriolet and VW boasted that it had created the first volume-produced diesel convertible. The fear that drivers would be troubled by diesel noise and smells with the top down proved unfounded and it was regarded as a refined long-distance tourer. However, while it was trialed for right-hand drive production, the British importers declined to take the diesel cabriolet, perhaps because most owners would not be driving long distances, but clattering slowly around fashionable parts of London.

Generally, though, a diesel car was no longer a fringe choice and every other manufacturer offered a multitude of options. In 1995 Volkswagen introduced a non-turbocharged, or normally aspirated, direct-injection diesel as the 64bhp Suction Diesel Injection or SDI and the following year, in the final period towards the next Golf, the Audi A4's 110bhp TDI became available, endowing the GTD with almost GTI-like power coupled to torque not far off that of the VR6, and developed from only 1,900rpm. The turbocharger had variable rate vanes which allowed exhaust gases to pass through continuously, even at low revs for better and quieter response.

This performance diesel was marked out by a red 'I' on the badging. In 1996, after introducing a TDI cabriolet, Volkswagen broke another taboo by making the 110bhp TDI engine available in the Golf GTI, badged rather lengthily as the GT TDI. On claimed figures it accelerated from 0–60mph in 9.3 seconds, three-tenths of a second quicker than the petrol-engined car and its acceleration in fifth gear from 50 to 75mph was even better at 11.1 seconds compared to 14.2.

TDI engines became immensely popular in Europe in the 1990s. In the German market it became the most popular engine of the Golf programme for three generations (four out of ten Golf cars had a TDI) although the technology behind the letters changed significantly. The Ecomatic, another diesel Golf development in the mid '90s, proved to be far less successful (see panel on page 162).

The Golf's market begins to change

In May 1994, what was now a routine milestone marker was passed as the 15 millionth Golf was produced. However, all was not well. Commentating in the British car magazine *Complete Car* (related to *Auto Motor und Sport*) Englebert Männer wrote that: 'A lot of people in VW head office had got used to the idea that the Golf and its saloon offshoot, the Vento would occupy the position of European best seller permanently. The first eight months have already seen a change, because the Fiat Punto has taken over pole position. The main reason for this being the decline of Golf vehicle registrations throughout Europe (an average drop of 20%).'

Part of this was due to wider factors. The boom following re-unification had turned to bust and worldwide recession in 1992/3. Volkswagen once more had to restructure its ways of working with a flexible plan to cut working hours when demand fell. There was a focus on making better use of the group's 16 platforms, 'lean' production methods based on Japanese systems were introduced into the new Mosel and Martorell (SEAT) factories and layers of management were axed to devolve more development responsibility to individual teams.

But the competition was intense and diversifying. With separate styling and names for three- and five-door versions of the same car the Fiat Bravo and Brava were said to be making a 'determined start' after a debut at Frankfurt in 1994, as was the Renault Mégane, which would start the medium-sized MPV (Multi Purpose Vehicle) trend with its 1996 Scenic version. Männer speculated that VW would respond with a Golf-based coupe to take up from the discontinued Corrado and 'possibly a Golf-based people carrier – if it becomes apparent that there is a demand for such multi-purpose vehicles.' Neither of these responses arrived for quite some time.

The more immediate challenge to the Golf's position was in house. As explained in more detail in the next chapter, Audi moved into the same sales territory as the high level Golfs with its own medium-sized hatchback based on the platform of what would become the fourth-generation Golf. This in turn would also be used as the

continued on page 164

↓ This 1997 TDI GL features the fully-body-coloured bumpers fitted to later Golf 3s.

The Golf Ecomatic

It was meant to be an environmental trailblazer, but the 1993 Golf Ecomatic was an idea too far ahead of its time and not user-friendly enough. Taking up the earlier ideas of the *Schwungnutz* automatic/Glider, Formel E and the Auto 2000 concept car, here was a Golf that not only cut out its own engine when sitting in traffic but also when coasting.

In 1989 Volkswagen co-operated with the State of Lower Saxony for the *Oko-Golf* (Eco-Golf) prototype, with a catalysed turbo diesel engine and automatic engine shut-down and restart. It was tested by the police. Four years later the Golf 3 Ecomatic went into series production. Coupled with the adoption of its TDI engines the company stated it was proof that it was on track to meet the 5.6 litre/100km (50.4mpg) corporate average fuel economy figure set by the German Government for 2005. By increasing the use of technology and lightweight materials it stated that it would have a car that could cover 100km on three litres of fuel (94mpg) on sale by the end of the decade. And it did with the Lupo 3L of 1999, a version of the Group's city car fitted with aluminium panels, an aluminium 1.2-litre direct-injection diesel engine and stop/start.

The Golf Ecomatic was launched at the 1993 Frankfurt show. It featured a 1.9-litre non-turbo diesel, which shut its engine off whenever it was not needed, such as idling in town traffic or going downhill, or even in the gaps between gear changes. You would come up to a red light, take your foot off the accelerator, the engine would cut and you would brake normally to a halt. Put it into first gear, the clutch

Only a badge at the back of this Golf told you it had an automatic stop-start system – the Ecomatic.

would re-engage and the engine would start. It was claimed to be capable of an average consumption of 4.6 litres/100km urban and 4.9 overall (61.4/57.6mpg).

Volkswagen claimed its own engineers had measured a 22% decrease in carbon dioxide and fuel consumption, while particulate emissions were down by 11%. The interior temperature of the catalytic converter stayed higher than the conventional diesel as with the engine running less, less cooling air was being forced across it.

It wasn't a conventional automatic (which would increase fuel consumption) but a five-speed manual gearbox where the clutch was activated automatically. A contact in the gear lever controlled its movement if the driver lifted his or her foot off the accelerator during shifts. It was the first system of its kind in the world to go into series production.

When the accelerator was released the clutch would automatically de-couple drive from the engine, activated by a vacuum servo. It would go into neutral for one-and-a-half seconds and then shut the engine off. The system was managed by an electronic control box called 'Digi Swing'. This worked from sensors around the car, which looked at coolant temperature, engine and road speed, and accelerator position to determine when to stop and start the engine and activate the auxiliary pumps. It matched engine speed against the gearbox output shaft speed to ensure smooth gear changes.

The Ecomatic reintroduced some of the features of Formel E cars more than a decade earlier, chiefly a button on the end of the windscreen wiper stalk but this time to override the system and keep the engine on permanently, rather than to shut if off. Also there was a row of extra lights in the instrument panel advising on the state of the system, engine braking and suggesting gear change points.

The press pack of the time took great lengths to reassure the public that this strange car was completely safe and easy to drive. If you switched the engine off to coast downhill you would still get engine braking and when reversing it was claimed you could manoeuvre the car to the last centimetre using the accelerator as usual as the engine shut-down was overridden.

A whole range of back-up systems had to be built in so that the car would still have heating, lighting, brake and power-steering assistance when the engine cut out.

↑ If the driver of an Ecomatic tired of the stop-start, they could override it via a button on the end of the windscreen wiper stalk. (Volkswagen Classic)

The main battery was described by Volkswagen as 'enormous', providing a store of power half as big again as a standard Golf – enough to leave the headlights on for nine hours. However, to avoid the current 'dipping' during the starting process and affecting on-board systems the Ecomatic switched to an auxiliary battery.

An electric vacuum pump made sure the clutch and brake servos were always at the correct pressure, being activated as the driver opened the door. The power steering was electrically driven and unlike normal hydraulic pumps did not run all the time, for example while the car was on a motorway. This provided another energy-saving measure. A further electric pump continued to circulate coolant around the engine when it had cut out.

Although applied to a diesel, Volkswagen said the system was equally suited to petrol engines, but the easy-starting properties of a warm diesel were an advantage. Volkswagen pointed out that restarting a warm engine put less strain on the starter motor whatever the fuel.

The engine, clutch and transmission were normal production units but the standard 64bhp diesel had been

The Golf Ecomatic (continued)

used instead of the new TDI unit because there would have been no space for its turbocharger and intercooler in addition to the Ecomatic's auxiliary pumps.

So the Ecomatic was just like a normal Golf, only extra special, its maker claimed and suitable for long and short distances. It was thought likely to be of special interest to local authorities or companies with lots of urban work – the beginning of a trend in fact.

The reaction from press and public alike was woeful. Launched in Germany in September 1993 sales were sluggish and production (once aimed to be 10,000 a year) at Mosel/Zwickau was scaled back. It was £750 dearer than the equivalent diesel Golf and by March 1994 only 3,500 Golf Ecomatics had been sold in its home market. German dealers were reported to believe many people didn't want to be the first to go for what was seen as an experimental car. Young people didn't think it fast enough, while older drivers preferred the economical direct-injection diesels.

The Ecomatic arrived in the UK in June 1994 with hope that over the following year 'a couple of thousand' would be sold, mainly to companies like the Post Office and The Body Shop. Ahead of this *Complete Car* magazine tested a German-registered example for its April 1994 edition and was not impressed: 'The car has a number of features many drivers will not tolerate; shutting down around slow corners, a shudder as the engine stops and insensitive throttle pedal. With a flurry of snow during our test we found the Golf sliding around as you can't pull away in anything but first gear. A stalk-mounted button allows the driver to turn off the cut-out system, which they may often do, thus making the exercise pointless.' Although the official fuel consumption test quoted a 61mpg urban, the magazine only achieved 43mpg over four days of London commuting. In a later test it managed an average of 40.2mpg.

After a year on sale in the UK the Ecomatic was withdrawn. While the Golf Ecomatic wasn't sophisticated enough to catch on, its ideas would have their time 20 years later as car manufacturers re-adopted the stop-start system (much better developed) as a way of reducing emissions, along with semi-automatic transmissions and electric power steering. The inertia flywheel and drive de-coupling became an essential part of hybrid cars, saving energy while switching between electric power and a petrol or diesel engine.

basis for other Volkswagen brand cars in an innovative strategy to share costs. 'The fact that Audi is going to supply a prestige Golf from mid 1996 makes things even more difficult,' Männer wrote. 'Because let's be honest, who would still want to buy a Volkswagen Golf GTI if, for slightly more money, he or she could have the much more attractive Audi A3?'

Indeed, once the Audi A3 was launched in 1996 the Golf GTI 16-valve was straight away found wanting in comparison tests. The Audi was of course more expensive but regarded as more stylish and sophisticated. Its engine choice included an impressive 20-valve 1.8-litre petrol engine with 125bhp, or 150 when turbocharged, as an alternative to both Golf GTIs. However, if you wanted a full four-seater and five doors the Golf was the only choice as the A3 was intentionally limited to three doors until 1999. But even if Golf GTI sales weren't what they were, the profits from the Audi A3 all ended up in the same place and if you wanted something more akin to a Golf 2 GTI there was now the Polo-based SEAT Ibiza GTI, with the familiar Volkswagen 1.8-litre 130bhp 16-valve engine or the bigger and cheaper SEAT Toledo GTI with the 2.0-litre 16-valve.

As was the custom, the last couple of years of the third-generation Golf saw a rash of special editions and equipment upgrades, which set the level for the next version. Body-coloured bumpers replaced the massive black items on the more basic versions, and in 1996 side airbags (a first in class) became available for the first time. In 1997 for most European markets the CL and GL badging was dropped to be replaced by Trendline and Comfortline.

Limited editions – which often stayed in the catalogues for some time – included tie-ups with world famous rock bands Pink Floyd, Bon Jovi, Genesis and the Rolling Stones. The Colour Concept cars splashed bright colours inside and out, and in 1996, to mark 20 years of the GTI a limited run of 1,000 GTI Anniversary models was offered with both GTI engines and the 110bhp TDI.

Bringing back what enthusiasts had been missing since launch, the Anniversary had special chequered Recaro front sport seats and matching rear seats bearing the GTI logo, red seatbelts front and rear, a half-chrome and leather golf-ball gear knob and a red stitched leather steering wheel and handbrake gaiter. The red theme was continued externally with a red striping on the bumpers and red brake calipers.

↑ In 1996, 21 years after first being unveiled (20 after sale), the limited-run GTI Anniversary was launched. Special edition GTIs appeared at five-year intervals after this.

← The GTI Anniversary's checked sports seats referenced the original tartan, and a stylised golf-ball gear knob appeared.

WOB GO 504
Volkswagen Classic

Golf 4
1997–2003

Affordable luxury

In the last few years before the fourth-generation Golf broke cover, the usual speculation as to what it would be like was backed up by hard facts as the products of the Volkswagen group's platform strategy, where differently styled versions of the same car would be built for different brands, started to emerge.

The 1994 Audi A4 marked the start of an ambitious plan to drastically reduce the number of platforms from the then 16 on which the group's vehicles were built. A new Passat followed in 1996 based on the Audi's B platform, its engine reverting from transverse to longitudinal installation. 'What appears to be a new VW could turn up a few months later in the guise of a SEAT, but for considerably less money,' Englebert Männer wrote cynically in *Complete Car* in 1995.

So all eyes were on Audi's all-new hatchback A3 in June 1996 because underneath it was the next Golf, with exactly the same dimensions in wheelbase, track and width. This platform, called the A4 platform (PQ 34 internally) was also destined to be the basis of the Škoda Octavia, the new SEAT Toledo and Leon and there was speculation of an aluminium-bodied Audi saloon that turned out to be the Audi TT coupe. Not forgetting the last-minute addition of the 'new' Beetle (see panel on page 170).

Audi's brand image was edging closer to BMW and Mercedes and the A3 was a Golf-sized hatchback for those who wanted to buy into that prestige. Until the new Golf was firmly established it was only made available as a three-door with a smaller range of engines but it was priced at comfortably more. The only immediate Golf 3 models to suffer in comparison were the GTIs, but they had enjoyed up to five years in production on their own.

↓ The 1997 Golf came to be considered one of the best styled, especially around the shape of the solid 'C' pillar, by then a non-negotiable feature.

A landmark style?

The third-generation car had re-defined the Golf to mean solidity, security and refinement although many had thought it too heavy looking. But by now Golf styling was expected to be variations of a theme. Evolution, not revolution.

Nonetheless in 1994 there was the customary styling competition, with six full-sized designs from the adventurous to the conservative, among them a Giugiaro design but this was judged too conservative. The in-house design won and it took 31 months from the styling freeze to the start of production.

Once more here was an all-new Golf that still looked like a Golf should look. Volkswagen claimed that: 'Research conducted amongst Golf owners throughout the world indicated that the car's recognisable and classless look was one of their prime reasons for choosing the model. Hence the decision was taken to retain many of the Golf styling cues in the fourth-generation car.'

Martin Winterkorn, head of quality assurance management from 2003 (and in 2007 appointed chairman of Volkswagen AG) monitored the development of the Golf 4. The chief designer was Hartmut Warkuß, an ex-Audi stylist and one of those who had backed the new Beetle. Before the Golf he had styled the 1996 Passat.

Walter de Silva, group head of design spoke to the author in 2012, as the seventh Golf was unveiled and the company began to portray the Golf 4 as the car which defined the 'DNA' of the Golf, the features that each further generation would inherit. 'The Golf was still successful but the Golf 4 had the same effect as the Golf 1 in terms of stepping up the pace. All those ideas were rationalised, even if the idea didn't immediately catch on.

continued on page 172

↓ All models had body-coloured bumpers and radiator grilles so it was harder to tell a GTI apart, except (unlike its predecessors) for the lack of any black trim and darkened rear lenses.

The New Beetle

At the start of the 1990s, Volkswagen sold less than 100,000 cars in America and there was talk of pulling out. In 1991, in an attempt to tap into styling that appealed more directly to the US market, Volkswagen opened its first non-European design studio in the Simi Valley, California, following the example of Japanese manufacturers. It was set up by J. Carroll Mays, an American who had been with Audi's advance studio since 1980.

The start of the new Beetle project was a brief to design an electrically-powered concept car, as environmental concerns were very current and California had some of the most stringent emissions standards in the world. Before long the shape of this car started to resemble the curves of the Beetle and the project was backed by corporate head of design Hartmut Warkuß and allowed to proceed to concept stage by Ferdinand Piëch.

There was a precedent for tapping into an idea from the past and rendering it as a modern motor car. The 1989 Mazda MX-5 sports car (Miata in America) had been painstakingly created in California to distil the ideas of the 1960s sports car into a modern yet 'retro' package. Mazda didn't have a heritage to base it on but analysed what had made drivers love British sports cars so much. It was a huge hit.

The Volkswagen Concept 1 – a nod to Type 1 – first appeared at the January 1994 Detroit Motor Show. Although absent since 1977, the original Beetle remained a fondly held abstract idea for Americans. It was highly unusual for Volkswagen to show a concept car that then became a production one (the Golf

Country was a small first example) and it conducted a great deal of customer research each time the concept was shown. Huge enthusiasm started to build and at the Geneva show in March a convertible version appeared.

In November 1994 it was approved for production and development began in Wolfsburg, although there was a reluctance to build the car there. For logistical and cost reasons the specialised 'New Beetle' would be built in Peubla, Mexico for American markets first and then Europe. The first Concept 1 had been based on the platform of the new Polo, but when it re-appeared at the 1995 Tokyo Motor Show it was appreciably larger. Piëch had decreed that if it was to go into production it should be based on the A-Class Golf platform then under development.

← The production Beetle initially sold rapidly in hatchback or convertible forms.

↑ The 1994 Volkswagen Concept 1 sat on a Polo platform but made production as the 'new Beetle' with a Golf underneath its bodywork.

Thus the new Beetle was the fourth car from the A-class platform although many of the fixed rules had to be broken to accommodate its styling and Volkswagen admitted to modifying over 50% of the underpinnings. The suspension and running gear was the same as the Golf but adjusted for the greater weight of the Beetle. The default engine was derived from the third-generation Golf GTI 2.0-litre although other petrol engines, including the V5, and the diesels were eventually offered.

In a wave of excitement, the new Beetle was launched in America in 1998 and Europe the following year, although the German market was cool in its reaction, not having quite the same nostalgia. A rash of other 'retro' or characterful styled cars followed of which the new Mini has been by far the most successful. The Beetle, however, suffered the fate of a fashion item. In the US it topped 88,000 sales in 1999 but tailed off somewhat as buyers who actively wanted one were satisfied. The idea of a people carrier styled like the old Volkswagen van was toyed with and then abandoned. The 'new' Beetle stayed in production until 2010 with only a mild facelift and was replaced by a new model in 2013, based on the sixth-generation Golf, with lower and wider styling to apparently appeal more to male as well as female buyers.

Ferdinand Piëch

Born in Vienna in 1937, Ferdinand Piëch is descended from Ferdinand Porsche's daughter and began work at Porsche in 1963 on experimental engines. Later in the decade one of his notable projects was the stillborn mid-engined Beetle successor EA266 (see Chapter 1), and he created the legendary Porsche 917 race car, which won at Le Mans in 1970 and 1971.

In 1972 Ferry and Louise Porsche banned all family members from management positions and floated Porsche on the stock exchange. Piëch went to Audi NSU Auto Union AG, heading technical development. The five- and six-cylinder Audi engines, turbocharging and intercooling were among his achievements, with the 1979 Audi Quattro the most significant car. He was proudest of the quattro four-wheel-drive system, galvanised bodies and aerodynamics. After sixteen years heading Audi research and development he was made chairman in 1988 and in 1993 took over from Carl Hahn as chairman of the board of management of Volkswagen AG. The first task facing him was a major re-organisation of American sales and production after a record sales low the year before.

'It was a bit of surprise that he actually got the job as chief exec of Volkswagen,' journalist Ray Hutton recalls. 'He was very autocratic at Audi and it was thought he was a bit too hot to handle as the chief exec, but he set off on this buying spree [of brands] and did all sorts of extraordinary things like putting the companies within the group in competition with each other – at one stage they had two V8 engines. He thought it was a good thing, "that's excellent, we'll find out which is the best one". But they were costing twice as much as they should have done.'

Widely accepted as a brilliant figure in the automotive industry, Piëch also became famous for filling journalists with trepidation, revealing very little in interviews and certainly not treating any kind of fool gladly.

Piëch continued what Carl Hahn has started tenfold; within ten years the Volkswagen group added Bentley, Bugatti, Lamborghini, Ducati motorcycles and Scania trucks to its portfolio. He made the car divisions extremely successful by sharing components under the surface yet keeping models distinctive.

The super luxury Volkswagen Phaeton of 2002 was regarded by some as Piëch's folly and it only sold in small numbers but was a superb flagship for the group built in a 'transparent' factory in Dresden. And its radical W12 engine was the basis of the all-new Bentley Continental introduced the same year to runaway success. 'Of course he did the Phaeton and one or two other projects, which because the company had so much momentum he got away with,' says Hutton.

He made managers attend test drives once or twice a month around the world and swap ideas. 'The way we handle our culture is unique,' he told *Fortune* magazine. 'In other car manufacturers, a leading brand or a leading group streamlines

'Warkuß was able to bring to the fore the key features of the Golf. A low line/stance with a very solid, robust pillar structure, excellent proportions and extreme linearity.

'The Golf 4 which has a very specific rounded cut of the doors can be seen as the true essence of car design. Nothing is redundant. I think that 1 and 4 – 7 as well – are really landmarks.'

Although the style was Golf-like there was a family resemblance to the Beetle and Passat in so much as the front door pillars had a gentle curve to them and the wheel arches were more pronounced to echo the Beetle. For the first time the tops of the doors folded over and blended into the roof panel.

In the side view the 'C' pillar was almost arrow-like in profile and the shut line of the rear bumper ran neatly parallel to the line of the lower half of the rear door on the five-door car. The almost-oval headlamps continued with single or twin headlamps inside but now incorporated the front turn indicators and front fog lights, giving the front end of the car a smooth look. Of course integrated twin headlamps made it even harder to distinguish a GTI from any other Golf other than by its badge. There was no red piping, no badging on the sides and alloy wheels were increasingly popular lower down the range. The most distinctive GTD or GTI markers were bumpers, door handles and side rubbing strips in the body colour rather than black plus darkened tail lamp lenses. Then again during the 1990s 'hot hatchbacks' had become a lot more discreet after an explosion in European car theft, which sent manufacturers back to reconsider car security.

Like every one of its rivals, the expectations of refinement, space and crashworthiness meant the new Golf was wider, longer and taller but the new styling managed to reduce the impression of bulk that the

the others. Here, it is an open market; you put your idea out, and the other brands can accept it or not.' An engineer through and through, his span of favourite projects ran from the 1-litre car project (the 94mpg Lupo) to the fastest car in the world, the Bugatti Veyron.

Whilst he was pushing through radical and often unpopular changes Piëch was engulfed in controversy when General Motors sued Volkswagen for hiring Ignacio Lopez, alleging he had arrived with stolen secrets. But he set Volkswagen on track to world dominance. As *Fortune* reported in 1999, when Piëch first arrived Volkswagen lost $1.1 billion; in 1998 profits rose 63%, to $3.6 billion before taxes with sales of more than 4.7 million vehicles, putting it close to Toyota as the world's third-largest carmaker.

At the end of 2000 Volkswagen was split into two brand groups; the 'sporting' brands would be Audi, SEAT and Lamborghini and the 'classic' brands Škoda, Bentley, Bugatti and Volkswagen. On April 16 2002, his 65th birthday, Ferdinand Piëch became chairman of the supervisory board, handing over daily running of the empire to former BMW chief Bernd Pischetsrieder. In a neat return to his roots, in his new role he saw Porsche come into Volkswagen ownership in 2012.

➔ A young Ferdinand Piëch pictured during his time at the family firm: Porsche. His influence as Volkswagen chairman became apparent from the Golf 4 onwards. (Porsche)

previous car had carried. It was 131mm longer than the Golf 3, 30mm wider and the wheelbase was 39mm longer to the benefit of boot capacity and rear leg room. At 1,439mm tall it was only a couple of millimetres taller.

The standard wheel size had gone up too, from 13 to 14in on basic cars to 16in on the top specification GTI.

The unladen weight range was stated as 1,163kg to 1,207kg, on average 60kg more than the previous car, but of course there was more equipment and it was a stronger bodyshell. With the increased length, boot space was bigger by 22cm, flat sided and with a lower loading height.

The bodywork's torsional (twisting) rigidity, seen as a measure of how well the car would cope with poor surfaces was now twice that of the 1974 Golf, which Volkswagen attributed mainly to laser welding and advanced bonding techniques to mount the windscreen and rear window. These also sped up manufacturing times, with the roof being welded as a single seam in 10 seconds.

Consistent gaps between panels – especially the gaps around the doors – were seen as a marker of a quality car and the new construction methods were claimed to allow consistent 3.5mm panel gaps around the Golf. This was a particular issue for chairman Ferdinand Piëch. Volkswagen engineer Rolf Trump who worked on every generation of Golf from the facelift for the second version, told the author how Piëch was closely involved as the talented engineer he was. 'He was all for precision and exactitude and quality and we had great quality – panel gaps were always his big issue.'

The drag coefficient was still a respectable 0.31, around the same as the best models of the previous car and two underbody trim panels smoothed airflow over the front and rear axles.

↑ **'New Golf is better to drive than its predecessor but still no driver's car,' said *Autocar*. (LAT)**

What lay beneath

The torsion beam rear axle was once again used but instead of being one inside the other vertically, the coil springs and dampers were located separately, with the springs positioned under the side-members. It meant a wider loading width in the boot for the hatchback and the forthcoming estate.

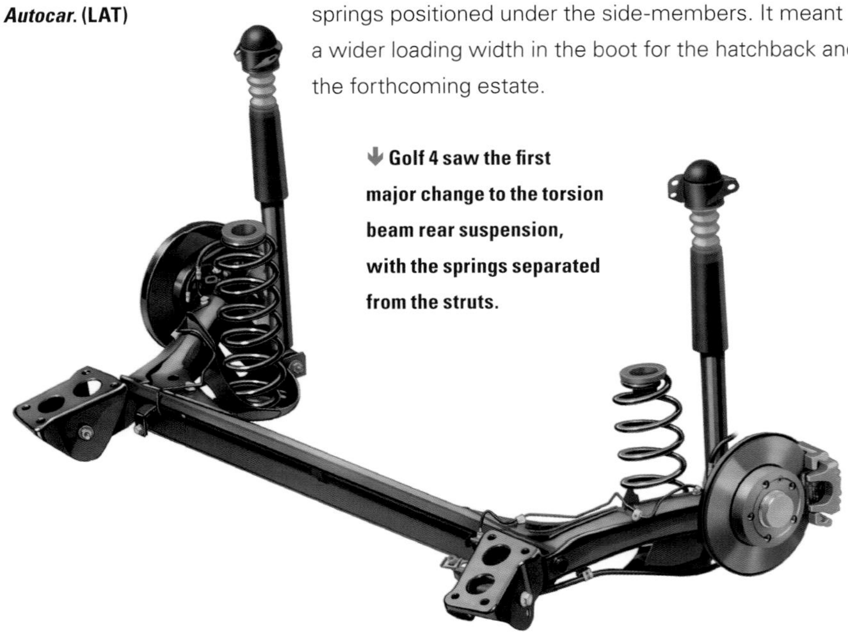

↓ **Golf 4 saw the first major change to the torsion beam rear suspension, with the springs separated from the struts.**

Front suspension by MacPherson struts and wishbones was now the industry norm, but the additional 'Plus' steering and suspension setting for the previous performance models was dropped, with one for all engines. The engine and running gear were mounted on a subframe both for insulating road noise from the bodyshell and crashworthiness. It was designed to direct the engine underneath the car in the event of a collision. Apart from the GTI, standard versions of the Golf were regarded as having soft, long-travel suspension set for the very good ride comfort that it provided. While road testers conceded that it didn't wallow as much around corners as the old car, and there were front and rear anti-roll bars as standard, they considered it did still roll excessively through the bends. The days when any manufacturer left even small cars with un-assisted steering were vanishing and all Golfs had power assistance.

It was of course exactly the same as an Audi A3 and road testers delighted in detecting the differences in settings – Audi firmer, Golf softer.

continued on page 178

Cloning the Golf

As Carl Hahn wrote in his autobiography, by the late 1980s it was clear that BMW and Mercedes were eyeing the medium-sized class, which the Golf had dominated. The 1994 BMW 3-Series Compact had been the first salvo and the ground-breaking but sadly flawed 1997 Mercedes A-Class initially appeared a very real threat. Part of the reaction was to take the Golf upmarket as the VR6 attempted to do, but the more radical decision was to create a Golf-sized Audi.

Audi's planned annual volume had stagnated at about 450,000 vehicles and Hahn and Audi chairman Ferdinand Piëch started to discuss an Audi model in the Golf class, meeting with the VW board every Tuesday from 1989, with Piëch bringing along his product planners, including Franz-Josef Paefgen (who would later head Bentley).

The initial idea of the Piëch/Hahn teams was a Golf platform with a typical Audi body, but with an Audi A4 front axle (longitudinal engine) and Golf rear axle. The first styling attempt was to simply chop the back end off an Audi A4 and give it a hatchback, as BMW had done with the Compact, but this was rejected in favour of an all-new car with a transverse-engined Golf drivetrain, a first for Audi. The first design study for the A3 was completed in autumn 1992 and passed for production in spring 1993.

But this was going to go far beyond the next Golf and a new Audi; 1993 marked the start of the Volkswagen group's first platform strategy. At that time – and it would change – Volkswagen essentially defined a platform as the floorpan, inner wheel arches, engine/transmission package and rear suspension. What went on top was called the 'hat' and these would be Audis, SEATs, Škodas and Volkswagens.

The PQ34 cars had the same wheelbase, track between the wheels and 20 'hard points' such as the centre of the floorpan, wheel-arch linings, suspension and engine mounts and body side-members. The aim was to share as many components as possible, even identical sunroofs; it went much further than metalwork and engines. Petrol tanks and seat frames would be

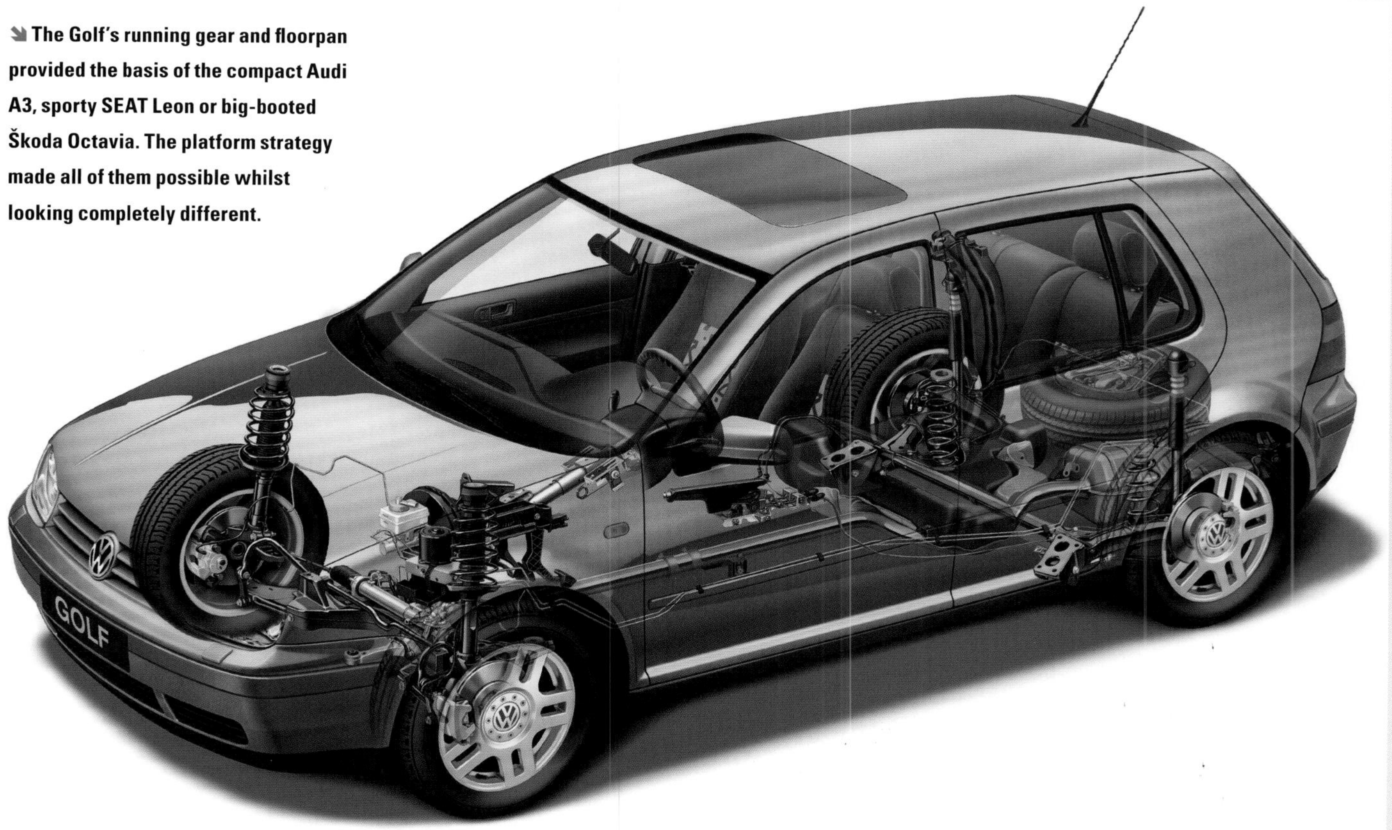

➘ The Golf's running gear and floorpan provided the basis of the compact Audi A3, sporty SEAT Leon or big-booted Škoda Octavia. The platform strategy made all of them possible whilst looking completely different.

Cloning the Golf (continued)

shared; dashboards would have a different design depending on the brand, but the internal components of the instrument cluster, the controls for the air conditioning or its compressor, wiring and ducting would be common. The differences would be in styling and suspension tuning according to customer tastes.

The pressed steel floorpans for all the brands were supplied from a central source in Germany and different front and rear sections added. So at one end you were able to have the Škoda Octavia with its vast boot (wheelbase 4cm longer than the Golf) and at the other the rather more compact Audi TT. The Audi A4 used a larger platform, the B platform, and was the basis for the 1996 Passat. Thus the Audi V6 replaced the Volkswagen VR6 and four-wheel-drive versions had quattro, not syncro drive. By reducing 16 platforms to four, Volkswagen expected to make savings of about £1.3bn.

The fourth Golf and the Audi A3 were developed in parallel with the Audi given the priority for launch over a year earlier than the Golf in June 1996, allowing it to become established, even if that meant unflattering comparisons with the Golf 3.

Volkswagen engineer Rolf Trump told the author how this first platform-sharing project demanded close working, with new Volkswagen chairman Piëch usually present. 'I was involved in some of the meetings he was in as well. He usually had meetings next to the car which was the subject of the meeting. Things were always discussed there, whatever the demand was, what was already taken care of for that particular car. He wanted to be sure that whatever he had given out as a demand had been met for that particular car.

'It was high value materials he was most interested in, that not only looked good but felt good, gave a good touch and feel for customers. So the dashboard was foam for example and we used very good leather for the steering wheel.'

Next on stream in summer 1996 came the Škoda Octavia, an early example of the 'democratisation of luxury'. Even though it was aimed at a cheaper end of the market it had Audi's much-praised 20-valve 1.8-litre engine.

At the launch of the Golf in 1997 Volkswagen admitted that 60% of the manufacturing value was shared with the A3. 'Twenty parts are crucial to platform management,' Horst Konig, in charge of the A-class platform told *Autocar*. 'We use one set of tool dimensions for every car built anywhere in the world on the Golf platform. We need board approval for any change; even drilling a hole is not possible without the board's okay.'

The days of the Volkswagen group depending on the Golf and losing customers to more prestigious or cheaper rivals were drawing to a close. Now it would have to compete with the three other Volkswagen brands, but as the costs were

The Audi A3 was a best-seller from launch, even restricted to three doors.

shared management could afford to be relaxed if there was an overlap of customers.

'So long as our market share is at the right level, any similarity is not relevant in a negative sense,' Erwin Stumpf, marketing manager for the A-class platform told *Autocar*. 'The bottom line is that it's good business for us.'

All the same, not everything worked in favour of the customer. British Škoda dealers may have wanted the new Octavia in 1996 when the rest of Europe had it, but because some of the right-hand drive components depended on the 1997 Golf they had to wait until 1998. At that time only 10% of sales were based on the four platforms, but the plan was to expand from 38 to 51 different passenger cars. As the platform strategy took off and continued to spawn more and more variations, the arrival of future generations of Golf was increasingly timed according to when the other brands wanted to launch their cars. The days of the eight- or nine-year Golf were well and truly over; six became the norm and even dropped to four for the sixth-generation Golf.

This was not a unique strategy and carried risk. Profiling Ferdinand Piëch in 1999 *Fortune* magazine pointed out that General Motors had been putting many cars on a few platforms for years, with the result that a lot of them drove and looked alike. It claimed analysts said customers confused the VW Passat with the Audi A4, but the boss had already claimed Audi A4 orders dropped less than expected in 1996 and orders for the two cars were 50,000 higher combined than the year before.

In the coming years, other carmakers would also move to common platforms, but the Volkswagen strategy remained ambitious and closely watched by the industry – what was meant by a platform would also evolve into a number of different ideas.

↑ The Octavia was a landmark car for Škoda.

← SEAT's 1999 Leon was the sportiest Golf clone.

↑ This was a Golf which felt more like an Audi. The cabin was even compared to a Mercedes. (LAT)

← The boot load height was the lowest it had been and a full-sized spare was beneath the floor. Luxury details included chrome load-lashing points and a power socket. It shared its 55-litre petrol tank with the Audi A3. (LAT)

Fascinating fittings

With Golf 4, the marketeers coined a phrase used by Volkswagen ever since; the 'democratisation of luxury'. There had long been a direct line of features which started on Audis and ended on Volkswagens, but with the greatly increased use of common components a trend began where once the Audi A3 appeared you could anticipate what further goodies the next Golf was going to get pretty quickly.

There was a real jump in the apparent quality of the Golf interior. Depending on the colour of the seat trim, the new Golf's dashboard could be specified in a contrasting lower colour, usually beige with the theme taken round to the lower halves of the door panels. A technique called 'slush moulding' gave a soft, grained feel to the top section of the dashboard while the lower sections, which you didn't usually touch, were made from a harder-surfaced plastic. It really did give the new Golf a 'mini Mercedes' look and when the new A-Class was compared, many found its cabin quality inferior to the Golf's.

The fourth-generation Golf was the first to be built using Volkswagen's new 'lean production' methods where independent companies developed and built individual 'modules' in and around the factories for assembly into the cars. They had to compete with in-house teams, which sometimes won. This led to more innovations, as *Automotive News* reported in 1997. The door modules were developed by Brose and Meritor to produce major savings in assembly time (claimed to be 30% down overall), the complex all-in-one headlamps were developed by Valeo and the soothing blue glow from the instrument panel at night – set to be a much appreciated Golf feature – was thanks to Siemens.

The hand of Ferdinand Piëch was at work in very small details that combined to give the Golf a premium feel, which it was to retain. A very small but often remarked fitment was a little damper in the grab handles above the doors so that if you released them they didn't clunk back into place but returned silently – this had come down from the Passat. Twin cup holders pivoted out of the dashboard and the rear console, the glovebox had a fluid-filled damper and was lined with a felt-like material as were the inside of the door pockets lest items jangle about on the move. All became Golf trademarks. The bonnet now rose gently on gas-filled struts rather than having to be lifted and hooked onto a stay. Such niceties cost money in production, but if the Golf was subsidising other cars in the group, economy of scale paid for them.

↑ Rear cup holders became a classic Golf detail, which contributed to the 'premium' experience. (LAT)

It was claimed to be built to the same standards as a Passat, or a Golf which felt like an Audi because it was one. Among the new luxury equipment, which would be optional or included, was an interior rear-view mirror with an automatic anti-dazzle function combined with a sensor which turned the windscreen wipers on if it detected rain. The options list also had electric front seats and a factory-installed satellite navigation screen, which doubled as an in-car entertainment unit. Keeping up with the competition, all Golfs now had a radio cassette player, and you could add an optional six-CD changer.

The door mirrors were now shared with the Passat as part of platform rationalisation. One was smaller on the passenger side of left-hand-drive Golfs and could be specified to lower itself to point at the kerb when reversing but British-market mirrors were the same size. While the rest of Europe stuck with Trendline, Comfortline and Highline, the UK had its own businesslike E, S, and SE trim levels when the range went on sale in May 1998, although had allowed itself a Highline on a version of the VR6.

Even though the prices had gone up, there was more equipment than the previous range so Volkswagen

would argue it was better value. And of course rival brands and their customers kept on driving up what an acceptable level of equipment was thought to be in a family hatchback. Air conditioning, electric front windows, CD players and central locking were on their way to becoming universal for Golf-class cars by the end of the decade. German buyers could have a winter options pack 'Winterpaket' with heated seats or a 'Technikpaket', which included an alarm and trip computer with even more information than before. Top models had 'Climatronic' air conditioning, which the user could set to maintain a specific temperature.

Car theft was now rife in Europe and the new Golf's security system was devised with the help of testers from the UK insurance industry. It included shielded door locks, rotating door and ignition locks and a new type of engine immobiliser. Taking care of your investment, the bodyshell was fully galvanised with a 12-year corrosion warranty and writing this book almost 17 years later, there are plenty of still-shiny Golf 4s on the road.

'Unless you simply must have the Audi A3's looks and charisma, it's impossible not to conclude that the Golf is rather better value for money,' said *Autocar* on its first drive in August 1997. 'Refined, yes, and superbly built, but not a naturally talented driver's car.'

There was to be no Car of the Year title for this Golf, beaten to first place by the Alfa Romeo 156. The line-up also included the revolutionary Mercedes A-Class but

by then it had suffered from its well-publicised stability problems. The views of the jurors were respectful of the Golf's progression to a 'premium' car but once more some were weary of it, and pointed out it was the third car to come off the same platform, the Audi A3 and Škoda Octavia having preceded it. 'The VW Golf is a fine car, but its concept is now 25 years old. I'd prefer a change,' wrote Steve Cropley of *Autocar*.

Delayed safety

The expected standard safety specification of any new car had of course moved on, and there was a more demanding safety imperative from buyers to be met rather than building to the latest regulations.

Through the 1990s and the Golf 3's life cycle public awareness and demands for safer cars that went beyond what was required by law had built relentlessly. The offset crash test into a block carried out by *Auto Motor und Sport* had become the accepted test manufacturers sometimes grudgingly engineered cars to meet.

A combination of European legislators and consumer groups set up an official testing and rating process for all new cars in 1997 under the banner of the European New Car Assessment Programme (Euro NCAP). Adopting the *AMS* tests, cars were also crashed to gain scores for occupant injury, for adults and children in front and side impacts, and their impact on pedestrians with further tests added over the years. The test results were made very public and it soon became a race to see which car would achieve the maximum four-star rating. The first to do so was the Volvo S40 in July 1997 and given that the previous generation had done well in the offset test the 1997 Golf had to have four stars.

So determined was Ferdinand Piëch that the new Golf would have its stars that when a weakness was found in the 'B' (central) pillar under Volkswagen's own side-impact test there was a last-minute solution to reinforce it weeks before production was scheduled in September 1997. Production was slowed and this had a huge knock-on effect. Dealer launch parties were planned across Germany for 10 October, but there were only 5,000 cars to share among 3,000 dealers who were expecting to get five or six show models. Some got none and had to be compensated. By the end of November domestic customers were being quoted delivery times the following summer.

It paid off when the Golf was crash tested by *Auto Motor und Sport* to the same standard as Euro NCAP in late 1997 and the following year in the official results. The five-door, which was tested with twin front and side airbags came through with a four-star rating.

As well as the subframe, which deflected the engine under the car in a frontal impact and reduced footwell intrusion by 27%, side-impact intrusion was claimed to have been reduced by 25% by the use of slanting side-impact bars in the doors, roof cross bracing and interlocking segments between the doors and sills.

Twin front airbags were now standard for all markets, and depending on market a pair of side airbags were built into the sides of the front seats, which became standard in UK cars later in 1998.

← It was imperative that the new Golf achieved a four-star Euro NCAP score in a combination of crash tests – the front offset is shown here.

Anti-lock brakes were now standard on every Golf with Electronic Brakeforce Distribution (EBD) to correctly proportion the assistance given to each wheel and this demanded the fitment of disc brakes all round. In the event of a crash locked doors would unlock automatically.

To add another acronym, EDL or Electronic Differential Lock was a development of traction control, monitoring the speed of the driving wheels and then braking the faster moving wheel if the difference exceeded a pre-determined value, transferring more drive to the gripping wheel.

A completely new feature was the standard fitment of Isofix mounting points for children's car seats. Rather than having to grapple with seatbelts to secure child seats in the car the new Golf had mounting points into which the latest generation of child seats would latch, securing them to the structure of the car.

A Volkswagen-Audi mix

Five petrol engines and three diesels were on offer for the 1997 Golf. It was more or less a full range and with the increased interchange of Audi A3 engines there was none of the delay which the Golf 3 had suffered. Multipoint fuel injection was now on all Golf petrol engines, and all versions had a five-speed gearbox at launch, with a four-speed automatic option later, then the first twin-clutch semi automatic.

A new 1.4 16-valve engine had been introduced in the 1994 Polo, now available as a five-door and almost exactly the length of the original Golf. This was a 75bhp all-aluminium unit (the first in a Golf), the valve gear was newly designed to minimise friction losses and there was a claimed 11% improvement in fuel consumption over the previous 75bhp 1.6.

The mainstay of sales was expected to be with the 100bhp 1.6-litre eight-valve unit carried over from the previous car. It was derived from the old group 1.6 engine but had been redesigned with an alloy cylinder block for use in the A3. This 1,595cc four-cylinder produced power equal to the old Golf 1.8 and featured variable intake manifold geometry, which changed the path of the air coming into the engine according to the engine load.

From launch in the British market you could have two types of GTI with 115 and 150bhp courtesy of two Audi 1.8-litre engines first used in the A4 and A3 with five-valve-per-cylinder technology. While enthusiasts were still impressed by a 16-valve engine (four valves per cylinder) Audi added a fifth. This meant that there were triple inlet and twin exhaust valves. All had to be proportionally smaller than before, demanding a new level of precision in manufacture, which Volkswagen found in Hungary.

The 115bhp 1.8 was unique to the British market with a GTI badge – in Germany it was offered in Highline trim. In the British market there was a logic in trying to replicate the old former two-tier GTI structure and both offered more horsepower than the outgoing models (125 over 115bhp and 150 over 130bhp) although there was an inevitable price rise to £15,515. However, the 'basic' GTI fell somewhat flat with the British motoring press, at the time quite enamoured of sports versions of the Peugeot 306 GTI. It was replaced by a 2.0-litre of the same power in 1999.

The popular direct-injection 1.9-litre diesels continued: non-turbo SDI of 68bhp (new for the UK), 90bhp TDI and the 110bhp TDI fitted to GT Golfs. This was also the engine's first showing in a UK Golf and *Autocar* magazine preferred it to the lower-powered petrol GTI, which it said was simply too softly sprung and not sporty or fast enough for the times. Of the GT TDI it said: 'VW has come up with a more effective GTI than the 20-valve petrol version. This is because it has more torque – a walloping 173lb ft at just 1,900rpm. So while the TDI doesn't really make the grade in the sprint to 60mph, its 9.7sec is still 0.3 better than the petrol Golf GTI. And it's a different story when it comes to in-gear punch and flexibility.' There was a new refinement, an electronically controlled shut-off in the inlet manifold, which cut the engine smoothly when turned off by key instead of the usual diesel jolt.

In the face of arguments that GTI was really becoming a trim level rather than a standalone car, the honour of the badge was left to the 150bhp 1.8 at first. After years of Volkswagen engineers keeping clear of them, there was finally a petrol-engined Golf with a turbocharger thanks to Audi. The five-valve-per-cylinder engine was judged by road testers to respond very well to turbocharging with a relatively small turbocharger, which gave no sensation of turbo lag and produced a wide spread of torque between 1,750 and 4,600rpm. The performance figures were respectable, with a claimed top speed of 139mph and 0–60mph in around eight seconds. But even though it was more tautly sprung than lesser Golfs, testers felt this was a rapid GTI but not a raucous one

with slightly remote-feeling steering isolating the driver from the action. It continued the trend that Volkswagen had identified with the last model. Customers wanted refinement above all, and as the GTI still came in five-door form (unlike many competitors) some chose it for practical reasons.

The 150bhp GTI was set apart from the British lower-powered version by 16in 'Montreal' alloy wheels and the 'I' part of the rear badge was red. Recaro seats, a glass sunroof and 'black wood' trim were also unique to this model.

Five and six

There was a second 150bhp engine in the range, this time an all-Volkswagen unit with a completely different character. Although the engine was now widely used across the Volkswagen group, the VR6 was initially absent from the fourth-generation Golf range, in its place an all-new 2.3-litre V5 engine, essentially a VR6 with one less cylinder.

Ferdinand Piëch had announced Volkswagen's intent to introduce a 2.1-litre V5 at the 1996 Vienna International Motor Symposium, where the company would customarily present future ideas. This was one that Piëch regarded as particularly important for extra sales and he had seen the proof as he developed the Audi five-cylinder.

'When we first developed the VR6 engine in the late '70s, we added a VR5,' Ernst Fiala – by now the retired head of research and development – told *Automotive News*. 'The 15-degree angle fits very well. You can build this type of small angle V-engine as a 3, 4, 5, 6 or 7 cylinder engine. You cannot go above that.' He added that Volkswagen had tried VR engines as diesels, but the small cylinder head became very crowded with valves, injectors and heating plugs. Two cylinders of the VR5 were tilted at the usual 15-degree angle in opposition to the other three.

The VR5 (the R designation was soon dropped) was intended to slot under the VR6, which was destined for

↑ At first the new V5 engine was the range-topper, here shrouded in covers. The two-stage inlet manifold was made of plastic. (LAT)

↑ **The VR6 became plain V6 and with standard four-wheel drive was a good tow car.**

further enlargement. Once the unique selling point of Audi, a five-cylinder engine was unusual but not unique in the Golf class. Fiat had introduced an inline five-cylinder in its Golf-class Bravo and Marea ranges from 1995.

The new all-aluminium engine – now 2,324cc – was launched somewhat prematurely in the Passat in early summer 1997 when it was reported that development had fallen behind because of the rush to get the car to market, and that it had been held back because of noise, vibration and harshness problems. It was pitched as an alternative to the 1.8 turbo engine, but Greg Kable, writing in *Autocar* found it 'suspiciously underdone', still exhibiting harshness at low speeds and being neither as flexible nor as economical..

When released into the Golf a year later, thankfully it seemed to have become a smooth and flexible engine, which when provoked gave a satisfying growl. It was pitched very much as a small luxury car and offered in Highline trim in Germany, badged plain V5 in England and could be had with a four-speed automatic with the Dynamic Shift Program (DSP) seen in the previous Golf, which was claimed to 'learn' your driving pattern and adjust the gear-change points accordingly. In late 1998 it was the top of the range Golf in the UK at £19,720 with very little on the options list.

Also launched in Europe in 1998, the Golf 4Motion V5 ushered in a replacement for the syncro four-wheel-drive system used by the previous two Golfs. The viscous coupling was replaced by a multi-plate clutch developed by Swedish company Haldex with engine software by Steyr-Daimler-Puch and branded 4Motion by Volkswagen. It was the beginning of a long association between Haldex and Volkswagen.

A part-time four-wheel-drive system as before, the Haldex unit was mounted at the rear of the car and once wheel slippage was detected oil pressure to a piston was increased, which engaged the clutches and started to transfer drive to the rear wheels (in normal driving 90% of power went through the fronts) until the torque was split equally between front and rear axles, but it could, as with syncro, send all the drive to the rear wheels in extreme conditions. The engine-management system worked in tandem with the anti-lock-brake and traction-control systems and could alter the engine speed. It could also lower the oil pressure to the clutch unit when parking or when the anti-lock brakes were being used and was claimed to be extremely quick in reacting. A driven rear axle demanded a new rear suspension and this had been developed alongside the regular car. The V5 4Motion was the first Golf to feature a multi-link rear suspension and the torsion beam across the rear of this Golf had gone, but it retained the separate spring and strut arrangement while the driveshafts were suspended on transverse links with a lateral radius arm attached to a subframe. The design didn't eat into boot space as the syncro system did and there was space for a fuel tank enlarged from 55 to 62 litres, which was just as well with an official combined fuel consumption of 26.1mpg. It had the novelty of a six-speed gearbox, starting to feature on high-performance cars on the basis that an extra set of ratios was the best way to exploit the different power bands of an engine and also as an extra ratio for fuel economy.

'In reality this Golf is vastly more capable than the two-wheel drive model,' said *Autocar* in July 1998. 'It still understeers in the wet, though notably less so than the Syncro. It's so immensely controllable it can be flung around as the driver desires. In the dry, however the chassis displays even more agility.'

Four-wheel-drive Golfs were still a marginal choice for UK buyers so the V5 4Motion was not exported. However, after the usual time delay this market did get an uprated version of the VR6 engine – now badged V6 – which was introduced in Germany in 1999. Now in production for eight years, a new cylinder head featured four valves per cylinder: 'When we started to deliberate whether to go for the four-valve version we really have to start employing watchmakers because it's such a fine and tricky task from the two- to the four-valve version,' a Volkswagen man told the author on a visit to Wolfsburg in 2012.

Power had increased from 190 to 204bhp and it was only offered allied to the 4Motion transmission with a six-speed gearbox. But even though these 4Motions were 130–140mph cars they were discreet rather than sporty. Elsewhere in the car world the four-wheel drive 200bhp-plus Subaru Impreza Turbo had come from nowhere to be a rally champion and cult performance car. In a few years the Golf V6 would be recast and the sporting four-wheel-drive Golf of the 1980s was to enjoy a revival. The V5 would also get a multi-valve cylinder head for the 2000 model year, releasing an extra 20bhp to bring its output up to 170bhp.

While it was only offered with a V6 engine for British buyers, German customers could pair 4Motion with the 1.8-litre petrol and 1.9 diesel engines as well. Even if these were not going to sell in great numbers the 4Motion system now had a wider application as part of the platform strategy than syncro. For the brand image it was essential that every model in the Audi range had a four-wheel-drive system, and that included the A3 and the TT even though they were the only models with a transverse engine. The Golf 4Motion beat the TT to the showrooms by only a few months. 4Motion was then rolled out to SEAT and Škoda.

Serious competition

Apart from lost earnings, Volkswagen might have wished the fourth Golf hadn't lost time coming to the showrooms when in 1998 Ford astonished the critics by replacing the dull Escort with the radical Focus.

With what Ford called 'New Edge' design, its high-mounted rear tail lights and swooping lines made it look like nothing else on the market. Massive investment

↓ Mainstream Golfs now benefitted from a 16-valve petrol engine.

had been made in customer research and it boasted many new features such as an electric boot release on the dashboard, a bonnet that could be locked by a key from the outside and radios designed in harmony with the dashboard. It had safety features equal if not better than the Golf and the way it handled completely enthralled the motoring press.

The Golf 4 had been tuned to give a fairly soft and comfortable ride. The Focus also had comfort but great precision in handling for the enthusiastic driver. One of the major investments Ford had made was in a multi-link fully independent rear suspension, not the industry norm – started by the 1974 Golf – of a relatively simple torsion beam linking both wheels to each other. More complex, and hence costly, multi-link rear suspension is considered to give the best combination of handling, comfort and space efficiency. What could be described as a multi-link design featured on the Golf 4Motion, but its production expense was only acceptable for a small-volume range-topper.

In addition, the Focus petrol engines were all 16-valve units and matched the Golf for power. No matter which

early 2000 and *Auto Motor und Sport* immediately put it up against a Focus. Section by section the Golf started to lose ground. Its equipment was described as meagre when compared to the Focus Trend, but it did gain by the fitment of Electronic Stability Control (ESP) with the new engine. 'Once again the Wolfsburg market leader has to be beaten by the Focus. The new 16-valve engine brings only a slight advance, a slight lowering of fuel consumption. ESP is indeed a safety factor but not one which raises its roadholding (chassis quality) over the Focus.'

Of all the elements of the new Focus it was Ford's rear suspension design that really made an impact in Wolfsburg and on the next Golf, changing its development plans. Key personnel from Ford appeared at Volkswagen, such as Dr Ulrich Eichhorn in 1993 who had worked on Ford chassis dynamics, and Karsten Schebsdat.

Cabriolet, estate and the PD diesels

A 'new' Golf cabriolet appeared in 1998 and this was a skilful re-working of the respected Golf 3 cabriolet introduced only five years previously. A fourth-generation Golf grille and smoothed front and rear bumpers contributed to a contemporary look with the number plate on the boot lid lowered to bumper level to accommodate a VW symbol as with the hatchback. Inside there was new seat trim, blue instrument panel lighting and Isofix child seat mountings. It remained in production until 2002 and was not to be directly replaced until the sixth Golf.

A new Golf estate followed in 1999, now a fully established part of the range. The hatchback's new design of rear suspension improved access and the load volume, at 1,470 litres with the seats down, was up by 45 litres. As it was supplemented by a Bora/Vento kombi the engine choice was restricted, with no V6 or top diesel versions. It was produced in Brussels, Wolfsburg and Mosel before transferring to Karmann in 2003 where it outlasted the hatchback for a further three years.

Another combination of initials was added to the Volkswagen lexicon in 1999 with the introduction of the 'PD' TDI diesels. This stood for *Pumpe Düse*, which translated as 'unit injector' and was of Volkswagen's own design. It was a new injection system that operated at far higher pressures than the rotary pump diesels used lower down the Volkswagen range and by other

← All was well for the Golf until it was deposed by the all-new Ford Focus (front right). This road test group of 1998 includes the Mazda 323 (front left) and Vauxhall Astra behind the Focus. (LAT)

engine it had, every Focus was deemed as sharp to drive as the other and the interior quality close to the Golf's. 'VW raises the bar with the Golf IV in terms of showroom desirability,' said *Autocar*. 'The Focus takes it a step further. Any potential customer, unsure of the styling, who drives or rides in a Focus will surely be won over.'

Golfs started to come second in road tests. The German press (and the Focus was a German-built Ford) was equally enamoured. A new 105bhp all-alloy 1.6-litre 16-valve engine for the Golf became available in

➔ Not a new Golf 4 cabriolet but a skilful blending of the Golf 4's front and rear styling onto the previous generation car.

← The new estate offered more space and easier access. The US and German markets got a Jetta Sportwagon/Bora Variant by grafting the frontal styling of the Bora/Jetta saloon onto it.

manufacturers. In PD engines the injector and pump were combined into one unit for each cylinder, where the system in the regular TDI engines had the fuel pressurised by a distributor injector pump and fed to individual injectors. Volkswagen claimed the higher injection pressures brought a better fuel and air mixture, resulting in higher torque but little or no change in fuel consumption. Introduced across the Volkswagen range, the first PD engines boosted the power of the 1.9-litre 110bhp TDI engines to 115bhp.

As with the other diesels, this was coupled to a catalytic converter and was claimed to out-perform the European diesel emissions standard due to come into force in 2000. Gradually rolled out in other engine capacities, the PD diesel found its way into Audi and other Volkswagen group cars. Golf diesels became ever more powerful. Between 2000 and the end of production the Golf GT TDIs could be had in 130 and then 150bhp versions, both with six-speed gearboxes. The latter started a petrol v diesel performance debate in 2002 with a claimed 0–60 in 7.6 seconds and a top speed of 134mph yet 54mpg on the combined cycle.

The first Golf R

At the Essen Motor Show in November 2001 enthusiasts finally got the Golf they wanted – the most powerful production Golf to that date. The Volkswagen Motorsport stand exhibited what it termed a concept car, an aggressively-styled three-door Golf with a deeper front bumper dominated by extra air intakes, a rear bumper with twin exhausts and 18in alloy wheels.

It was Volkswagen's response to cars such as the Subaru Impreza Turbo WRX, the Mitsubishi Evo and the 212bhp Ford Focus RS launched in 2001, one year later than planned, a turbocharged road racer which put all its power through the front wheels via a specially developed limited-slip differential.

The same year Volkswagen Motorsport had been renamed Volkswagen Racing, to concentrate all its efforts on developing a circuit racing championship, the Volkswagen Racing Cup. In a similar way to Renault and Ford's sporting divisions it set itself up to produce small volumes of very high performance versions of its road cars. For Volkswagen this was initially set to be called the RSI line (like the racing Beetle RSI) but it opted for

↑ By 2002 diesel Golfs were serious GTI alternatives, with power outputs up to 150PS (this is a 130). The (breathe in) Golf GT TDI PD 150 was the most powerful diesel hatch in this market, with *Pumpe Düse* or 'unit injector' technology.

↑ **A specially designed exhaust system with twin chrome tailpipes marked the 2002 R32 as well as new front and rear bumpers and side sills.**

the letter R plus the engine capacity as AMG used with Mercedes. It was the equivalent of the 'M' badging used by BMW and in future years applied to other Volkswagens and go-faster accessories.

The Golf R32 was officially launched at the Madrid Motor Show in May 2002 as a flagship model sitting above the GTI range. A new level of performance was provided by a 3,189cc version of the narrow-angle V6 without the aid of a turbocharger. A bigger cylinder bore and longer stroke took maximum power up to 237bhp at 6,250rpm with continuously variable exhaust and valve timing. This was not, however, a specially race-tuned engine but an existing unit also used by the luxury Phaeton and the large Touareg off-roader. The exhaust system though was specially tuned to enhance the engine's sound.

The R32 had a claimed 0–60mph time of 6.5 seconds and a top speed of 153mph and used 4Motion four-wheel drive with suspension lowered by a further 10mm compared with a standard Golf V6, more responsive steering (from the Audi TT) and throttle responses, plus ESP. The interior featured aluminium trim, Konig sports seats with integrated backrests and extensive use of the 'R' logo. Befitting a Golf that cost some £22,000 when it went on sale in the UK in late 2002, climate control, xenon headlamps and rain-sensing wipers were also standard.

↑ Leather sports seats, still with side airbags, featured the new sports 'R' brand.

This Golf was certainly into the premium price territory. Road testers mused that this might be the car to bring back some of the lost 'honour' of the GTI. In October 2002 *Autocar* was impressed again by the composure brought about by the 4Motion multi-link rear suspension even though there were stiffer anti-roll bars and springing. '…get further into that sharp throttle on a good road and it really works – so well in fact, that we're left wondering why we've had to wait until the Mk4 is almost obsolete before getting one that handles properly.'

While the standard gearbox for the first-generation Golf R32 was a six-speed manual, from 2003 German buyers could specify a new type of automatic gearbox, also shared with the Audi TT. The Direct Shift Gearbox (DSG) was a new type of fully automatic gearbox, sometimes described as two gearboxes in one. It divided the odd and even number of gears (in this instance six) into two separate shafts each with their own clutch. As Volkswagen describes it, when you turn the engine on and select Drive mode, one shaft selects first gear while the second shaft puts the next gear on 'standby'. As the gearbox changes to second, the second shaft is engaged and the original shaft reaches third. As you shift upwards and then downwards the sequence continues. The next gear is always 'ready'.

Bora

In January 1997 what appeared to be a Golf coupe appeared at the Detroit Motor Show, the 'Volkswagen CJ Coupe'. It was said to represent both the front end of the new Vento for '98 and also a new Golf coupe.

In reality the coupe never appeared, but the Golf-based Bora saloon (still Jetta for the US market) was pretty much the same car with four doors. The Bora was another exotic wind name, no longer used by Maserati.

Although the British motoring press was determined to see the Bora as a dressed-up Golf it did finally break with 'Golf with a boot' styling with its own rear doors and the distinctive curved roofline taken from the new Beetle to the Passat, emphasising that the Bora was a smaller version of the latter.

In 1999 a Bora estate was introduced in the German market in addition to the Golf estate, visually differing only in the front-end styling. Only available with the larger engines, it was targeted more at the 'lifestyle' customer but drew criticism that this was stretching the brand too far. 'Thanks to the platform strategy it does not cost us anything at all,' Piëch said at the time. It made rather more sense as the first Jetta estate for the US market in 2001.

↑ The Volkswagen CJ concept that appeared at the 1997 Detroit Motor Show gave rise to speculation that it was the basis of a new Golf coupe to take up from the Corrado, but it was just the front end of the new Jetta/Bora, ahead of sale.

↓ The production Bora (Jetta in the US) was a more standalone design than previous Golfs-with-a-boot thanks to a distinct roofline and rear doors.

← Although the R32 was not a big-selling Golf its DSG automatic gearbox design would spread across the range over the next decade. You could shift up and down between the plus and minus symbols.

The gear changes in a DSG 'box were meant to be far quicker than a traditional automatic, with none of the power loss or increased fuel consumption (it was claimed the entire shift process was completed in less the four-hundredths of a second). You could drive them in fully automatic mode or by tapping the gear lever forwards and back. DSG went on to become widely applied across Volkswagen cars, latterly with seven speeds. Similar kinds of gearboxes were adopted by other manufacturers.

Originally due to be a limited series of 5,000 (2,300 were eventually sold in the UK), such was the European reception given to the Golf R32 that it was exported to America in 2004 after the regular Golf had been superseded by the fifth generation. It planned to sell 5,000 as a counter to the Impreza and the Mitsubishi to attract attention to the brand ahead of the next generation of Golf and did just that at 4,935 in one year only.

Less headline grabbing, 2002 saw a further development in Volkswagen petrol engines with the introduction of what Volkswagen/Audi termed Fuel Stratified Injection (FSI). This was the principle of direct injection for diesel engines applied to a petrol engine. FSI used a high-pressure injection system to inject fuel straight into the cylinder head, its fine atomisation giving cleaner burning and better fuel efficiency as the compression ratio was much higher.

Mitsubishi had been first to introduce this principle into its petrol cars in 1996 and Audi introduced FSI into its ranges first. Volkswagen started with a 1.4-litre Polo FSI and in 2002 as the fourth Golf was nearing the end of its run it gained its third type of 1.6-litre engine, an FSI (although not for the UK) with power increased from 105 to 115bhp yet a claimed improved combined consumption from 41 to 46mpg. Still a 16-valve engine, it reverted to a cast-iron rather than aluminium block for the higher pressures. FSI was to become widespread on VW group engines in the next decade.

What then of the GTI, overshadowed by the R32? Volkswagen determined that 2002 marked the 25th anniversary, working on 1977 being the first model year it was on sale, and produced a special edition. This time it was more than a matter of cosmetics as it became

↑ **With 180bhp the 2001 model-year GTI Anniversary (25 years) was the fastest GTI to that point, limited to a run of 3,000.**

↓ **The GTI Anniversary featured Recaro 'Le Mans' sports seats and a golf-ball gear lever once more.**

the fastest Golf with a GTI badge available with either a 1.8-litre turbocharged 180bhp petrol engine used elsewhere in the Volkswagen group or the 150bhp TDI PD diesel engine. Both were coupled to a six-speed gearbox with the first five closely spaced and the sixth a higher cruising ratio. The GTI Anniversary was distinguished by 18in BBS alloy wheels and Recaro seats inside with red piping plus various red interior trim items and race-inspired aluminium pedals.

In April 2002, when Bernd Pischetsrieder took office as chairman of Volkswagen AG European sales had reached 2.8m the year before. Over its six-year run, the fourth Golf contributed 4.3m sales and started a new strategy of platform sharing, but it was not unassailable. A small Golf-sized MPV had not appeared to counter the success of the 1996 Renault Scenic, nor a sports utility vehicle, and the project to build the former was behind schedule. As *The Times* newspaper reported in early February 2003, 2002 was not a perfect year for Volkswagen or the Golf in relative terms. The Peugeot 206 knocked it off the top European seller slot and a fall in the popularity of the Golf was said to have helped trigger a profits fall of nearly 10%. The next Golf had as hard a task as ever keeping on top of the pile.

← In April 2002 Volkswagen claimed it had made motor-sport history with the first-ever British track appearance by a diesel-powered racing car. The TDI Racer was modified to produce 165bhp.

↓ Golf catches up with the Beetle in half the time. The 21,517,415th Golf rolled off the line in Wolfsburg on 25 June 2002. It was a V5 for a customer in Hamburg.

↑ Some old Golfs never die. This 2007 Brazilian Golf is a local restyling of the Golf 4 with new front and rear light clusters from the Golf 5. It was also imported into Canada for a time as a base model. The Chinese market had its own version taking the Bora name. Volkswagen squeezed extraordinary value out of the Golf 4's platform with Chinese-market new Bora and Lavida saloons in 2008.

WOB GO 505
D
Volkswagen Classic

Golf 5
2003–2008

Highly developed

By 2003 and the launch of the fifth Golf, its market had changed for good. 'When we launched the Golf in 1974, it had just 10 rival models,' chairman Bernd Pischetsrieder remarked. 'Today there are 130.'

Thanks to the 1996 Renault Scenic every manufacturer in the lower-medium (Golf) class had to supply a mini multi-purpose vehicle (MPV). This was essentially a tall hatchback, the same length as the regular car it was based on but with raised seating, multiple storage compartments and rear seats that folded, slid back and forwards, or in some cases came out altogether. The large MPV once popularised by the Renault Espace was now of lesser importance and taken care of by the Volkswagen Sharan, developed in partnership with Ford.

The first Scenic was a massive hit, selling as much as the Mégane hatchback on which it was based plus its other variants put together. The market it created sent every manufacturer back to the drawing board for their own versions. Volkswagen had been expected to produce its Golf MPV based on the fourth generation in 2000 but Opel beat it to the market with the Zafira in 1999. This boxy Astra-based vehicle surprised everybody

by being a seven-seater with two extra seats that folded into the boot floor. This stalled the Volkswagen MPV project and the initial response was the 2002 Touran, more van than Golf-like ('Touran' from 'Tour' and 'Sharan'; the ending '-an' used to indicate Volkswagen's multi-purpose vehicles). Styled in-house, the Touran did indeed have a major connection to the van world as much of it formed the basis of the 2004 Caddy. However, it could be had in five- or seven-seat versions and boasted 500 choices of what to do with them. In some regions, such as Japan, the car was called the Golf Touran, but a further more Golf-sized vehicle was still to come.

← **The 2002 Touran was Volkswagen's first attack at the booming mid-size MPV market, aimed at the larger family.**

The Touran did, however, ride on the new Golf platform, internally known as PQ35. This was a further development of the platform strategy and had fewer 'hard points', or fixed dimensions, which governed the body shapes that could be put over it. The wheelbase and the track could now be varied so cars in the class above and below could share more components. Thus the 2004 Volkswagen Passat reverted to a transverse engine because it sat on a stretched version of the PQ35 platform (PQ36), although Volkswagen preferred to speak of 'modules' because common floor stampings were less of a cost saving compared to individual components. They were also largely invisible to buyers or motoring journalists who loved to point out which switches on an Audi wound up on a Škoda.

Group cars were able to make increasing use of shared engines and transmissions, door-lock mechanisms, brakes and axles. The plans for new models grew even greater. As well as PQ35-derived Audis, SEATs and Škodas, boss Bernd Pischetsrieder told *Autocar* in 2003 that Volkswagen was lacking the variety of its competitors, and needed a smaller MPV than the Touran, a sports utility vehicle (SUV) to complement the big Touareg, another convertible to go with the Audi A4 and possibly a Golf-based roadster. 'All this must be done by 2006, and even this is not quick enough. But when it is done, we will be exhausted.'

Hidden investments

So the first PQ35 product was the Touran, the second the Audi A3. Both previewed the two most important engineering changes for the new Golf: multi-link rear suspension and electro-mechanical power steering, as well as new FSI petrol engines. The A3 gained the Volkswagen narrow-angle V6 engine for the first time.

The simple but highly effective torsion-beam rear suspension, which Volkswagen's chief engineer had once called 'ridiculously cheap' and had been copied in one form or another by all the Golf's rivals, was now not good enough, thanks to the Ford Focus.

As detailed in the previous chapter, with its multi-link rear suspension the 1998 Focus had rewritten the rule book on the level of engineering sophistication buyers could expect from a family hatchback. Road testers, who of course were naturally keen drivers and pushed a car to its limits, were besotted by most aspects of the Focus but especially its ride and sharp responses. The Golf

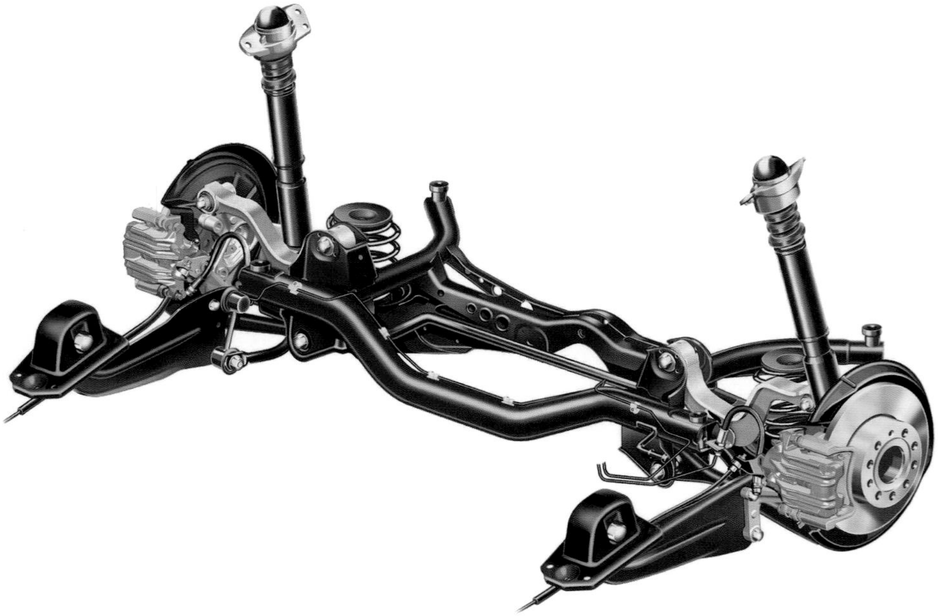

↑ **Compare the complexity of the Golf 5's multi-link rear suspension with the previous version on page 174. Given that a Golf never changed radically this was a minor revolution.**

had always been regarded as a good car for enthusiastic driving but now the Focus seemed a lot better. Worst of all it was cheaper than a Golf. So, as the fifth Golf was in its early development stages, a considerable investment was made for a multi-link rear suspension, and quickly. It was a matter of prestige, although the 2003 Opel Astra stuck with a torsion beam.

Considered to be best for both comfort and handling, multi-link is a more complex arrangement where the rear wheels can move fully independently of each other as they are carried by their own units, similar to the wishbone design of some front suspensions, and can be tuned to give a certain amount of rear-wheel steering. Each wheel unit was in turn suspended on forward-facing trailing arms. Like other designs, the Volkswagen rear suspension unit was mounted on a subframe across the car, which carried the spring for each wheel and a separate strut.

'We had a great head of production at that time, Dr [Folker] Weissgerber,' long-time Golf engineer Rolf Trump told the author in 2012. 'Of course you always want to have the best of everything which is sometimes difficult and difficult for the customer to pay for. We negotiated with Dr Weissgerber and told him if we only chose the expensive multi-link axle production could be realised in quite a cost effective manner. So we got one great axle.'

Of course the cost was mitigated by spreading the suspension around the Volkswagen group brands, but one of the trade-offs in the Golf was reported as a downgrading of lower plastic parts of the interior to hard-feeling material rather than the softer 'slush moulded' upper dashboard. Testers noted too that instead of being hidden, the runners for the front seats were now visible when far forward or back. Ironically, later as the sixth generation was readied for 2008 introduction Volkswagen would concede that it had found the Golf 5 far too expensive to build for its liking.

The second major mechanical change on the new Golf was electro-mechanical power steering. Instead of a pump with hydraulic fluid driven by a belt from the engine, the power steering was driven by an electric motor. Only in use when the vehicle was being steered, it varied the level of power assistance according to speed, thus maximum when parking, minimum when cruising. It also better absorbed kickback and had a stabilising effect in crosswinds. Perhaps most importantly though, because the pump ran only when needed there was also a saving on the official fuel-consumption figures, reckoned to be about 1.2mpg on average over an engine-driven pump system. Electrically-assisted steering was set to become widespread across the industry.

Styling continuity

If there had been significant mechanical changes, for styling the fifth Golf carefully picked up and enlarged features of the fourth and drew on some details of current Volkswagens such as light unit styling from the Touareg and Phaeton. Compared with the previous model the slope of the bonnet was more pronounced as was the v-shape that ran forwards to the headlights. The waistline along the tops of the door also rose towards the rear of the five-door to give it a slightly more wedged-shaped profile.

The rapid downward movement of luxury features in the Volkswagen range continued with additional turn indicators built into the lower part of the electrically-adjusted wing mirrors, more visible for pedestrians and the tips were visible from the driver's seat, a useful reminder on motorways. Practical observers noted that these were going to be expensive to replace if they were hit.

Some styling elements such as the large headlamp units and the circles within the tail-light units drew

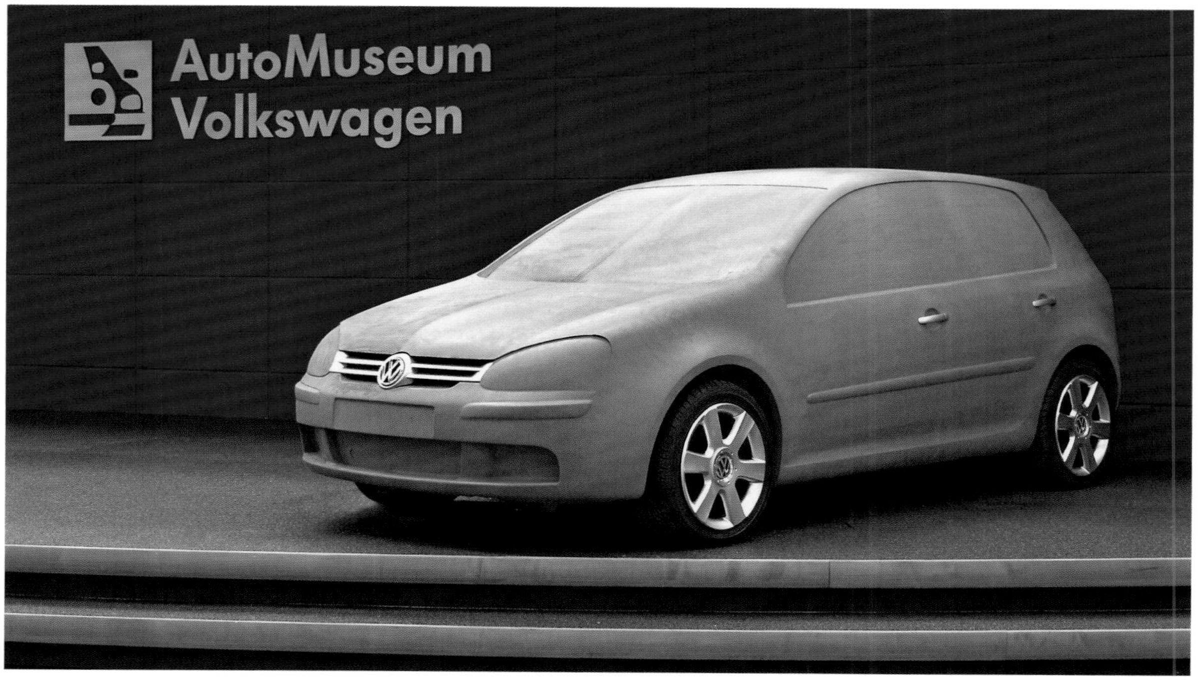

↑ The smooth look was aided by windscreen wipers that parked themselves out of sight behind the rear edge of the bonnet when the ignition was switched off.

← The design of the Golf 5 was set by the time of this 1999 clay model. Hatchbacks were growing taller, and the new best-seller followed the trend. (Stiftung AutoMuseum)

↑ **The rear side window styling on the three-door kicked up to convey a more 'sporty' look.**

comparison with other cars such as the Peugeot 307, but maybe the 307 was trying to look like the Golf? You could also look to contemporary rivals with a Golf-like solid 'C' pillar like the new Opel Astra and Toyota Corolla. As ever, if you wanted a Golf then you bought a Golf, if you wanted fashion, there was the curved-roof Citroen C4 and the Renault Mégane with its love-it-or-loathe-it protruding tailgate.

The boxier European Honda Civic approached MPV levels of interior space, with a flat floor and short dash-mounted gear lever, and in the Golf's search for the desired passenger space, mainly for those in the rear, it too grew once more. At 4,204mm it was 57mm longer than the Golf 4 and 24mm wider at 1,759mm (without wing mirrors). It was 1,483mm high (up 39mm), and the wheelbase had grown by 67mm to 2,578mm for 52mm extra rear legroom. On the other hand the boot volume was slightly smaller with seats up. There was criticism that when the rear seat backs were folded they sat higher than the level of the boot floor behind them but a flatter load bay was reserved for the Golf Plus, which followed shortly afterwards.

As an aside, the effect of nearly 30 years from the first Golf and four subsequent generations had seen the model grow, but even if every road test gave the impression the latest car was becoming an ocean liner, the size difference wasn't that extreme. The biggest increase had been length, with the 2003 Golf almost exactly half a metre longer than the 1974 car, then about 15cm wider and just over 7cm taller. People were getting bigger and so were all classes of cars to accommodate them and their belongings in high safety. The new bodyshell design was boasted to have improved static torsional rigidity by 80%, having laser-welded seams over a total length of 70 metres compared with five metres in its predecessor, yet weighed only 11kg more. Adding extra equipment as well, a petrol-engined Golf 1.6 five-door weighed in at 1,220kg compared to 1,200kg for the previous car and 1,195kg for the now six-year old Ford Focus.

FSI and TDI engines

After their debut in the Polo, Audi A3 and late-model Golf 4, the Volkswagen Group Fuel Stratified Injection (FSI) petrol engines were rolled out across the brands alongside further-developed TDI direct-injection diesel units.

By the time of the Golf 5 the German method of expressing engine power in PS – short for Pferdestärke for metric horsepower – was becoming increasingly used in the British market over BHP. PS is not quite the same as BHP for brake horsepower, being between one and two units higher, but English-language publications often transposed the two. Although British-market engine choices were badged in PS terms, British magazines started to make the downwards conversion to BHP because that's what people still understood and they were still dealing in miles per gallon rather than litres per 100km. Just to add further confusion European manufacturers also used the newer kilowatt rating (KW) for engines but most people still associated it with electrical power; so a 55KW Golf was also a 75PS Golf or a 74bhp Golf...

The new entry-level Golfs had the carry-over 1.4-litre 75PS (later 80) petrol engine, which, as usual, most testers deemed to be too slow, but January 2004 saw a new 90PS 1.4 FSI engine added. Also continued from the previous generation, a 102PS (100bhp) 1.6-litre was offered in some markets, but from 2004 a 115PS FSI unit appeared – the same power of the basic British Golf GTI 1.8 a decade previously. It differed from the 1.4 by offering variable valve timing. This changed the behaviour of the inlet valves (when they opened and for how long) depending on engine load and speed, helping emissions and improving the development of torque.

Top of the Golf FSI engines was a 1,984cc unit already seen in the Audi A3 and A4. It too offered what once had been top-range turbocharged GTI performance of 150PS (148bhp) achieved at 6,000rpm. The next GTI had not yet emerged but was known to be set for over 200PS. But while power was up so too was promised fuel economy. Official combined fuel economy for the old 1.6 was 37.2mpg but for the more powerful FSI it was 44.1. Whilst still not as economical as a diesel, the FSI engine narrowed the gap. All Golfs over 100PS now had a six-speed gearbox, which also improved economy and made high-speed cruising more relaxing by lowering the engine speed.

Because of the greater combustion pressures at work, road testers often found the FSI engines to sound slightly coarser under load, but *Autocar* found the 2.0-litre better than the 1.6 in that respect with a maximum speed of 131mph and a 0–60 time of 8.6 seconds; again once very respectable GTI territory but with a test touring average of 38.1mpg.

FSI engines could run on 95-octane petrol but were designed to run best on cleaner sulphur-free fuel, which was not widely available in the UK in 2003. Owners found – and VW recommended for the 2.0 – that for best overall performance 98-octane super-unleaded should be used. Whether or not the engines lasted longer on this more expensive petrol was a frequent subject of debate on internet forums.

All the Golf engines were designed to comply with the 2006 Euro 4 emissions standard and much to the dismay of car manufacturers those standards were getting rapidly tougher. As well as the accepted harmful gases, European vehicle legislation from the mid-2000s focused on progressively stricter carbon dioxide (CO_2) emissions in addition to harmful substances, CO_2 having been identified as a component in global warming.

In the UK, for cars made after March 2001 vehicle road tax became related to the amount of CO_2 an engine produced in grams per kilometre (g/km) rather than engine size. At the time of the Golf 5, a headline figure for any manufacturer of popular cars was something around 120g/km, and the Polo 1.4 diesels were the best Volkswagen performers at 124. The best performing Golf engine at launch was the 1.9 TDI at 143g/km.

Diesel was booming in the European market in 2003, taking 43.7% of all sales and the Volkswagen group was a dominant engine producer and innovator – it had even introduced a 313PS V10 diesel in the Phaeton and Touareg. By 2007 Golfs could be bought in five different outputs of diesel engine, only two less than the petrols.

The Golf 5 saw a new 2.0-litre (1,968cc) TDI with a 16-valve cylinder head offering 140PS and meeting Euro 4 emissions standards. Whilst it was 10PS down on power from the Golf 4 GT TDI, it was praised for its refinement over the eight-valve 1.9, a broad spread of power from 1,750 to its 4,000rpm limit, and claimed combined fuel economy of 52.3mpg. It later became available in 170bhp guise. The diesels were all now *Pumpe Düse* 'unit injector' engines.

From 2004 some diesels could be fitted with a

particulate filter, increasingly fitted to diesel cars' exhaust systems from 2000 onwards to trap and periodically burn off the very small soot particles not caught by the catalytic converter. In early 2004 a 75PS 2.0-litre SDI version without a turbocharger was added as an entry-level diesel. During Golf 5 production the 1.9TDI units were available in 90 or 105PS versions.

Throughout the Golf 5's career a conventional six-speed torque-converter automatic gearbox was an option with the 1.6 petrol engines and the non-turbo 2.0 FSI but from 2004 diesels could be ordered (for 1,325 Euros) with Volkswagen's six-speed dual-clutch Direct Shift Gearbox (DSG), which then became available on the new GTI and the TSI petrol engines from 2006. The revolutionary DSG had two wet clutches, one clutch controlling the 'odd' gears plus reverse, the other operating the 'even' gears, meaning the next gear up or down was always ready.

A tough start

Entering a tough European market and having lost the engineering advantage to the Ford Focus, Volkswagen gave the Golf 5 a long run to its autumn 2003 debut at the Frankfurt Motor Show. Publicity started with the 'Big Golf Show' at the Wolfsburg Arena in June, the same month when Golf production overtook the original Beetle at 21,517,415 units. In August, anticipating high demand, production was started simultaneously at the Wolfsburg, Brussels and Zwickau plants. From 25 August until the press launch on 9 September the mayor of Wolfsburg allowed his town to be renamed 'Golfsburg'.

Thanks to its new suspension and steering the press view was, on the whole, that the Golf was now back on the top rung, but the competition was fierce. The Focus was on its way towards replacement and while Japanese Golf rivals such as the Toyota Corolla

↓ There was a debate that some cabin plastics were downgraded but the blue-lit dials remained. This late-model UK Match is highly specified with audio and telephone buttons on the wheel.

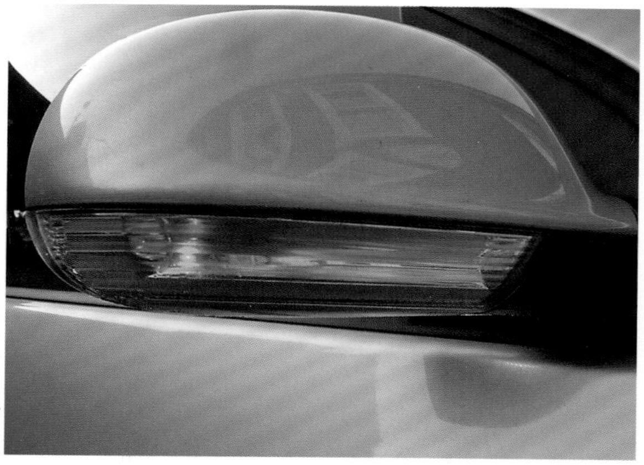

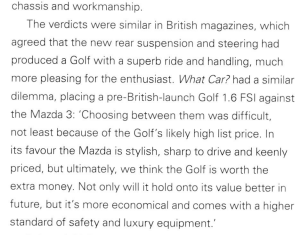

had never swayed the critics very much, the Mazda 3 was a more interesting proposition. Designed and styled to appeal to European tastes it was based on the floorpan and suspension of the Ford Focus as at the time Ford owned a majority share in the company. Good to look at, fun for enthusiastic drivers and well built, the 2004 Car of the Year judges had been impressed enough to rank the Mazda 3 joint second with the new Golf.

Testing a 1.6 FSI Comfortline alongside a Peugeot 306, Renault Mégane and Mazda 3 in 2003, *Auto Motor und Sport* approached the Golf almost wearily, listing the reasons why buyers might look elsewhere after the Golf 4, which had not proven reliable in the magazine's reader satisfaction survey, coupled to the new model's conservatism and high price. Japanese manufacturers were top for reliability and Renault was routinely producing cars with five-star Euro NCAP scores – what was unique about the Golf?

Even though the rival cars were loaded with far more equipment, the Golf still pleased with its details; the fully lined luggage compartment, the fine adjustment of the seating, the way the car was styled so the windscreen wipers weren't in the driver's vision when not in use. It came first for the quality of its new chassis and workmanship.

The verdicts were similar in British magazines, which agreed that the new rear suspension and steering had produced a Golf with a superb ride and handling, much more pleasing for the enthusiast. *What Car?* had a similar dilemma, placing a pre-British-launch Golf 1.6 FSI against the Mazda 3: 'Choosing between them was difficult, not least because of the Golf's likely high list price. In its favour the Mazda is stylish, sharp to drive and keenly priced, but ultimately, we think the Golf is worth the extra money. Not only will it hold onto its value better in future, but it's more economical and comes with a higher standard of safety and luxury equipment.'

At launch Volkswagen had forecast 600,000 sales a year of the new Golf with an additional 180,000 Tourans but it was a hard first year on sale. Buyers' expectations of what a basic Golf-class car should include continued to grow, with Trend being the entry level Golf in most European markets and badged 'S' in the UK. A five-star Euro NCAP rating (scoring the highest 12-point rating

↑ Even more pleasing details: (left to right) wing mirrors that indicated and lit up the path, a bottle opener to divide the front cup holders and the VW badge on the tailgate was now the handle to open it, unlocked only by a button on the key fob. (Author)

↑ **The new suspension seemed to pay off with a ride described as 'exemplary'. (LAT)**

in 2004) was supported by a combination of electronic systems that intervened if the car appeared to be out of control, described by a raft of acronyms. Anti-lock brakes (ABS) were standard, as was an Electronic Stabilisation Programme (ESP). This sensed any tendency for the car to slide and could apply the brakes from one to four wheels. The car's systems could also sense if it was being emergency braked and increase pedal pressure while activating the ABS. If a crash happened, all Golfs had front airbags, side airbags for front and rear passengers and anti-whiplash head restraints. An engine immobiliser, remote central locking, front electric windows, a CD player, height and reach adjustable steering column and driver's seat height adjustment also featured as standard.

Although the 2003 Golf was judged to have built on its 'premium' feel, Volkswagen's ability to sustain a premium price came under pressure. As reported in *The Times*, German Golf registrations were down 45% in December 2003 while VW's European sales in January 2004 were 11% down on the previous year. In February Volkswagen said it would have to close three of its German factories for four extra days over Easter to reduce numbers. Despite the presence of internet brokers it refused to discount Golfs but responded by increasing equipment, adding Climatic semi-automatic air conditioning (which maintained three set temperatures) to the basic 1.4, worth 1,225 Euros.

On sale in the UK from early 2004, there was some adjustment in April 2005 when prices were reduced and equipment added. The British Golf S gained Climatic air conditioning, SE five-door models added rear electric windows and a convenience pack of automatic headlights and dimming rear-view mirror with rain-sensing windscreen wipers and front footwell illumination. Cruise control was an option and added to the later 'Match' specification. Higher grade models had Climatronic automatic air conditioning, which could maintain individual temperatures for driver and passenger.

Golf Plus

As the hatchback settled into its marketplace, the belated Golf-shaped answer to the rise and rise of the medium MPV – especially the new Ford-Focus-based C-Max – was introduced at the Bologna Motor Show in December 2004. Volkswagen described it as a 'reinvention of the traditional hatchback'.

As the name implied, the Plus was more Golf, but it didn't share any common body panels and had its own dashboard design. Apart from the wheelbase and the width all the other dimensions had changed, primarily height. The Plus was 95mm taller than a Golf for an extra 20mm of headroom. The seating position was raised and the rear bench, split 60/40, could be moved forwards independently to extend the load space or fold flat but not removed. There were flip-up tables on the back of the front seats, cup holders recessed into the back of the armrest/ski hatch, a storage bin between the front seats and drawers under them. A roof console was available as an extra. In total 34 places in which to lose things.

↑ Almost 10cm taller, the Golf Plus appeared a regular Golf pulled up by its roof. The only common top body parts were the door mirrors, door handles and the badges.

↓ By virtue of a floor that could be dropped or raised, the Golf Plus boot could be configured to form a flat load bay with seats folded.

Most models had a variable boot floor, which allowed a storage compartment below it (above the spare wheel) or could be lowered to add an extra 120 litres to the 395 litres of luggage space with the rear seats in place. A lever folded the seats flat to the floor for a full 1,450-litre maximum capacity.

To drive, the Plus was much the same as a Golf hatchback with suspension reworked to take account of the extra height, with extra wheel travel and larger anti-roll bars. Priced at a few hundred pounds more, and offered with more or less the same engine range as the mainstream Golf (VW stopped short of a GTI) the Golf Plus was considered a worthwhile addition to the range and added some of the Golf sales volume to return it to number one in Europe by December 2005.

For some, however, the conservative looks of the Plus meant it lacked the cachet of the regular Golf and in Germany it earned the nicknames of '60 plus' or *'Senioren-Golf'* (elderly Golf) as some of its buyers appreciated the high stance and ease of access. The SEAT version, the Altea, was allowed a more adventurous look.

However, in 2006 an attempt was made to increase the 'lifestyle' credentials of the Plus in a CrossGolf version. Following a fashion for cars gaining raised suspension and the styling of off-road vehicles but without four-wheel drive, the CrossGolf was based on the Golf Plus but with its ride height raised by 20mm, BBS 17-inch alloy wheels, matt black blistered wheel arches, a restyled lower front bumper with an air dam framed by a set of fog lights, silver roof rails and plastic rubbing strips down the side. Not quite sure about this proposition, Volkswagen UK renamed it the Golf Plus Dune and sold it as a limited edition of 400 1.9TDIs in 2007.

As to real four-wheel-drive Golfs, with the growth in small sports utility vehicles such as the Toyota RAV-4 and the Honda CR-V buyers had far more choice than a discreet Golf and Volkswagen belatedly joined the market with the Tiguan in 2007. Meanwhile, from

↓ There had been speculation of a Golf 'Marrakesh' but the Plus was given pseudo off-roader looks to become the CrossGolf or Golf Plus Dune.

late 2004 the Haldex four-wheel-drive system was introduced on the Golf 5, once more under the 4Motion label. The system always put 10% of drive to the rear wheels and as much as 50%. Mounted on the rear axle, it was linked to the plethora of electronic traction systems, said to be quicker to respond and needing less servicing. However, the old bugbears of extra weight and lost boot space remained.

There was an optional rough-road package featuring harder suspension and 20mm increased ground clearance, and an engine protection plate was also available but there were no great claims at being an off-roader, better for crossing wet fields and snow. For an extra 1,500 Euros German buyers could have a 4Motion with the 2.0 FSI and 1.9 and 2.0 TDI engines. Sold with Sport and GT badging in the UK with only the 2.0-litre engines, the sales forecast was a modest 600 a year and the petrol-engined 4Motion was withdrawn from sale in May.

↑ Until the advent of the Tiguan, the Golf 4Motion was the Golf for rough roads, but not off-roading.

↓ The 2007 Tiguan was Volkswagen's second sports utility vehicle, aimed at the likes of the BMW X3. Based largely on the Golf platform it was longer and taller with Passat front and rear suspension, Golf Plus-derived interior and Haldex/4Motion drive.

The Volkswagen Eos

By the time production of the Golf cabriolet – a long-lasting facelift of the third Golf – ended in 2002 fabric hoods had fallen from fashion. Reviving an idea from 1950s America, the 1996 Mercedes SLK had combined the appeal of a fixed roof and an open-air experience by a folding metal hardtop, which pivoted into the boot via an electric and hydraulic system of cables, motors and pumps. The Peugeot 206 Coupe Cabriolet (CC) brought the idea to a lower price class in 2000, then the Golf-sized 307 CC and Renault Mégane CC followed in 2003. With Ford and Opel planning similar cars Volkswagen was bound to follow.

These hard-top coupes retained the front panels of the hatchback but had bespoke bodywork from the windscreen backwards and a large rear deck. Inevitably all were heavier and more expensive than traditional convertibles. When the roof was retracted luggage space was substantially reduced.

Volkswagen's interpretation of this fashion was shown first as the Concept C at the spring 2004 Geneva Automobile Salon then appeared little different in production form at the following September's Frankfurt show, with the name Eos for the Greek goddess of dawn.

Although it sat on the Golf platform the Eos used a mixture of Golf and Passat components and was visually less derived from the hatchback than its rivals. Audi had the soft-top A4 in the price bracket above and Volkswagen was still catering for the affordable four-seater cabriolet market with the new Beetle, so it could afford to distance the Eos from the Golf and push it upmarket. At 4,407mm long it was placed between Golf and Passat.

Former Audi designer Peter Schreyer was credited with the styling but both the SLK and the 206 CC had been designed by Murat Günak, head of design at the Volkswagen brand group from 2003 to 2007.

The folding hard-top was made up of five parts, and was claimed to fold into a smaller space than other cars as a result. With the roof closed, boot capacity was 380 litres; with the roof 'off', 205 litres, and owners had to make sure a cover for the luggage section was fully in place before pulling the large chromed lever between the front seats. The complicated ballet for opening or closing was claimed to take 25 seconds and the Eos was initially unique in its class as the only convertible coupe with a full-length tilt and slide sunroof fitted as standard, which gave the interior a glassy feel.

➔ Roof up, luggage capacity was huge but rapidly diminished. The glass centre section can be seen on top.

⬋ Like others of its kind the folding of the Eos roof structure was balletic and could only be carried out while stationary with space above and behind.

The Eos was built not by Karmann, which at the time built the Mégane CC, but at Volkswagen's Autoeuropa factory in Portugal, which had been building the Ford Galaxy/Volkswagen Sharan people carrier.

The engine range started with the 1.6-litre 115PS petrol FSI engine and included the 200PS 2.0-litre from the Golf GTI and the 3.2 V6 although the extra weight of the roof machinery blunted performance a little.

The Eos was generally respected by road testers, regarded as a good-looking and well-executed example of its type, although after a few years it wasn't hard to find internet postings from owners unhappy that the roofs in their cars leaked – a problem shared with competitors.

A new Golf cabriolet appeared in 2011 and a second-generation 'new' Beetle convertible the following year. The Eos received a facelift with the latest corporate front and rear styling, and at its launch Volkswagen head of design Klaus Bischoff was quoted saying the Eos would not be replaced when it ended its production run as the company did not need three four-seater open tops in the same segment: 'The trend for hard-tops seems to be disappearing again,' he said. 'I don't mind, I like canvas tops.'

⬇ If a rollover was detected, substantial posts were ejected from behind the rear seats in milliseconds.

↑ **With unique frontal styling the fifth Golf GTI was certainly the most extrovert to that point. The word 'Golf' was absent from the outside or inside.**

Return of the GTI

A radical rethink had taken place over the Golf GTI, regarded as damaged goods by enthusiasts after the over-discreet and over-large range of engines the badge had been applied to with the Golf 4. For the first time, rather than launching the GTI alongside the regular range at Frankfurt in 2003 Volkswagen instead held it back but showed a 'concept' GTI, which, as a technique for building interest for the real thing, worked extremely well.

Referencing back to the first GTI of 28 years previous, the concept car was of course red, and had a black radiator grille in the new corporate V-shape previewed on the Volkswagen Concept R, a two-seater sports car concept shown also at Frankfurt but which never made it to production. The red stripe round the grille was back, as was a tartan pattern on the seats with GTI logos embroidered into them. The three-spoke steering wheel also featured a GTI badge. There was black trim along the sills and rear window frame too. Beneath the new grille were three large air inlets in the bumper surrounded by a honeycomb structure.

At the rear, there was a spoiler and twin exhaust pipes. Red brake calipers were visible through the newly designed 18-inch alloy wheels. 'We want to get back to a more purist approach like that taken with the original GTI," said Bernd Pischetsrieder in 2004. 'The new car will be more than an additional trim level.' Volkswagen's head of design, Murat Günak, added: 'This Golf GTI comes full circle – it unites the origins and future of an ingenious idea.'

To have any credibility, extra PS was required for a new GTI. The Ford Focus RS, Honda Civic Type-R and Renault Mégane Renaultsport were beloved by the car magazines, all 200PS-plus cars. There was internal competition too from the Škoda Octavia vRS and from SEAT, cultivating a 'sporting' personality with its Leon

Cupra models. To match the Cupra R alone (with the older 1.8-litre, 20-valve turbo engine) the fifth Golf GTI would have to have a power output of at least 200PS and indeed that's exactly what the 2003 'concept' had, a turbocharged version of the 2.0-litre FSI direct-injection petrol engine combined with an intercooler.

'And the product launch date?' asked the concept press release playfully. 'Let's just say: If it's high-tech and outstanding performance, with the GTI philosophy in mind, that people are looking for, they will find it all at the 2004 Motor Show in Paris.'

One year later the new GTI was unveiled in exactly that way, with very little difference in looks or specification and driven by the European press at the Paul Ricard racing circuit in the South of France in October 2004.

Now there was an official set of performance figures; a claimed 0–62mph (100kph) time of 7.2 seconds and a top speed of 146mph. Whereas the Honda Civic Type-R gave its best performance at very high engine revs, the new GTI's power was delivered in the user-friendly fashion of its predecessors, pulling strongly and smoothly throughout with no hint of turbo lag. Its maximum pulling power of 207lb ft was available from 1,800 to 5,100rpm. The direct-injection system had been tuned to give a different blend of air and fuel entering the cylinders for performance over economy.

'While the 1.8T is a bland, unexciting performer', wrote John Barker in *Evo* magazine in November 2004, 'the 2-litre direct injection FSI is stimulating and effervescent, a pleasant surprise given the turbo's delivery is capped to give linear torque between 1,800 and 5,000rpm. There's nothing linear about the delivery, though, and underpinning its strong, responsive performance is a genuinely engaging induction note. Somehow VW's engineers have given this turbo engine a normally-aspirated voice – a guttural, appealing bwarp that swells with bass on large, low-rev throttle openings and then gradually thins out to a keen bark that reaches a natural peak and suggests an upshift.'

A sophisticated rear suspension was already provided and the GTI sat 15mm lower than other Golfs with stiffer anti-roll bars, shorter, stiffer springs and revised dampers. A larger 16in (as opposed to 10in) brake servo was used, while the brake discs also increased in size to 312mm at the front and 286mm at the rear. All were ventilated and covered by red brake calipers. The power-assisted steering was recalibrated to give more 'feel' and, as on lesser Golfs, the ESP could be switched off if you wanted to throw the car around and were confident you could handle extra understeer and a more abrupt turn into oversteer.

The six-speed gearbox had more resilient synchromesh to handle the power of the GTI. An option of great interest was the first automatic gearbox – the DSG unit – to appear on a GTI and the first petrol-engined fitment in a Golf 5. This was offered

↑ The new GTI 'Interlagos' cloth was a chequered design approaching the original tartan or full leather was an option.

at a not inconsiderable £1,325 extra (incidentally a 1:1 conversion from the German price in Euros).

First appearing on the 2003 Golf R32, by August 2004 almost 60,000 DSG systems (called S-Tronic by Audi) had been produced at the Kassel gearbox plant for the Golf, Touran, Audi TT, Audi A3, SEAT Altea and Škoda Octavia. Volkswagen had applied for over 70 patents for the gearbox technology and commentators were hailing it as the gearbox of the future.

Traditional automatic gearboxes were not considered desirable options for performance cars as their torque converters absorbed power, didn't always change smoothly or quickly enough and used more fuel. However, Ferrari had turned this thinking on its head from the late 1990s when it introduced a sequential manual transmission (SMT), drawing on its Formula 1 cars.

There was no clutch pedal and cars like the 360 Modena could be driven as an automatic or drivers could change gear – in theory more quickly than a manual with a clutch pedal – by using a pair of levers or 'paddles' to go up or down a gear. It wasn't a traditional torque converter automatic but a fully computer-controlled manual gearbox with a normal clutch. When the paddles were flicked, the engine revolutions were adjusted to match and each gear was engaged with varying degrees of smoothness, which challenged the driver's skills. Alfa Romeo offered its version, called Selespeed, from 1999.

So the ground was laid for acceptance of DSG in a sporting car and it offered major advantages from an SMT, where there was still an amount of delay when changing up through gears because the drive to the engine was being cut by the clutch each time a gear was selected. In a DSG twin-clutch gearbox, just before the need for a change was detected (and this could be for

← Golf GTI 5 meets the original. Double the power but 1,350kg to about 900.

economy or performance driving) one clutch disengaged while the other was engaging, both in a few hundredths of a second, so the transmission always preselected the next gear to be used. With a DSG gearbox there was in theory no perceptible interruption in traction and no jolting during gearshifts.

A Golf GTI fitted with DSG could be left to run as an automatic or the driver could change up and down themselves by flicking the gear lever forwards and back. For an extra £515 this could be done by a pair of paddle-like levers behind the steering wheel and most GTIs fitted with DSG were specified with paddles. Volkswagen UK estimated 30 to 40% of UK GTIs would be specified with DSG. The UK was still the second largest market for the GTI.

According to Volkswagen's own performance figures a DSG gearbox could change more quickly than a person using the manual gearbox, with 0–62mph in 6.9 over 7.2secs. When tested by *Evo*, its figures revealed it was half a second slower but slightly more economical, with a combined mpg figure of 35.3 – 0.4mpg better than the manual car. However, the shifts were not quite as imperceptible as claimed.

Priced from £19,995 for the manual gearbox three-door, the new GTI went on UK sale in January 2005. Prospective buyers had been able to configure their GTIs on a dedicated website and arrive at the dealer with a reference code, so the order books were already filling helped by numerous plaudits from car magazines. Specification was complete for this top-of-the-range Golf and satellite navigation, a multi-function steering wheel, gas-discharge (Xenon) headlights and a six-CD changer were among the options. 'Monza' 17in alloy wheels were fitted as standard, with optional 18in versions.

↑ **In yet another reference to the first Golf GTI, the 2007 Golf GTI Pirelli special was shod with the famous tyre maker's most advanced product.**

↓ **Inside, the GTI Pirelli's seats mimicked a tyre tread pattern.**

The GTI brand having been re-established (and to underline this there was no GTD), the production run of the fifth generation saw two factory special editions. As expected, 30 years of GTI was marked by a 2006 batch of Golf GTI Edition 30s, 2,264 of which sold to UK buyers for £1,935 over the regular car. This brought some cosmetic changes to the exterior and interior such as the 'golf ball' dimpled gear knob, which over the years had been fitted and withdrawn several times. It also brought 30PS more power, taking half a second off the 0–62mph time at 6.8 seconds and pushing the claimed top speed up to 150mph. Tuning companies could, however, liberate more power by re-programming the engine management system for less money.

May 2007's mass GTI gathering at Wörthersee in Austria saw the GTI Pirelli special edition, harking back to the first-generation Golf special of 1983 with its 'P' pattern alloy wheels. The GTI Pirelli was of course shod with the new Pirelli P-Zero performance car tyres on 18in wheels and had seats with a tyre tread pattern. On German sale from October 2007, it came in blue, black or a bright yellow 'Sunflower' hue (not for the UK).

GTI W12-650

Only eight weeks before May 2007's Wörthersee festival chairman Martin Winterkorn tasked his engineers to come up with something special. The result was spectacular.

The GTI W12-650 design study was a highly modified Golf GTI three-door bodyshell covering a mid-mounted bi-turbo W12 650PS engine in the same specification as the Bentley Continental. Sitting in an aluminium subframe the 5,998cc W12 was effectively made up of a pair of narrow-angle V6 engines laid alongside each other and made from aluminium to reduce weight.

This was a fully driveable car, albeit with some limits on the speeds it could achieve in each gear to save the tyres (drive was to the rear wheels only). 'We know that Mr Piëch lives in Austria so he's always there,' said exterior designer Marc Lichte at one of its many outings. 'We knew that if we presented a car like this it should work.' The W12-650 was robust enough for a publicity tour around car magazines and TV shows like *Top Gear*, with a claimed 0–62mph (100kph) in 3.7 seconds and a potential maximum speed of 202mph. There was talk that if there was enough interest then more would be built, but it became an exhibit in the Volkswagen museum complex in Wolfsburg.

↓ The wild W650 just about resembled a Golf. Its 16cm of extra width accommodated a mid-mounted engine, bespoke drivetrain and side-mounted cooling systems.

↑ Vast fans were needed to cool the mid-mounted 12-cylinder engine.

↑The second-generation Golf R32 was less overtly sporting than the GTI and had a similar shape grille/bumper assembly with a chrome effect. Headlights were high-spec xenon gas units.

The second R32

The second iteration of the V6-engined Golf R32 appeared at the 2005 Frankfurt Motor Show. Its predecessor had gone a long way to reinvigorating the image of fast Golfs and with the relaunched GTI franchise, some commentators felt that a headline power figure of 250PS (up by 9 from the first R32) was not all that interesting. Tuners such as Oettinger could extract 280PS from the GTI albeit minus the security of four-wheel drive.

There had been speculation that when the R32 arrived it would have the 300PS 3.6-litre V6 of the later Passat R36 and company indecision over this, according to US magazine *Car and Driver*, accounted for no Golf R36 and an R32 delayed into the American market until the 2008 model year.

As well as a bigger engine it was also carrying the extra weight of the Haldex 4Motion four-wheel-drive system, again essentially sending most of the drive to the front wheels unless required at the rear. On official figures it was still just about the fastest Golf with 6.5 seconds to 100kph (62mph) compared to the GTI's 7.2 seconds (manual) and matched its 146mph top speed. And the power was delivered with the satisfying burble of a six-cylinder engine. The appeal was the same as its predecessor; discreet power in a compact and luxurious car and the only direct competitors were the Audi A3 3.2 Quattro with the same engine and the Alfa Romeo 147 GTA with only front-wheel drive.

Sitting 20mm lower than a regular Golf on 18in alloy wheels, the R32's unique styling featured an aluminium full-length grille and a new front spoiler, centrally-positioned twin exhaust pipes, darkened rear lenses, new front spoiler with imposing air scoops, plus a full-depth painted rear bumper and signature blue brake calipers. Inside there was leather and aluminium-effect trim, and racing-style Recaro bucket seats with twin holes for a racing harness were available from £945.

The price difference was not that great compared with a GTI, with a UK starting price of £23,745 for the 3-door manual. 'But biggest, fastest and most expensive isn't always best,' wrote Golf aficionado John Simister in *The Independent*, 'and the R32 feels overweight and over-engined. Buy a Golf GTI instead. You know it makes sense – and, even better, it satisfies sensibility.'

Rabbit returns

Volkswagen of America's dealers had a long wait for new models including the Golf, once more against a background of falling sales. The mainstays were still the Passat and Jetta, and the newest version of the latter was launched in March 2005, five months ahead of its European debut. The Golf – referred to as the Jetta's hatchback version – remained a far less significant car than in Europe and arrived in the US the following year when Volkswagen of America used the GTI as the image maker once more. In an 'edgy' press stunt Golf GTIs were left around the roads of Los Angeles surrounded by police cars ahead of the January 2006 LA Motor Show, suggesting they had been pulled over for speeding.

The bigger surprise though was the re-adoption of the Rabbit name after 22 years. Perhaps because of the wave of Volkswagen nostalgia created by the new Beetle, or perhaps because of retro American cars like Chrysler's PT Cruiser, Volkswagen of America skipped back to the 1970s and named the fifth Golf the Rabbit. The *Financial Times* reported in April 2006 that this brainwave had come from Volkswagen's new Miami-based advertising agency, which had successfully introduced the BMW Mini into the USA. 'It's not an April fool's joke,' a VW spokesman said. 'The agency has a solid belief that the Rabbit name provides us with interesting opportunities for brand and marketing.' This baffled commentators as the original Rabbit had started well only for sales to collapse as it was 'Americanised' and badly built.

The other notable aspect of the US Jetta and the new Rabbit was the adoption of a new 148 (US) horsepower, 2.5-litre, five-cylinder engine as the basic engine instead of the former 115bhp 2.0-litre four-cylinder. Extra power was needed for the larger and heavier Jetta, and to keep up with similar-powered versions of the Honda Civic and Ford Focus. Developed 'for the North American driver' it was about torque, 90% of which was claimed to be available between about 1,750rpm to 5,125rpm.

It bore no relation to the now-discarded European V5 engine but claims that it was half of the Lamborghini Gallardo's V10 were not quite true. However, there was a connection in that it shared the same 82.5mm bore and 92.8mm stroke and it used the aluminium-alloy 20-valve cylinder head found on one bank of the Lamborghini unit combined with variable intake-valve timing. But for all this it seemed to underwhelm domestic road testers when fitted to the Rabbit and they complained it was unrefined although they still found the car fun to drive. The five-cylinder's power was upped to 170bhp (US) for the sixth-generation US Golf but the Rabbit revival was short-lived, lasting just three years. As ever, the Jetta proved more popular, regularly posting annual sales of 90,000 to the Rabbit's best of 40,000 (including GTI).

FSI becomes TSI

Before and after the arrival of the GTI, European Volkswagen ranges had contained Sport and GT models as sub-GTI sports hatchbacks, but the 2006 Golf GT was far more significant as it ushered in a major development in Volkswagen group petrol engines.

Frankfurt 2005 saw the announcement of TSI engine badging. Reviving the ideas of the *G-Lader* of the 1980s,

↓ TSI meant a small turbocharger placed close to a direct-injection petrol engine. It was to become standard Golf engine technology.

the new Golf GT's FSI 1.4-litre engine was dual-charged through a combination of an engine-driven supercharger plus an exhaust gas turbocharger arranged in series. The belt-driven supercharger operated at lower engine speeds, with the turbocharger coming in as the engine speed increased (the supercharger disengaged at a maximum 3,500rpm in this case). The result was claimed to be excellent driveability and performance throughout the range with no turbo lag and high maximum torque. During its mid-1980s rally heyday Lancia ran the Delta S4 on similar principles.

The combination of these technologies enabled a small capacity engine with a high compression ratio to cruise at part load on high gearing, combining improved performance with lower fuel consumption. It marked the start of a general automotive trend to reduce fuel consumption and emissions by downsizing engines, meaning reduced friction losses and engine weight but with performance and flexibility added by a turbocharger or supercharger.

The new 1,390cc TSI engine could be set to produce either 140 or 170PS. The 170PS version was claimed to have the same peak power as the 2.3-litre V5 once had but with 20% lower fuel consumption, returning 38.2mpg on the combined cycle. It also produced torque of 177lb ft from 1,750 through to 4,500rpm. Compared to the 1.4 FSI it used a reinforced cast-iron cylinder block to withstand higher combustion pressures, plus modified six-hole injectors. This was distantly descended from the trusty EA111 series of engines, which dated back to the 1974 Golf but had an EA211 designation.

The use of TSI spread across the Volkswagen group, with lower-powered cars using engines equipped just with intercooled turbochargers. In 2007 the 115PS 1.6-litre Golf FSI engine gave way to a 122PS turbocharged TSI 1.4. Its combined consumption increased from 42.2 to 44.8 mpg and carbon dioxide emissions fell from 161g/km to 149g/km.

So even though cars had become bigger and heavier with the decades, the entry-level 2007 Passat was a 1.4-litre – the smallest since the early 1980s. Engine capacity began to have less and less meaning as a marker of a car. Ford would take downsizing even further in 2011 when the Focus was offered with a direct-injection turbocharged 1.0-litre engine that could still produce 125PS.

↓ For Europe the Golf GT had the same power as former GTIs and was significant for the first use of a 'twin-charged' TSI engine.

The late estate

After the Golf's two-pronged entry into the MPV market with the Touran and the Golf Plus, the traditional estate or kombi appeared to have been forgotten with the Golf 5. In fact the Golf 4 estate had remained quietly in production with a mild facelift and new engines at Karmann until May 2006.

At the Geneva Motor Show in March 2007 a new Golf estate broke cover, and according to Georg Kacher writing in *Car*, it had been delayed for almost two years. 'Initially, we thought that the Touran and the Golf Plus could together cover the estate car segment,' said Ulrich Hackenberg, then recently appointed board member in charge of engineering. 'Obviously, this was a mistake. Having sold over 1.2 million Golf variants since 1993, the customer base clamoured for a replacement.'

Built in Peubla, Mexico alongside the Jetta with which it shared frontal styling, the new variant was 352mm longer than the hatch so load space went up to a maximum of 1,550 litres with rear seats flat; an increase of 80 litres. There was a luggage compartment divider to stop small objects moving around and a 12-volt power socket. Like the 4Motion the variant was not a big seller in the UK and confined to two petrol and one diesel engine choices.

↑ With the Touran and Golf Plus on offer, the estate was not a big seller in the UK. In 2008 2,800 were forecast to go mostly to business users. Roof rails were standard.

↓ For the fifth-generation Golf saloon Volkswagen abandoned the Bora name in Europe and it became Jetta for all markets, built in Peubla, Mexico. Rear styling especially linked it to the Passat.

Blue: the new green

Although all its engines were becoming more economical the Volkswagen Group still wanted to be seen as an environmental innovator and in 2006 introduced the Polo BlueMotion, the spiritual successor to the Lupo 3L with a theoretical 72.4mpg from a modified 1.4-litre TDI three-cylinder engine, aerodynamic adjustments, longer gear ratios and a diesel particulate filter (DPF).

Essentially, BlueMotion was the 21st-century version of Formel E, but why blue? In early 2006 Volkswagen and Mercedes (ChryslerDaimler as the whole company was then known) announced they were both going to use the term Bluetec to promote the technology of low-emission advanced diesel engines for passenger cars and trucks.

Mercedes was aiming to make its diesels meet stringent new American emission requirements for diesels and one component was a system that injected a fluid called AdBlue into the exhaust upstream of the catalyst. This was claimed to reduce nitrogen oxide (NOx) emissions. A key ingredient of the fluid was urea, which is the main nitrogen-bearing component in urine. AdBlue of course sounded much better than urine and the liquid was contained in a tank and topped up at services. In 2008 Volkswagen introduced similar technology to the US-only version of the Jetta.

However, Mercedes at first chose not to badge its cars Bluetec (it eventually became BlueEfficiency badging) and Volkswagen said it wasn't going to either, but then invented its own term, BlueMotion, for cars that included some or all of the latest fuel-saving modifications.

The Golf 5 BlueMotion appeared at the September 2007 Frankfurt Motor Show. Available for the German market at the end of the year and in Britain the following March, it was the fourth Volkswagen with an optional package of fuel-saving modifications such as revised aerodynamics, optimised gear ratios, a new turbocharger and hard-compound tyres.

All Golf BlueMotions were fitted with the standard 105PS 1.9 TDI diesel and there was little to recognise one apart from its badging. It sat 15mm lower and the underbody received more trim to smooth airflow. The radiator grille was partially covered and in all this reduced the drag coefficient to 0.30 from 0.32. It also ran on 195/65 tyres at higher pressure and the combination meant the top speed rose from 116 to 118mph. The gear ratios in third, fourth and fifth were higher and this too was claimed to reduce consumption. Like the old Formel E system, an instrument panel indicator suggested the best gear to be in. The engine idle speed was also set lower. The Passat BlueMotion was the first to add a stop-start system in late 2008.

The claimed Golf BlueMotion combined economy figure was 62.8mpg compared to 56.5 but as ever it was a case of doing your sums if you wanted to know if this fuel-saving showcase would pay off. The advantage for London commuters was clearer, as with CO_2 emissions of 119g/km it qualified for low-emission-vehicle exemption from the daily congestion charge to enter the centre of the city. The snag was that when the Golf BlueMotion was introduced into the UK market in summer 2008 Volkswagen UK had lowered the price of the standard diesels to compensate for a lack of supply of the much-praised 1.4 TSI petrol engine, so the BlueMotion could cost as much as £1,290 more than the regular car. But all these additions worked. Testers found the 60mpg was quite possible although both *Car* and *Autocar* commented that the 1.9TDI was now starting to sound noisy, especially at idle, relative to rival diesels with more up-to-date common-rail injection engines.

BlueMotion went on to become the label for the lowest-consumption version of most Volkswagen models, while SEATs could be EcoMotive and Škodas Greenline. Other manufacturers also introduced 'eco' models.

The other Golf technical highlight of late 2007 was the introduction of a seven-speed DSG gearbox for 1.4-litre TSI petrol and 1.9-litre TDI diesel engines. It was designed for smaller engines of up to 170PS and 184lb ft torque, and differed in a significant way, being a 'dry clutch' unit in that its twin clutches didn't sit in a bath of oil for cooling like the six-speed and the fact of being a seven-speed automatic was claimed as a world first. These two features were claimed to be good for both power and economy, and the unit itself was lighter. It also had a 'hill hold' function.

The lower gear ratios were more closely spaced for better take-off and in-gear acceleration while the higher ratios were lengthened to reduce loading on the engine and maximise economy. Fitted to the Golf 1.4 TSI, compared with the six-speed manual version, the new

seven-speed DSG was claimed to bring a 10g/km CO_2 saving from 149g/km in the manual and a fuel economy improvement of over 3mpg (combined 44.8mpg for manual and 47.9 for seven-speed DSG).

The DSG automatics were so efficient that they were independently recognised as environmentally-friendly technologies and magazine road testers could find little to fault the driving experience, letting them run as automatics or changing via paddle shifts. However, after several years in service DSG reliability was called into question by unhappy owners on internet forums and recalls in some markets.

The seven-speed DSG was the last significant introduction for the Golf 5 and in June 2008 the industry was already looking forward to seeing a sixth interpretation that autumn. The fifth Golf had entered a difficult market and the period had been marked by Volkswagen battling to save costs caused by factory closures and restructuring.

The value of the dollar against the euro left the company once more debating whether to end Golf sales in America or start building it there once more. The *Wall Street Journal* reported that the company had struggled to make money with the Golf 5 and it had only been profitable from 2006. The next Golf was, according to the paper's sources, set to be 1,000 Euros cheaper to build by carrying over the same platform. However, if the Golf 5 had proved to have the shortest production run to date at five years, this was about to be beaten by the next car.

↑ The fuel-saving BlueMotion sat as low as a sports Golf for less air drag. Its partially obscured radiator grille meant twin fans were needed.

WOB GO 506

Golf 6
2008–2012

The in-betweener

Generation 6 or generation 5.5? Even as the new Golf for 2008 was being launched there was talk that this car, with a large amount of carry-over components and hard to distinguish from its predecessor (even for a Golf), was a stop-gap model to keep it at European number one while a totally new Golf was under development.

In September 2008 *Automotive News Europe* (ANE), reporting from the eye-catching launch venue in Iceland, claimed that details were already beginning to emerge of the seventh-generation Golf, due as soon as 2012, built on an all-new platform with a range of more fuel-efficient engines. German magazine *Automobilwoche* (automobile week) claimed to have seen a company dossier that gave the new Golf only until December 2011. Volkswagen was apparently concerned that rapidly rising fuel prices would demand a lighter Golf with more power-train options than ever before, faced with hybrid and electric models from key competitors.

'The first step in downsizing is not to increase the size of the new model,' was as much as design head Walter de Silva was going to tell *ANE* and he confirmed that he and his team were already working on the Golf 7. Development on the radical MQB platform (see Chapter 8) had indeed started.

At five years the Golf 6 had had the shortest development cycle in the model's history. The norm had been around six, with the design frozen four years before first production. To the untrained eye it was quite difficult to distinguish what was new, but Volkswagen claimed that 60% of the components had changed. What hadn't changed though was under the surface and that remained well engineered and respected.

Buyers needed a reason to choose another Golf and Volkswagen needed to be ready for the new Astra of 2009 and the new Focus (built heavily on the base of the last one) of 2010. The Golf needed to claw back profitability and the 2008 version was reported as being

↓ Iceland was the eye-catching backdrop for the 2008 Golf 6 launch. The striking 18in alloy wheels were called 'Bilbao'.

5% cheaper to build. In contrast the more expensive Audi A3, which shared its base with the Golf 5, was allowed an uninterrupted run from 2003 to 2012. One of the production savings for the 2008 Golf was a reduction of the number of European plants it was built in, dropping Brussels assembly (after a great deal of protest in Belgium until the Audi A1 took its place) to leave Wolfsburg and Zwickau.

The front end of the new Golf had been redesigned for faster assembly and the doors were welded rather than clipped together, which was also faster. Elsewhere the Volkswagen group was making savings in production and purchasing, but the Golf 6 was also more cost-effective by virtue of the capital expenditure in the multi-link rear suspension having been spread across many group vehicles over the last five years, as well as the re-equipment of the production lines. Until November 2008 the Golf 5 and 6 were able to be assembled alongside each other at Wolfsburg. Unlike the Golf 4, which was still produced outside Germany, once the 5 was gone it was gone for good.

All of the external panels of the Golf 6 had been changed apart from the roof, but the designers were constrained by using the same 'hard points' of the Golf 5 so the wheelbase, door pillars and seating positions could not move. The sixth Golf carried over the 2,578mm wheelbase of its predecessor and was actually about 5mm shorter with its new bumper designs.

'It is more accentuated than its predecessor with precisely defined lines and edges and with finely proportioned flared surfaces and recesses,' said de Silva and pointed to the first and fourth Golfs as reference points. It had in fact had a last-minute nose job.

When new chairman Martin Winterkorn took up post at the start of 2007 he asked de Silva to head design for the company. A good friend of Giugiaro, de Silva came via Alfa Romeo and SEAT. He first took stock of models about to be launched such as the Scirocco and Passat CC. 'We looked at a number of models and in terms of design the situation was worrying,' he told the author in 2012. 'The final design of the Golf 6 had completely changed the front, the face of the car, so I widened the grille and referred to Giugiaro's line linking the two headlamps. I said we can't afford to lose that. Had we left things unchanged, believe me, we would have had a disaster.' Perhaps though, the end result was a little too subtle for some. 'The Mk6 is tightly drawn and tidy in the traditional Golf manner, but it looks more like a Mk5.5 than a model worthy of new generation billing,' said *Autocar*. The new corporate nose banished the bold, sometimes chromed grille, which had been fitted to performance derivatives of the previous car and the Jetta. It was a retreat into conservatism.

At first glance the interior also looked the same but again had been subtly refined. The overall shape of the dashboard was the same as the Golf 5 but it was positioned slightly higher and featured more soft-touch grained plastics. The speedometer and rev counter were now in cowled binnacles with silver trim around them (like the Passat CC) and there was an optional touchscreen for the radio. It was noted wistfully that the instrument panel no longer glowed blue at night but white.

The interior door panels were redesigned so the armrests swept up to meet the base of the windscreen and the electric window switches were higher placed. The seats were slightly redesigned to offer more back and leg support and could be moved further back for taller drivers. It all felt a little bit more luxurious than the last Golf, the press decided, rather exaggerating how the plastics in the previous car had felt so much cheaper.

↑ White, not blue backlit dials sat in recessed, individual cowls behind a three-spoke steering wheel with the option of controls for entertainment and communications. This is a 2010 British base 'S' trim.

↑ Still a Golf but with the new conservative corporate Volkswagen front and rear styling. Headlamp washers emerged from the squares below the headlights if the 'Winter Pack' was fitted.

Premium for the people

Launching the Golf in Iceland provided an unusual experience and dreadful road surfaces on which to test the improved rolling refinement – the key improvement claimed for this car. Journalists were treated to rides in the Volkswagen flagship Phaeton limousine and bosses spoke of the 'Phaetonisation' of features, which had come down the family tree to the humble Golf. This headline-grabbing technology was usually optional – and not for all markets, especially the litigious US – but gave a sales advantage compared to rival cars even if this was often short-lived as they gained similar features.

Mid-specification Golfs were now equipped with rain-sensing wipers, automatic headlamps and cruise control, and some markets (not the UK) could now specify the latter coupled to a function called ACC automatic distance control (ACC for Adaptive Cruise Control). Working with the cruise control, a laser sensor located above the rear-view mirror and five laser beams scanned the distance to the vehicle ahead as well as its speed. The car would then maintain a set speed and a safe distance between 30 and 210kph (18–130mph). It seemed a little complicated, the driver being able to select 'normal', 'sport' and 'comfort' modes. First seen in the mid-1990s, BMW had launched a similar system the year before and this new Golf feature had been seen in the Passat CC.

Volkswagen was already experimenting with a 'self-driving' Golf. Shown to the press in 2006, the GTI 53+1 was a test bed where electronic systems would control the throttle, steering and brakes (having electro-mechanical steering made this possible). The less science-fiction manifestation of this was Park Assist, first introduced on the Touran. If the driver wanted to parallel park they pressed the Park Assist button and two ultrasonic sensors would scan the space as the car went past to see whether it was big enough. The driver then stopped the car, selected reverse and let go of the steering wheel. The car steered itself but the driver still

could deactivate the system immediately by taking over the steering or by braking. A rear-view camera, which popped out from behind the Volkswagen roundel on the boot lid, was also available as an option. It transmitted an image and graphic guidelines to the dash-mounted radio or navigation screen to assist with parking.

There was nothing much to improve on the Golf's suspension, so the biggest change was a DCC Adaptive Chassis Control option, again filtering from the Passat CC and new Scirocco. It allowed the driver to select from normal, comfort or sport modes to change suspension, steering and accelerator response settings for any particular journey. Testers regarded it as interesting but a little superfluous.

Compared with the price and equipment adjustments that Volkswagen had juggled with on the 2003 Golf, this new-found refinement and extra equipment equated to only a small price increase in the UK market. On sale from January 2009, the cheapest UK-market Golf was £13,150 and an equivalent three-door Focus a little more, although heavy discounts were available. Golf prices on the whole had risen by about £100.

For the first time air conditioning was now standard on every Golf and standard safety was augmented by a knee airbag for the driver, bringing the total number of airbags to seven. A new head restraint system designed to reduce whiplash injuries and rear seat belt detection sensors were joined by new, more advanced Electronic Stabilisation Programme (ESP) software. All Golfs had body-coloured bumpers (without the black lower half rear bumper of the previous car), door handles and electrically heated and adjustable door mirrors, still with built-in indicators.

Every new Golf buyer also got a much quieter car with levels of interior calm judged to be from the luxury class. Subtle changes to create this included a completely new design of door and window seals, a new damping film sandwiched between two layers of windscreen glass

↑ When lit, the broad rear lights formed a distinctive pattern of a row of semi-circles.

A tale of two Jettas

The new Jetta of 2010 was as far away from a booted Golf as it had ever been. Teasingly previewed as the New Compact Coupe at the January Detroit Motor Show, its hybrid drivetrain was of more significance than the styling, which morphed into an undramatic four-door saloon later in the year.

Although the dashboard was the same, this new Jetta shared no panels with the Golf and sat between the hatchback and the Passat in terms of size, its wheelbase extended by 70mm to 2,648mm over the Golf for better rear legroom. The boot was cavernous.

Even though they were built in the same factory in Puebla, Mexico there were big differences between European and American Jettas, the latter determinedly built down to a price. The European Jetta retained the Golf's multi-link rear axle but US models got a specially developed torsion-beam rear axle and the electric power steering was deleted in favour of cheaper hydraulic power steering. Even the gas struts holding the bonnet open were withheld.

The petrol engines of the US Jetta were unique to its market: a 2.0-litre four-cylinder and the previous generation 2.5-litre five-cylinder. Even the dashboard was downgraded. However, if you specified a GLI, most of the missing equipment returned along with the GTI engine – a four-door GTI. It shared an intriguing gadget not afforded to European buyers called the 'Soundaktor', an audio file that played from a speaker under the bonnet to give a more rumbly engine note under acceleration. Whether it convinced was keenly debated on internet forums.

As part of Volkswagen of America's new sales offensive the new Jetta really hit the mark with 2011 sales of over 150,000 compared to 97,000 the previous year. European sales were, as usual, tiny (UK 2011 target: 3,000) and it had few direct rivals. The motoring writers, as usual treated it with respect, indifference or hostility.

While a Golf hybrid remained an experiment in Europe, Volkswagen launched a petrol/electric Jetta into the US market in late 2012, its second after the Touareg hybrid. The Jetta was competing against the Toyota Prius, Honda Civic hybrid and the range-extending electric Chevrolet Volt.

Itself new to the US market, a 1.4-litre 150PS TSI petrol engine and seven-speed DSG automatic were coupled to a 20kW electric motor in parallel hybrid, with a decoupling clutch, which disengaged the engine for pure electric drive (or when coasting or braking), the electric motor (for higher speeds or when the battery charge was low), or combined the two, adding 20PS to the peak power, comparable to the 2.5-litre Jetta. Under pure electric power the Jetta Hybrid could be driven at speeds of up to 70km/h (44mph) and over a distance of two kilometres (1.3 miles), depending on conditions. The car would switch between petrol and electric drive automatically or manually and it employed regenerative braking like the Golf BlueMotion.

Taking advantage of the Jetta's vast boot, a lithium-ion battery was located behind the rear seat bench, creating a raised section of the floor. There were dedicated instrument displays and a blanked radiator grille with hybrid badging, but otherwise it resembled a regular model.

In the US it was priced some margin above a Jetta GLI diesel but on official figures (of which all car magazines were becoming increasingly sceptical) the hybrid was claimed to return 45mpg (around 54mpg imperial) compared to 34 (40 imperial) for the TDI. From the outset it was clear that the Jetta hybrid would not be sold in the UK although it was introduced to the German market in April 2013.

and a new engine mounting system. The wing mirrors were redesigned to eliminate wind whistle (and stay cleaner) and there were 20 sections of noise insulation, including in the front pillars and the front bumper. The bonnet was double-skinned and insulated.

Car of the Year 2009 judge John Simister wrote: 'The new Golf has moved on less, sharing more major components with its immediate predecessor than any previous Golf. It's quiet, civilised, pleasing if unmemorable to drive and it has an interior of class-busting quality. But a significant new car? No.'

More TSI and a new TDI

The 2008–9 engine choices for the new Golf were four petrol and two diesel units, heralding a wholesale move to smaller-capacity turbocharged engines, which lowered emissions at the same time as keeping weight gain elsewhere in the car under control.

Carried over from the Golf 5 were the 1.4-litre 80PS or 1.6-litre 102PS, plus the 1.4-litre TSI power plant with 122PS and a turbocharger (expected to be the best-selling petrol engine) or 160PS with supercharger and turbocharger. The latter replaced the 170PS unit of the

➔ The Volkswagen New Compact Coupe (NCC), unveiled at the 2010 North American International Auto Show in Detroit, was more important for its hybrid drivetrain than styling.

← The sixth-generation Jetta was a larger car that decisively broke with its Golf origins.

previous Golf GT. There was now no need for the 150PS 2.0-litre FSI unit. In Germany the Golf Aktionsmodell was an oddity with a 1.8-litre 170PS turbocharged petrol engine lasting only for 2009.

New engine and gearbox technologies were claimed to lower fuel consumption by up to 28% and all petrol and diesel engines met the 2009 Euro 5 emissions regulations. All bar the base engine could be paired with the six- or seven-speed DSG automatic gearbox.

The Golf 6 diesel engine choice was at first only the 1,968cc turbo diesel with 110 or 140PS, the trusty 1.9 having been withdrawn. This featured a new fuel-injection system, which had already been introduced on the Tiguan. Increasingly criticised for its noisiness, Volkswagen was in the process of moving away from its *Pumpe Düse* or 'unit injector' design of the last ten years, where the injector and pump were combined into one unit for each cylinder, and to the common-rail system being used and refined by its competitors. The injection pressure was generated in a high-pressure fuel reservoir referred to as the 'common rail' as it supplied all the injectors to each cylinder. This enabled a higher

↑ **The ever more frugal Golf BlueMotion was marked by a new front bumper, sill extensions, lower ride height and relocated air ducts behind the grille.**

pressure again for more efficient combustion and quieter running. Still labelled TDI, the new-generation diesels also each had two balancer shafts to damp down vibrations. A particulate filter, which had been an option on the last Golf diesels, was now fitted as standard to meet emissions requirements. Emissions were on a steep decline – the 2.0 TDI was now claimed to emit 119g/km of CO_2 while returning a claimed 62.7mpg on the combined cycle, about 6mpg better. This was the same as the late-introduced BlueMotion, thus the expectation was that the 2009 version would better this figure. As before it could be teamed with the 4Motion four-wheel-drive transmission, but this was not imported to the UK where the Tiguan was satisfying that sector of the market.

Coupled with the new diesels, the in-house petrol-fuelled competition from the TSI units was getting stronger on flexibility and fuel economy and the design was winning awards. The twin-charged version was a favourite for many road testers. 'It's as if VW has thrown engineering at this car in a way that only Honda could match,' wrote *The Telegraph*'s Andrew English. 'It's virtually impossible to tell when the supercharger cuts out and the turbo cuts in, and the urgent push of the engine is smooth and linear.'

Although it had been a popular aftermarket conversion in some European countries for some years, in December 2008 Volkswagen presented the first factory-built Golf able to be driven by petrol or liquid petroleum gas (LPG), the 1.6-litre Golf BiFuel. Rather than the usual bulky tank which took up boot space, an LPG tank was fitted into the spare wheel well and the driver could switch between both fuels. The use of LPG cut emissions and its price was subject to tax breaks in some markets, but it was not a big-selling option. With a claimed range of 273 miles on LPG the total range combined with petrol was around 700 miles. In 2009 the Golf Plus became available as a BiFuel car.

More downsizing

Illustrating that this Golf had to take its new engines when they became ready for use in other ranges, the TSI engine migration was completed in May 2009 when Volkswagen presented a 1.2-litre 105PS TSI unit at the 30th Vienna Engine Symposium. Fitted to the Golf and Polo ranges, it once more used petrol direct injection and a turbocharger, and delivered the performance of a 1.6-litre engine and greater engine flexibility with maximum torque developed at a notably low engine speed of 1,500rpm. Volkswagen claimed 'rigorous friction optimisation' and lightweight construction with an aluminium crankcase and a newly developed combustion process combined pulling power, high fuel economy and low emissions. Now engine size meant very little in the Golf catalogue. The 1.4-litre FSI engine continued in production in 80PS form as the engine for the cheapest versions.

At the same time a new common-rail 1.6-litre TDI engine was presented in outputs from 75 to 105PS and with its modular structure was the basis for all future four-cylinder Volkswagen diesel engines. As well as the claimed economy benefits, an improved reduction in CO_2 emissions was aided by the diesel particulate filter with an oxidation catalytic converter sited close to the engine.

This engine was now given to the next BlueMotion Golf, previewed as a concept in 2008 and ready for sale in summer the following year. It adopted the repertoire of changes seen on the previous model such as low-rolling-resistance tyres, optimised aerodynamics and revised ratios in the five-speed gearbox (the 2.0 TDI had six).

After the 1970s experiments, Formel E in the 1980s and the unpopular Ecomatic of the 1990s the 2009

Golf BlueMotion also marked the return of a stop-start system on a Golf, where the engine cut out automatically to save fuel. Now finally seemed to be the right time for consumer acceptance of the engine switching itself off. The European car industry was embracing cheap-to-buy systems from the likes of Bosch and Valeo as the solution to a European proposal to cut average CO_2 emissions from new cars by 18% to 130g/km or face heavy fines. BMW rolled out stop-start on the 2007 Mini while the Passat BlueMotion was the first Volkswagen with the new-generation stop/start.

This time the engine would only cut out if when coming to a halt the driver depressed the clutch and selected neutral. When the clutch was released the engine would shut down and a 'Stop-Start' symbol was illuminated on the multifunction display. To move away the driver depressed the clutch again to select first gear and the engine automatically restarted. The system could be deactivated by a switch if it became too irksome.

It did without the complicated emergency backup battery of the Ecomatic through what was termed regenerative braking. During deceleration and braking, the alternator's voltage was boosted and used for bulk recharging of the car's battery. This meant it was possible to lower alternator voltage, under acceleration or driving at a constant speed or switch off the alternator entirely, reducing engine load and improving fuel consumption. Thus the claimed combined fuel consumption of the Golf BlueMotion was 74.3mpg while emitting only 99g/km of CO_2, abut 10mpg better than a regular Golf diesel. Road testers found it gave little away to its driving pleasure. 'The BlueMotion ups the eco ante, while sacrificing nothing in everyday performance over a normal non-true blue 1.6 TDI Golf,' wrote *Car*'s Gavin Green. While the Golf BlueMotion was the flagship eco-car, buyers could opt for elements of its technology under the BlueMotion Technology label on other versions.

That said, as well as a host of diesel imitators the Golf BlueMotion now had a different kind of competition in the shape of the futuristic hybrid petrol Toyota Prius, in its third generation for 2009

↓ In May 2009 the Golf 5 estate was updated with a new front tied to the Scirocco, new Golf and fifth-generation Polo with redesigned headlamps and front and rear bumpers. The Touran and Golf Plus received similar facelifts and the latest engines.

and boasting 89g/km. On a cost basis alone the comparison was quite narrow. *Auto Motor und Sport* pitted a second-generation Prius against a Golf 1.6 TDI in December 2008 and the Golf just about won overall. But it noted that the diesel engine was still worse for pollutants. As detailed in Appendix 1, Volkswagen had been experimenting with hybrid cars for years – a hybrid Golf TDI had been shown in 2008 – but in production had sought more straightforward solutions to fuel economy. A catalogue hybrid Golf was still something for the future.

Built on strong foundations: the sixth GTI

Helped by a government bonus for owners trading in old cars for new (also running in the UK) German Golf sales were running high in early 2009, providing a confident background for the launch of the next GTI in spring. This time, however, there was another sporting option in the shape of the new Scirocco (see panel on page 236).

Following the successful strategy adopted for the Golf 5 GTI, the new hot hatchback was launched as a 'concept' at the October 2008 Paris Motor Show in pretty much the same specification as it would go on sale in 2009.

The vertical three-piece centre grille had been banished from the sporting Golfs and other Volkswagens with the new more conservative frontal styling, so there was less to mark out a GTI in a rear-view mirror than before. There was of course a red stripe around the top grille (the show and publicity GTIs were white, to best illustrate this) with a deep honeycomb air dam framed by vertical fog lights pushed out to the edges to emphasise width. At the rear, a diffuser sat between an all-new exhaust system with twin tailpipes along with a subtle rear spoiler atop the tailgate and smoked rear light lenses. There were black extensions to the lower part of the sills, but that was the extent of the extra additions to the bodywork. Red brake calipers, and the 'telephone dial' design of 17in 'Monza' alloy wheels were carried

↓ Unlike the previous generation, the GTI did not have its own grille styling but the red stripe remained.

over with 18in items optional. Inside, red and black tartan sports seats with red stitching and headrests featured the 'GTI' logo and a flat-bottomed multifunction steering wheel was new.

Although it shared the same 1,984cc capacity as the previous GTI, the engine for the new car was part of a new range, the EA888 series, which had been developed by Audi as a family of larger engines for the North American market, capable of high performance and better emissions. Again turbocharged with direct petrol injection, it had an iron block and alloy cylinder head, modified pistons and piston rings, an improved oil pump, new induction system and a high-pressure fuel pump. In a bid to reduce servicing costs the turbocharger and oil cooler were easier to access. It was also a selling point for some owners that the valve gear was run by a timing chain rather than a belt, considered to be much longer-lasting. The variable valve intake system was newly developed by Audi. Also fitted to the Scirocco, this was officially a TSI engine – not a TFSI. As before, the GTI could be specified with a six-speed manual gearbox or six-speed DSG automatic.

The all-important headline power was 210PS (10PS extra) delivered between 5,300 and 6,200rpm for a claimed 0–62mph in 6.9 seconds (the same claimed for the previous car), but with emissions falling from 189g/km to 170g/km in the manual version and economy improved from a combined 35.3mpg to 38.7mpg.

In the GTI tradition, bespoke springs and dampers were linked to a ride height lowered by 22mm at the front and 15mm at the rear. The Adaptive Chassis Control system (DCC), featuring pneumatically controlled damper units, was offered for the first time on the GTI.

Keeping the front wheels in the direction the driver intended was an electronically controlled differential called XDS, a distant relation of the system first introduced on the GTI G60 in the early 1990s. Sensors detected when the inside wheel was not sufficiently loaded and applied braking pressure via the Electronic Stabilisation Programme (ESP) in order to restore

continued on page 238

↓ The GTI tartan was called 'Jakara' and the dashboard was a darker shade of black called 'Titan Black'.

A new Scirocco

Even though the Volkswagen range – especially variations of Golf – had mushroomed between 2000 and 2010 there was no choice of coupe and a handful of two-seater sporting concept cars had come to nothing.

The 1982 Scirocco had lasted in production for ten years, still picking up buyers but latterly regarded as antiquated and priced below the highly respected Corrado (1988–1995). The two-door Jetta concept cars had seemed to promise Golf coupes only to disappoint by being little more than a preview of the latest corporate grille.

So when a dramatic-looking concept car named Iroc (a clue) was shown to the press in Berlin in late August 2006 and then publicly at September's Paris Motor Show it created huge excitement. Finished in Viper Green metallic paint, one of the colours in the 1976 Scirocco range, the Iroc's long roof and steeply sloping rear concealed two full-sized rear seats and reasonable boot space.

The Iroc was slightly longer (36mm) than the Golf at 4,240mm and its wheelbase over 100mm longer at 2,680mm. As concept cars often do, it sported huge 19in wheels and an outlandish interior. It was touted as having a new Volkswagen 'face' and the honeycomb pattern of the radiator grille was put forward as a link to the 1976 Golf GTI.

When it appeared in production form in March 2008, the gaping grille was gone. Styled by a team led by chief designer Klaus Bischoff, one of Walter de Silva's first edicts was to graft a new, more conservative, corporate grille onto the front, albeit with the

↑ The Iroc concept's blue lighting didn't make production but its instrument binnacle previewed the 2008 Golf's.

← Over a decade after the Corrado had gone, the 2006 Iroc was clearly a concept car destined to become a production coupe, powered by the twin-charged Golf 1.4 TSI engine.

VW roundel on the bonnet. The rear-end styling stayed largely the same. The dashboard, while more conservative than the Iroc, was the same as the Eos and the two cars were built in the same factory in Portugal.

Now firmly based on the PQ35 Golf platform it had shrunk back to the standard 2,578mm wheelbase, but this still allowed it to remain a full four-seater. It was a small amount longer than a Golf GTI but 6.5cms lower. The dramatic stance was retained by a track 29mm wider than the Golf at the front and 62mm at the rear.

This packaging did not allow it to be fitted with the 4Motion four-wheel-drive system. Engines and transmissions were initially carried across from the faster Golfs although not always with the same power outputs. It launched with the 200PS 2.0-litre TSI engine from the Golf 5 GTI then the twin-charged and turbo-only engines down to the 122PS 1.4 as an entry-level car. An R version was launched alongside the Golf equivalent. Equipment levels largely mirrored the Golf's.

During the gap between concept and reality a healthy interest had built up in the new coupe, cemented by rave reviews of its handling and prices, which started at medium-range Golf money. 'Volkswagen should clean up with the Scirocco,' wrote *Autocar*. 'Until now, if you wanted a really good-to-drive £20K car you'd have to buy a hot hatch rather than a coupe. But the Scirocco has created a new niche class of its own – and gone in straight at the top of it.' Although it hadn't been engineered for North America, over 200,000 examples had been sold in Europe by 2013 and an all-new version based on the MQB platform was expected for 2015.

↑ The dashboard was derived from the Eos, built in the same factory in Portugal.

→ The production Scirocco was faithful to the concept car but the grille was toned down.

↑ **An electronic differential was optional to help provide maximum grip when cornering in conjunction with the Electronic Stabilisation Programme (ESP).**

traction. 'A good part of the precision within the steering can be traced to the adoption of an optional electronic differential for the first time, because Volkswagen has done an excellent job of quelling any torque steer without resorting to a mechanical limited-slip diff,' wrote Greg Kable in *Autocar*.

As the Golf GTI went on German sale in March 2009, the GTD diesel made a return at the Leipzig Motor Show after having skipped a generation in the UK. The 2.0-litre common-rail TDI engine gave 170PS and while it wasn't as fast as the GTI, with 0–62mph (100kph) in 8.1 seconds and a top speed of 136mph the payoff was a claimed average fuel consumption of 53.3 mpg. It featured all the chassis modifications of its petrol equivalent apart from the XDS electronic differential (less necessary for its lower power). There were few external differences compared with the petrol GTI too. It lost the red highlights around the grille for chrome and the alloy wheels were 17in 'Seattle Black'. Inside, the tartan seat pattern was grey, white and black, rather than red, white and black.

Farewell Golf V6

With the general policy of downsizing, it was clear that the days of the V6 Golf were numbered and from the 2008 launch of the Golf 6 there was, in Europe, no prospect of any more than four cylinders. Enthusiasts might have hoped that the Audi TT RS of 2009 might have donated its turbo five-cylinder engine to the next generation Golf R, but it was not to be.

Developed by Volkswagen's special projects wing, Volkswagen Individual and launched alongside a Scirocco R at Frankfurt 2009, the new Golf R carried a 2.0-litre TSI four-cylinder engine, so couldn't lay claim to being an R32 by virtue of capacity. However, with the addition of a turbocharger it boasted 270PS compared to the R32's 250.

Illustrating the complexity of Volkswagen's engine programme this was not a hotter version of the Golf GTI engine but a different unit, derived from the EA113 engine from the fifth-generation GTI, not the EA888, essentially that of the Audi S3.

Evo reported that according to Volkswagen Individual it was because it lent itself more readily to tuning. The R engine had a reinforced block, new alloy cylinder head, uprated pistons and con rods and high-pressure fuel injectors. The turbocharger ran at a boost pressure of 1.2 bar, claimed to be an unusually high figure. An uprated oil cooler sat behind the front air dam to cope with the increased heat.

Like the Audi, power was channelled through a six-speed DSG gearbox to all four wheels via a Haldex system, now in its fourth generation. The system fitted to the R32 had relied on differing wheel speeds between the front and rear axles to engage the four-wheel drive, but that fitted to the Golf R was claimed to be quicker reacting thanks to faster coupling of the drive to the rear wheels by a hydraulic accumulator, which was kept 'pre charged' so there was no drop in pressure. The improved system also limited torque when needed to maximise traction. It was possible for all of the drive to be transferred to the rear wheels in some situations. New front brake discs and calipers were joined by uprated suspension lowered by 25mm with revised spring and damper rates and new anti-roll bars. The ESP was revised to offer two stages designed for track use (owners were increasingly using their cars on 'track days'). The electro-mechanical power steering system was adjusted to sharpen responses.

Thanks to the physically smaller and lighter engine there was more space in the engine bay. The Golf R was

↑ The GTD made a return to UK price lists for the sixth Golf, distinguished from the GTI by its alloy wheels and an absence of red trim around the grille.

→ GTD interior was more muted than GTI but shared its design of sports seat.

← Becoming more discreet, (and publicity shots showed more practical five-door cars) the Golf R had new front and rear bumpers with LED running lights at the front and a diffuser at the rear housing a pair of central exhausts.

↓ The Golf GTI Edition 35 featured a bodykit incorporating new side skirts and a revised front bumper. Bi-xenon headlights with LED daytime running lights came from the Golf R.

↑ **Hood up or down, the 2011 Golf cabriolet was a neat design and now unusual in its class for having a fabric roof.**

35kg lighter (albeit still much heavier than a GTI) so had a better power-to-weight ratio. It was claimed to be the fastest accelerating Volkswagen ever produced, with a 0–62mph (100kph) time of 5.7 seconds. Although not top of most owners' lists, the claimed combined cycle of 33.2mpg was around 4mpg better than the R32 and CO_2 emissions of 199g/km were down from 257g/km.

Once road tested by the magazines there was no complaint about any loss of flexibility minus two cylinders. The turbocharged Golf R came over as a much more eager car, starting to deliver its increased maximum torque of 258lb ft (compared to 236lb ft) at 2,500rpm continuing to 5,000rpm where the V6 had tailed off at 3,000. These were figures that mattered. 'The Golf R has also got terrific pace and tractability, coupled to a memorably effervescent engine and a sport-biased chassis that exudes confidence, composure and, perhaps most importantly, genuine enthusiasm,' wrote Richard Meadon in *Evo*.

UK prices for the R ranged between £28,930 and £30,820 and equipment was reasonably generous although it was observed that there was now enough choice on the options list to create a £40,000 Golf.

A further version of the EA111 engine was fitted to the 35th anniversary GTI, which made its debut at Wörthersee in June 2011, its power output of 235PS siting it between the regular GTI and the R and also making it the most powerful production GTI to that point. It was distinguishable by a revised front bumper, distinctive lightweight 18in alloys, '35' signatures inside and out and, yes, a golf-ball gear knob.

The Golf cabriolet returns

With the Golf Plus and the estate being face-lifted versions of the previous generation Golf the only truly new derivative of the 2008–2012 Golf was the welcome return of the soft-top Golf cabriolet, absent from the catalogue since 2002. On sale for summer 2011, it was for the first time ever a full convertible, without a rollover bar, forsaking the *Erdbeerkörbchen* – or strawberry basket – nickname of old. The Golf cabriolet didn't supplant the Eos, which sat in a slightly higher price bracket (the Beetle convertible having been dropped in the UK), and was around 20cm shorter but still a reasonable four-seater. Production returned to Karmann in Osnabrück or rather Volkswagen Osnabrück, as it was now wholly owned by the company as an assembly facility for smaller-volume cars.

↑ **The return of the GTI cabriolet was welcomed.**

→ **As safe as expected, the new cabriolet had automatically deployed rollover protection, front and side head/thorax airbags and a driver's knee airbag.**

Ford and Opel/Vauxhall had dropped folding metal hardtop versions for their new Focus and Astra, leaving the Golf with few direct rivals apart from the BMW 1-Series cabriolet and the 2008 soft-top Audi A3, built in Hungary, which provided much of the structural basis. Sharing the same wheelbase, the front panels were carried over from the Golf hatchback but everything rearwards was new, with a far more steeply angled windscreen.

Body engineering having moved on from the 1990s, the rollover bar was no longer needed to keep the structure from flexing over poor surfaces and the windscreen could bear the weight of the car in a rollover accident. As well as the usual quota of airbags and the hatchback's anti-lock and skid control systems, in the unlikely event of a rollover a pyrotechnic charge shot two metal posts from behind the rear seats to protect rear passengers. Audi had opted for fixed roll over hoops behind the rear headrests of the A3.

There were reinforced window frames and structural modifications to the underbody, side panels, cross-members and doors to endow the new car with a class-leading level of torsional rigidity, according to Volkswagen.

To come close to the hatchback's level of hush the fabric roof had an additional exterior skin, as well as new window and door seals. As it had always been, the rear window was heated and made of glass.

The roof could be lowered electrically in a claimed 9.5 seconds including on the move at speeds up to around 18mph, and a wind deflector could be fitted across the top of the back seat area when two were travelling to reduce buffeting at high speeds. Unlike its predecessors, when it was folded the hood sat flat on the rear deck as the final section that attached to the windscreen was rigid, so it needed no separate cover. There was less boot space intrusion with 250 litres of available space; top down the Eos counted 205 litres for luggage and the Audi A3, 260.

The new Golf cabriolet was available with three engines from launch: a 1.2-litre TSI 105PS, 1.4-litre TSI 160PS and a 1.6-litre TDI 105PS. DSG and BlueMotion Technology modifications such as stop-start could be specified with the diesel engines. In the UK prices started at £20,720, about £1,000 less than the Audi A3.

If the road testers found this contemporary and weighty Golf cabriolet to be a little short on sportiness, the spring 2012 finale to the Golf 6 range was the return of the GTI cabriolet, not seen since the 1980s. It used the same engine as the hatchback and a weight penalty of 138kg lowered the performance figures, but this was still a very fast soft-top albeit an expensive one at £29,310, on a par with the Golf R and BMW and Audi rivals. With the Golf 7 anticipated for the autumn, the cabriolet was set to continue production and be offered in an even more powerful and expensive guise.

For a stop-gap model the Golf 6 had met the challenge of keeping Volkswagen at the top of the hatchback league. By May 2012 nearly three million had been produced (including Golf Plus) over almost four years.

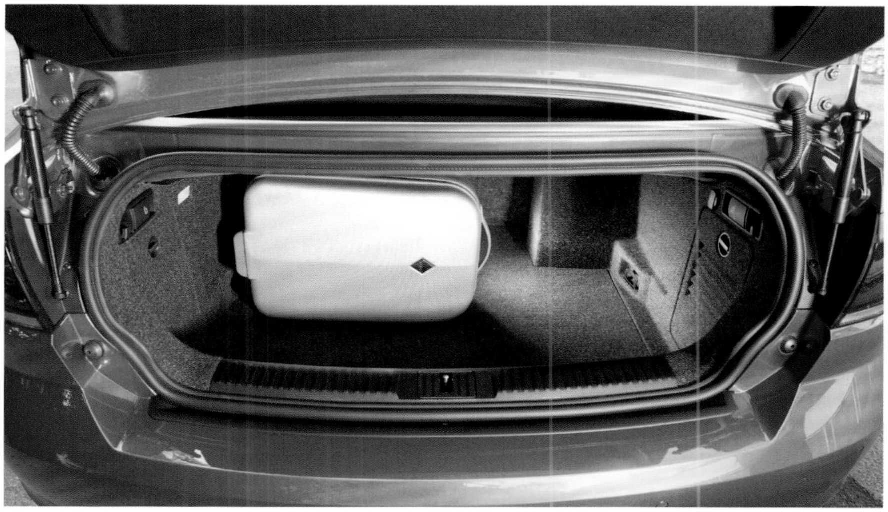

↑ Offering more space than the larger Eos, the cabrio's boot folded and split 50/50.

← In March 2011 Volkswagen Osnabrück GmbH (formerly Karmann) was once more making the car it helped to create. Then it employed 1,800 people and was preparing for overflow production of the Porsche Boxster and Cayman.

WOB GO 507

Golf 7
2012

Definitive?

Summer 2012 and a presentation of the latest Golf to 700 selected guests at Berlin's national gallery in early September before a full public showing in Paris. A parade of Golfs from 1974 arrived in the hall before the big moment as number seven entered through a mist of dry ice. This Golf was at first glance reassuringly familiar but in fact almost all-new: safer, quieter and above all more economical and lighter. 'It's not just the next Golf' one of the print adverts said.

As before, the Audi A3 had been a curtain raiser, first and foremost for the new platform on which it and the Golf were constructed, the widely anticipated MQB system *Modularer Querbaukasten*, translated as Modular Transverse Matrix (see panel on page 248) for more detail). Although customers may not have been all that interested by this, it was a potent corporate symbol of Volkswagen Group innovation and laid out its future plans. Taking component sharing to new heights, MQB provided the basis of cars from Polo to Passat size with petrol, diesel, hybrid, dual fuel or electric power and significantly drove down weight. It could expand or contract in nearly every dimension. 'Normally we already have the engines and platform ready and we develop a new top hat and interior,' Stefan Yung, technical project manager for the Golf, told *Automotive Engineer*. 'But this Golf was, as we say in Germany a *grüne wiese* – a greenfield project.'

In 2011 the Volkswagen Group had set out 'Strategy 2018' aimed at positioning the Volkswagen Group as a 'global economic and environmental leader' – and that meant beating Toyota and General Motors, first and second at the time.

In the 38 years leading to the Golf 7, this family hatchback had played the biggest part in transforming a company teetering on the brink in 1974. At the time of the Golf 7's debut, the first three-quarters of 2012 had seen 3.6 million Volkswagen cars sold, up 9.7% over the previous year. A million Audis had been sold in Europe and North America. The group had finally taken

↓ By 2012 and Golf 7, Volkswagen was proud of its continuity and heritage. Here the trademark solid rear three-quarter panel or 'C' pillar can be seen in all its permutations.

over Porsche, its 12th brand. Group sales to September 2012 stood at 6.9 million vehicles with ever-increasing manufacture in China. Impressive figures in a climate where new car sales were considered to be shrinking. For context, in the painful year of 1974, as US sales plummeted and the Golf started to take hold, group sales had still been around 3.3m with only two brands (not counting NSU) and a far smaller range of cars.

Expected to be the benchmark car for its class once more, the Golf faced new rivals other than the Focus and Astra, especially in the higher price segments. In 2012 Mercedes gave up on two generations of the boxy but space-efficient A-Class to produce a more conventional front-drive hatchback much more along the lines of the Golf and BMW was fielding a second-generation version of its rear-drive 1-Series in hatch, coupe and convertible versions, but the biggest volume threat was from Korea. Hyundai's i30 and its sister car the Kia C'eed were designed and built in Europe (the latter styled by former VW designer Peter Schreyer) and were seen as closing the gap on quality and driver appeal at a lower price.

↑ A Golf is presented to the press at the Paris Motor Show 2012, with the GTI again previewed as a 'concept'. (Author)

However, Volkswagen claimed that thanks to the component sharing made possible by the MQB system it was not any more expensive to own this all-new Golf. At launch in Germany a 1.2 TSI 85PS Trendline (S in the UK) cost 16,975 Euros, exactly the same as the superseded 80PS car. Buyers were in addition getting features such as a 5in touchscreen display, a stop-start system and an electronic parking brake.

But there was plenty of price competition within the Volkswagen Group and the motoring journalists' favourite game of spotting the differences between a Golf and its siblings was in play early on. The new SEAT Leon had been unveiled in June 2012 and went on sale later in the year. At the Paris show the Volkswagen Group took an entire hall for its brands so you could wander from Audi A3 to Golf to Leon and to Škoda. SEAT was struggling with falling sales in the recession-hit Spanish market and the Leon was seen as a crucial car to its survival, accompanied by a new Toledo (a re-badged version of the Škoda Rapid, which also used many Golf parts). Unlike the previous generation, the Leon was also to be offered as a three-door and as an estate, inviting further Golf comparisons. A new Škoda Octavia built on the MQB platform appeared at the March 2013 Geneva Motor Show.

MQB – magic letters?

In one sense the concept of a shared base on which different types of car are built is as old as the car itself. When the chassis was separate you could plonk anything you wanted on top, but the advent of the integrated steel bodyshell (or monocoque) meant the floorpan dictated where the wheels, windscreen, engine and seats had to be. As customers wanted more variety so the number of platforms multiplied.

Because of its pre-war origins the Beetle lived on with a separate chassis but with the Golf – particularly the fourth generation – Volkswagen was a pioneer in designing a monocoque substructure capable of being the base for anything from sports cars to estates. The first Golf, Jetta and Scirocco came from the same floorpan and with every generation of Golf every other Volkswagen had a bit more Golf componentry in it.

The philosophy behind MQB – standing for *Modularer Querbaukasten*, (Modular Transverse Matrix) – dates as far back as 1993 when Ferdinand Piëch (see Chapter 5) started the Volkswagen Group's first platform strategy to spin off Škodas, Audis and SEATs from a Golf structure.

Dr Ulrich Hackenberg, made company head of development coordination in 2013, was reported to have been nurturing the MQB idea for three decades. He had worked on technical development since he joined Audi in 1985 and became best known for developing the new Bentleys. Back at Audi, he developed the 'modular longitudinal system' in use from 2007, at which point Volkswagen CEO Martin Winterkorn finally committed to develop the concept for the whole group. MQB was formally announced in February 2012 as the future basis for the Volkswagen Group A0 to B segment cars, from the Polo to the Volkswagen (Passat) CC.

Although the practice of sharing hidden componentry such as door locks and window motors was not new, MQB took the idea of a platform much further. Cars from the 1990s had been on the whole obliged to share the same wheelbase, track between the wheels and 'hard points' such as the centre of the floorpan, wheel-arch linings, suspension and engine mounts and body side-members.

MQB swept these constraints aside. While much of the frontal structure containing the engine mounts, suspension and the pedal positions were the same, beyond these the length, width, height and seating position of a car could all be changed, thus for example the new Škoda Octavia's wheelbase was 50mm longer than that of the Golf. You could make different cars from different brands in different sizes on the same production line.

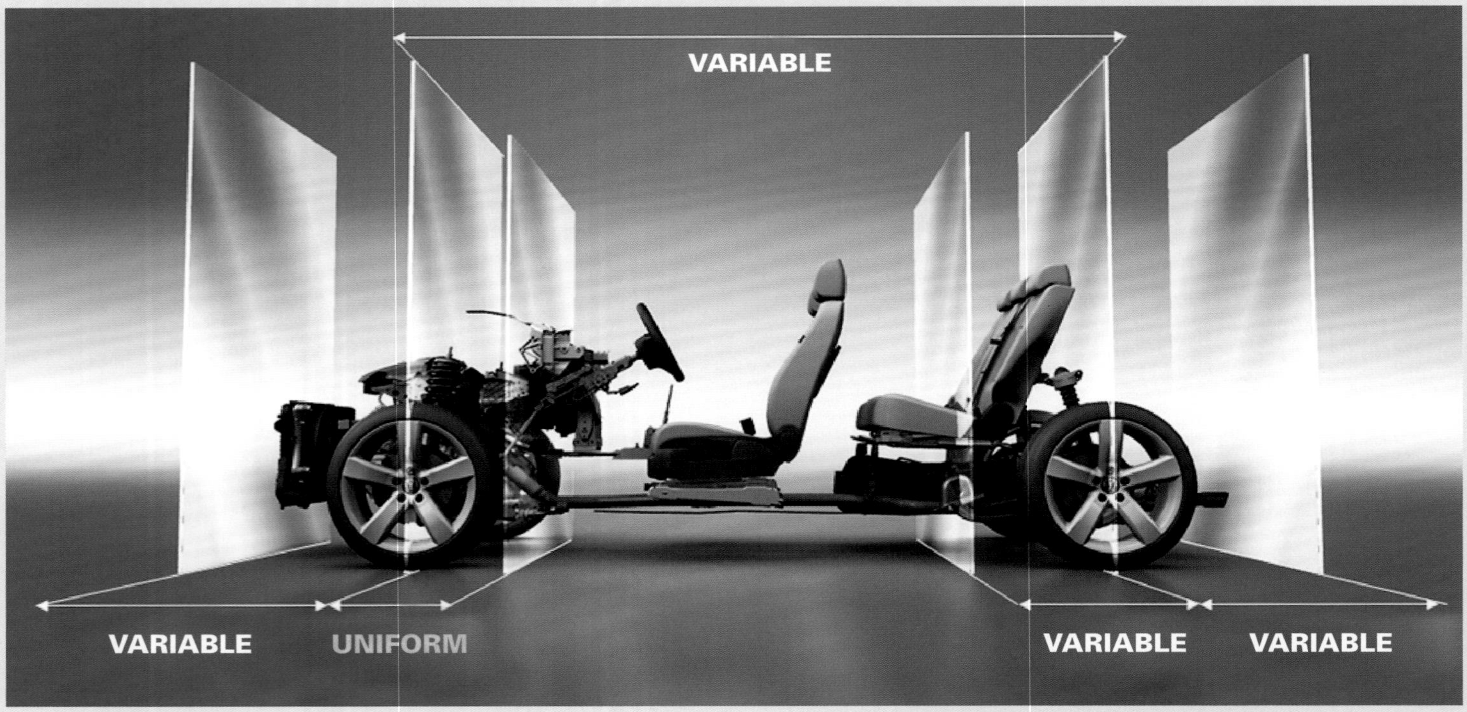

➔ Its home still very firmly in Wolfsburg, the new Golf had the latest production techniques applied to it. Rotating cradles helped comfortable assembly.

⬋ This illustrates the degree to which the platform for the new Golf could cater for many different sizes and types of vehicle.

The era of one factory being home to one model was ending. If demand for one car fell, another would take its place.

One of the key characteristics of MQB was the uniform mounting position of all engines. The new EA211 and EA288 series was claimed to have reduced the group's engine and gearbox variants by approximately 90%. Gearboxes, steering systems, electronics and infotainment systems could all be mixed and matched, as could exhaust-gas treatment components (catalysts, particulate filters) to meet varying legislation. Although completely different in looks and size, a Volkswagen Passat and a SEAT Leon could in future comprise up to 90% shared parts from the window motors to the air conditioning.

To be implemented over four years from 2012, MQB also demanded that Volkswagen's factories were re-equipped, bringing a total cost estimated at more than $60 billion. The first product was the Audi A3, the next far more important in sales terms, the Golf. The next-generation Škoda Superb, bigger than the Octavia and the Passat would also use MQB as would future products built at Volkswagen's American and Mexican plants.

The competition

Although many Volkswagen parts had been interchangeable since the late 1990s and Piëch's drive for commonality, rival carmakers took a long time to catch up. According to Reuters, in 2008 Renault and Nissan executives lifted the hoods on several VW Group vehicles side by side. 'They had the same engines, the same clutches, the same ventilation – all identical parts,' said an executive who attended the presentation. 'It was a level of commonality that didn't exist at Renault-Nissan.' In 2011 Peugeot-Citroen (PSA) board members were reportedly shocked when technicians took apart the front ends of two different VW cars and swapped most of their components.

Forced by recession and the need to build 'global' cars, other manufacturers developed their own platform strategies and felt obliged to showcase them. Thus Peugeot-Citroen based its 2013 Golf-competitor Peugeot 308 on the Efficient Modular Platform 2 (five wheelbases, four track widths) and in 2013 Renault-Nissan announced the Common Module Family, which would be used across five continents in more than ten countries to 2020, the first use covering 1.6 million vehicles a year and 14 models.

MQB – magic letters? (continued)

The ambition and the risks

Volkswagen's plan was to build 40 vehicles from MQB, accounting for annual production of more than four million cars. The scale was massive because so was the Volkswagen Group. 'This year we're likely to be below the 1 million mark regarding vehicles based on the MQB,' chief financial officer Hans Dieter Poetsch told *Boersen-Zeitung* in September 2013. 'The number should double to nearly 2 million vehicles in 2014. For 2016, we are expecting about 4 million vehicles.'

As well as the flexibility of MQB, this scale of use impressed analysts. In 2013 global financial advisor Morgan Stanley examined the 'titans' of the auto industry (Toyota, General Motors, Volkswagen and Hyundai-Kia) and reported that VW and Hyundai were already making most cars per platform (about 600,000) and that MQB could potentially save Volkswagen $18 billion a year by 2019. And it was only part of the story; MQB covered only transverse-engined front-drive models from the Polo. There were other platforms designed on similar principles for others; the NSF (New Small Family) would be for small cars based on the Volkswagen Up, Audi used MLB for cars with longitudinal engines and front-, four- or rear-wheel drive – including Bentley, while Porsche had MSB, a sports car tool kit.

What was the benefit for the customer? They didn't need to know what MQB or any of the other acronyms stood for but Volkswagen explained that it meant more choice, enhanced comfort and more features once reserved only for luxury cars. It made cars safer and protected the environment through weight saving and allowing alternative drivetrains. "No-one really cares that an A3 and an Octavia are basically the same under the skin. "It is all VW" is not really a problem if VW is a highly respected company,' Says British automotive analyst Jay Nagley.

Some analysts though warned there was a danger in spreading luxury features to lower-priced brands such as Škoda as it would dilute its 'cheap and cheerful' niche and cannibalise sales of more expensive and profitable brands. Perhaps the biggest danger was in using a component across very many models, which then developed a fault and triggered a massive recall – a fate that befell Toyota.

↑ With the Spanish brand SEAT struggling, the new Leon was allowed to provide increased in-house competition for the Golf with a greater choice of body styles.

← The Audi A3 was the first MQB product, launched ahead of the Golf but at first only as a three-door. Its styling was similarly evolutionary.

Same but quite different

If you looked hard, here was an apparently lower, sleeker Golf. The Golf 4 was once more referenced as a benchmark in styling and it appeared as though the 2012 version was what it might have looked like had it continued without diversion into the rounded forms of the 2003–2008 series.

As ever, the dimensions were constrained by where Europe's favourite hatchback sat in the Volkswagen pecking order, but at 4,255mm the seventh Golf was 56mm longer than its predecessor, with a 59mm longer wheelbase at 2,637mm.

The MQB platform allowed the front wheels to be placed 43mm further forwards, which helped interior space and also gave the stylists the chance to be relatively radical within Golf constraints. At the Berlin press launch Walter de Silva was joined by lead exterior designer Marc Lichte and Klaus Bischoff, Volkswagen head designer. 'Visually, the passenger compartment has moved towards the rear, creating what is called a "car-backward" impression,' said Bischoff. 'That's what we call the proportions of premium-class vehicles, on which the bonnet is long and the passenger compartment a long way towards the back. On the new Golf we thus have proportions that you otherwise only get in higher-class segments of the market.' It was also 13mm wider at 1,799mm, and 28mm lower at 1,452mm. There was a claimed 10% improvement in the drag coefficient at 0.27, the lowest ever for a Golf. If you looked closely, one styling feature had returned from the Golf 1 and 2; an extra pane of glass above the door mirrors in the angle between the windscreen and the top of the door.

As was the tradition, customers and commentators either loved the Golf's looks because they had only subtly changed, or hated them for the same reason. A Golf had not been crowned European Car of the Year since 1992 but was once more victorious in 2012, the first of a string of accolades. 'Honestly, I wouldn't know what to criticise about this car,' wrote German judge Ulla Elmer. 'Among the finalists it seems the most complete one to me. Some may call the body design uncharismatic or even boring, I find it perfectly classless.'

'The current Golf is a remarkably well designed car because it expresses all the philosophy of VW,' Patrick Le Quément, former group director of corporate design told the author in 2012. 'It has gone beyond being robust, touching on perfection in terms of suggesting extremely good fit and finish. It looks extremely precise, like German engineering.'

Enforced weight loss

As predicted in 2008, the billions invested in MQB had been aimed at reducing weight across the range and improving emissions, both to meet legislative requirements and to cement Volkswagen's image as an environmental leader. By 2015 the average CO_2 figure of all cars sold in Europe had to be 130g/km and would be 95g/km by 2020. Radical solutions had to be found and high-volume Volkswagen models had to subsidise the thirst of Bugattis and Lamborghinis.

The new Golf press material gave a selection of examples where components had shed weight. The air conditioning weighed 2.7kg less through changes in the thickness of various system component walls, reduced-diameter pressure lines and a new heat exchanger. The new seats saved up to 7kg depending on version, especially the rear backrests with lighter latch mechanisms. The bare bodyshell weighed 23kg less.

The fuel tank had shrunk from 55 to 50 litres, which was fine as the fuel economy had improved once more, but this also helped to reduce some weight figures as it held less fuel for official measurements. Relative to the competition, *Autocar* listed the kerb weight (with a full tank) of a new UK-market Golf 2.0 TDI SE at 1,354kg compared to a similar Ford Focus at 1,421kg. The comparison was not quite so marked against the 1,395kg of a BMW 118d Sport.

However, comparing old to new Golf on UK brochure specifications, a 2008 1.4 S (122PS) three-door had a stated unladen weight of 1,205kg and a 2012 1.2 S three-door (122PS) 1,225kg. This was not all it seemed as both car's unladen weight was measured 90% full of fuel but the 2008 car had no driver (deemed to weigh 68kg). The 2012 car, in accordance with the then current EU directive, added that driver and 7kg of luggage. The actual like-for-like weight was in fact 1,205 vs 1,150kg minus a small amount of fuel.

So although much quoted in road tests, the 100kg headline weight figure took some unpicking. Perhaps all the customer really needed to know was that the new Golf used less fuel by whichever means. It also has to be said that other carmakers started to make similar weight loss claims with each new model.

A minor engine revolution

The greatest overall weight loss was claimed to be the Golf's new range of petrol and diesel engines, which could weigh up to 40kg less mainly by all-aluminium cylinder blocks replacing cast iron. They were either major redesigns or all-new series. Only the six- and-seven speed DSG automatic gearboxes came across unchanged from the previous generation.

The new EA211 series replaced the EA111 engines, but those themselves had been vastly developed since their 1974 namesake had appeared. In the Golf 7 the EA211 series was first presented in 1,197 or 1,390cc displacements, all with turbochargers and intercoolers (developed with Bosch Mahle and Mitsubishi Heavy Industries).

The path to the EA211 had started with the twin-charged 1.4 TSI engine of 2006. It was a complete redesign based on an aluminium cylinder block. The exhaust manifold was integrated into the cylinder head to speed up warming times and help exhaust gas flows with a smaller-diameter turbocharger reducing weight further.

A Golf tradition where the smaller engines were mounted differently to the larger ones came to an end as EA211 rotated from the traditional position where the exhaust manifold had faced forwards to be inclined rearwards towards the bulkhead. It meant the driveshaft and gearbox mounting position could be standardised. Dozens of small design changes had been made so the engine took up as little space as possible, with items like the water pump bolted directly to the engine instead of a bracket. As had been the case on previous BlueMotion models 'reducing internal friction' was much bandied around and to this end the chain driving the overhead camshafts on the late versions of EA111 was replaced by a toothed belt, which Volkswagen assured sceptics would last the life of the vehicle. The EA211 family also included three-cylinder engines for the Volkswagen Up.

The Golf launch line-up was a 1.2-litre TSI 85PS eight-valve unit from the Polo, later joined by a 105PS version, then a 16-valve 1.4-litre TSI with 122 or 140PS. Combined fuel economy figures for these ranged from 54.3 to 57.6mpg with CO_2 emissions from 113g/km to 120. Illustrating that power outputs for these engines was governed primarily by the engine-management unit, German tuner ABT pretty soon offered reconfiguration of the 85 to 105PS and to 165PS from the 140.

Engine downsizing was now common even among luxury brands, which increasingly had the facility to shut down banks of cylinders at lower and cruising speeds. Now there was a Golf with a 1.4-litre turbocharged EA211 engine of 140PS featuring Active Cylinder Technology (ACT). From 2012 the system started to be used across the group from the Polo to the Lamborghini Aventador. However, Volkswagen UK opted to offer the ACT engine as the only petrol unit for the high-spec Golf GT model (the equivalent was Highline in Germany, which also offered ACT in the next trim down, Comfortline).

Working between an engine speed range of 1,400 and 4,000rpm (so over a broad range of road speeds

including 70 to 80mph) the fuel supply to the middle (second and third) cylinders would be shut off and the intake and exhaust closed by electromechanical actuators engaging a specially shaped part of the camshaft, then fire up again should the driver press the accelerator hard. These mechanical switchover processes were claimed to take place within one camshaft rotation – depending on engine speed, 13 to 36 milliseconds. The engine-management system adjusted the ignition and throttle settings to smooth the transitions and the road testers concurred that the change was indeed almost imperceptible with only a dashboard light showing when two-cylinder mode was operating (although some found it didn't happen very often). When the ACT unit was voted best new engine of 2013 Volkswagen made the point that it was only possible with the TSI concept of petrol direct injection plus turbocharging. The claimed combined fuel consumption figure of this petrol engine bettered some diesels at 60.1mpg.

The twin-charged 160PS TSI engine was no longer fitted to the Golf and the next highest petrol-powered version in the new line up was the 2.0-litre EA888 unit from the previous generation, with a new cylinder head design destined for the GTI and a standard power output of 220PS with a 'performance pack' option of an extra 10 with upgraded brakes and a limited-slip differential.

Although the difference in emissions and economy was becoming less marked between petrol and diesel,

↑ The production Golf BlueMotion once more drove down diesel consumption and in November 2013 one example managed 93mpg. Aerodynamic aids were less marked than Golf 6.

↑ **At the unveiling of the Golf BlueMotion in Paris, pressure group Greenpeace unfurled a banner reading Volkswagen *nous enfume!* (Volkswagen makes us smoke!) at the top of the stand to muted effect. It had argued the company was opposing tougher emissions laws. (Author)**

many countries enjoyed a price advantage at the pumps. There was also a range of Volkswagen TDI engines that earned a new designation of EA288. The switch having been made to common-rail fuel injection with the Golf 6, the induction system for the turbocharger benefitted from some of the new design features of the petrol engines and reached operating temperature more quickly.

All 16-valve four-cylinder units with turbochargers, the diesels ranged from a 1.6-litre with outputs of 90 to 110PS to a 2.0-litre offering 150 to 184PS in the GTD. Combined fuel consumption was 62.8 to 74.3mpg with the base 1.6 emitting just 98g/km of CO_2. With each new generation of Golf Volkswagen set itself the task of making the basic diesel emit the same as or less than the previous BlueMotion with all its modifications. In any case, the 'BlueMotion Technology' badge was now liberally spread around the boot lids of Golfs and all models were fitted with a stop-start system and battery regeneration plus a visual indicator of the best economy gear to be in within the multifunction computer in front of the driver.

Nonetheless, there still had to be a flagship economy Golf and the next BlueMotion was unveiled as a concept in Paris 2012 then fully at Geneva the following March. Sporting the usual suspension lowered by 10mm, a blocked-out radiator grille and spoilers on the roof and C-pillars, the claimed fuel consumption was 88.3mpg on the combined cycle and CO_2 emissions were 85g/km. The 2007 Golf BlueMotion had returned 62.8mpg with emissions of 119g/km. The 2012 iteration was also endowed with a six-speed gearbox for the first time.

How close did it get to that 88mpg claim in real life? In autumn 2013 *Autocar* matched it with a Ford Focus Econetic and a Toyota Auris hybrid. Illustrating a growing customer annoyance at the disparity between fuel figures from official test procedures and regular driving, the magazine returned an overall figure of 66mpg, although by wafting along at an inconvenient 50mph over nearly 16 hours, 82.6mpg was attained. If you were a UK buyer you would then have to factor in a £1,215 price premium over a regular 1.6 TDI. Turning to other methods of propulsion, electric and hybrid Golfs were, after decades of experiment, not far away (see Appendix 1).

With the Golf 6 having sold on its refinement, the seventh had to maintain this serenity while not resorting to heavy sound-deadening materials. However, as the car was virtually all new many components such as the engine induction systems, suspension and subframes benefitted from acoustic tests as they were being designed. It was recognised that with less wind noise and outside noise kept out by the sealing of the bodyshell the occupants of a new Golf might notice more ancillary noises such as the heater blower or the turbochargers, so these were tackled directly. The sound damping film between two layers of windscreen glass was carried over.

Low-tech: return of the torsion beam

For the first time ever, the Golf was offered with two types of rear suspension. The front suspension stayed true to the MacPherson strut and lower-wishbone principle while at the rear there was either a multi-link set-up or a 'modular lightweight suspension', which marked the return of the simple torsion beam, albeit engineered to the latest standards. Applied only to Golf models with power under 122PS, there was a manufacturing saving and the MQB system was flexible enough for both types of suspension to be fitted on the same production line. There was also a weight saving of 11kg over the multi-link unit.

Given that Bernd Pischetsrieder had felt obliged to follow the Ford Focus and endow the Golf 5 with its first multi-link rear suspension as a matter of prestige, and only the cheaper US 2010 Jetta had been downgraded to a torsion beam, this was potentially more difficult to explain to Europeans on the high-tech Golf 7.

Indicating that the changeover point to multi-link rear suspension according to engine power was perhaps more down to price and marketing than the abilities of the torsion beam, the SEAT Leon was fitted with it for versions of over 150PS and the Škoda Octavia only received it for the 220PS vRS, a Golf GTI in Škoda clothes. 'Around 75% of all Mk7 Golfs sold in the UK will have simpler suspension,' *Car* magazine noted. 'You might not notice the difference on an 84bhp 1.2, but the bean counters in Wolfsburg will.'

High-tech

While the market for large family cars like the Ford Mondeo was in terminal decline as buyers turned to Golf-sized hatchbacks and MPVs in their desire for fuel economy, there was an inverse appetite for luxury features. While only four years earlier the Golf 6 had appeared to offer all the comforts of a mini-Phaeton, the 2012 Golf could be specified with even more technology and the standard equipment list grew yet again.

All dashboards had touchscreen systems as standard to operate the DAB digital radio, CD and MP3 players plus a mobile phone, starting in the UK with a 5.8-inch colour display system and rising to satellite navigation with an 8-inch colour display. It operated with the same kinds of finger gestures people were using on their mobile phones, sensed the approach of a finger and presented the choices available.

Where once there had been a large lever only a small square button indicated the presence of a handbrake. Instead of being activated by a cable, the brakes to the rear wheels were activated by two electric motors once the button was pulled upwards. To drive away you pressed the brake pedal and flipped the button again.

This starter British-specification Golf S dashboard is far from austere. The centre console was now angled more towards the driver. Colour touchscreen was standard and your iPod/phone could be connected and hidden in a compartment below.

↑ Like mobile phones, the touchscreen worked by swiping and pushing movements of the fingers, and could be used to display album artwork.

→ The radar sensor for City Braking and Adaptive Cruise Control had to be heated to keep it clear of ice and snow.

↑ Like some of its rivals, the new Golf banished the handbrake lever for a small button.

An auto hold function applied the brake if the car rolled while stationary and would enable the driver to perform a hill start. Again this was a feature that had trickled down from upper-range Audis, the Passat and Tiguan. The 2009 Opel/Vauxhall Astra also featured an electronic handbrake, so there was keeping up to be done.

The benefits of a button handbrake were more space in the centre console and a further contribution to vehicle weight loss. However, such gadgets were not universally liked by car buyers, some of whom bemoaned their complexity and potential repair costs. A 2012 survey of 21,000 British Automobile Association (AA) members showed many longed for simpler cars; 70% (mostly men) saying they could do without an electronic handbrake.

Of course the MQB Golf platform enabled easy sharing of such technology but it was rationed by brand. The Audi A3 had the same parking button as the Golf but when you went down the pecking order the SEAT Leon and Škoda Octavia had a traditional lever.

Golf passive safety was catered for by seven airbags as before with standard anti-lock brakes and ESC stability control extended to provide the same electronic differential lock previously fitted to the GTI and GTD, which was claimed to improve traction and handling through bends. Called XDS, an uprated version was fitted to the new GTI and GTD.

All new Golfs came with a multi-collision brake system, which had come via the Passat and Audi A3. Activated by signals from deployed airbags, after a collision the brakes were automatically applied to minimise the chance of a second impact if the car was hit again. From Comfortline/SE trim upwards a system detected the possibility of an accident, pre-tensioned the seatbelts and closed the windows and sunroof.

So MQB didn't just allow various types of body structures, it allowed a plethora of electronic systems to be shared around. To begin listing a few of the new technical names for gadgets on the Golf 7 (each given capital letters), Automatic Distance Control (or intelligent cruise control) was now a radar-based system available on UK market cars where the car would cruise at a set distance from the vehicle in front. It was combined with Front Assist, which on its own could warn the driver if they were getting too close and at low speeds City Emergency Braking would halt the car. If a DSG gearbox

↓ The Golf 7 was judged to have succeeded in combining performance, economy, refinement and good handling. Awards arrived almost immediately. (LAT)

↑ **The company claimed a boot sill height of 665mm was the lowest in the Golf segment. The slots at the sides of the boot enabled the height of the floor to be raised or lowered, depending on the load. (LAT)**

→ **Rear legroom was increased by a longer wheelbase but a central tunnel remained in the floor for four-wheel-drive variants.**

was fitted the car could start itself up and drive away. Insurance companies liked this very much and in Britain the insurance groupings were lowered across the range.

A Driver Alert System, as on the Passat, could detect signs of tiredness in the driver while a camera-operated Lane Assist system kept the car in a specific lane while the Dynamic Light Assist system dropped the headlamps onto dipped beam automatically when it detected another car approaching on full beam.

For the first time, driver profile selection allowed the user to select Eco, Sport, Normal and Individual modes by changing the throttle mapping and engine management to their chosen style. Bringing back the old concept of freewheeling, when a DSG gearbox was fitted on the Eco setting it dropped into coasting in neutral under certain conditions. The Park Assist option had evolved to offer parallel parking and reverse parking at right angles to the road.

The reception

As soon as the road tests were out it was clear that Volkswagen had a success on its hands once more. All were respectful and some were not so much road test verdicts as eulogies. Andrew English of the *Daily Telegraph* and a Car of the Year judge wrote: 'And then you drive the Golf… and everything else feels that bit less well thought out, less well put together and just a bit (not much, but a bit) less good.'

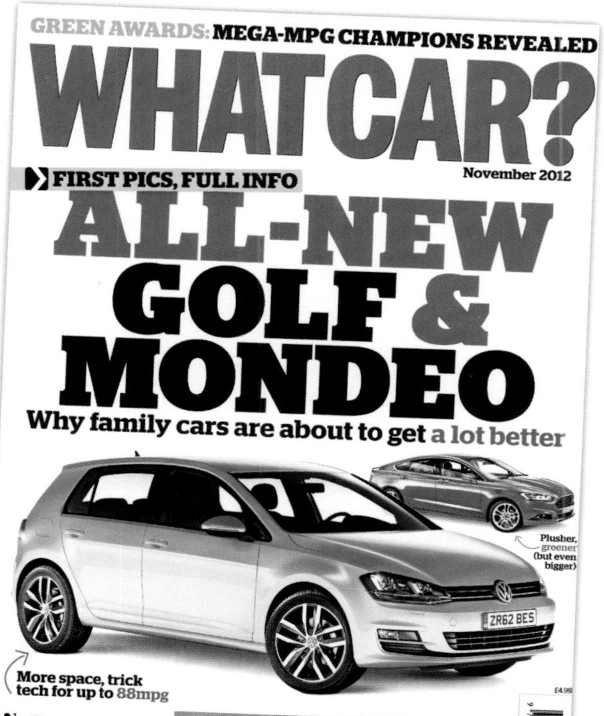

← When Europe's top-selling car is renewed, it's front page news. (Author's collection)

The famously unforgiving Jeremy Clarkson found it impossible to say anything bad about his drive in a Golf 7 for the *Sunday Times*: 'Honestly, reviewing this car is like reviewing a floorboard. It's impossible to say anything other than: "it does what it's supposed to do."' In a contest which had been running for over a decade the worst people could say was that a Focus was still more involving to drive.

By mid-January 2013 when it had newly gone on sale in the UK, European Volkswagen dealers had taken over 100,000 orders for the new Golf. As might have been anticipated, Leon versus Golf was a popular contest with minute examinations of specifications, likely depreciation and quality. 'The new SEAT Leon has all the raw ingredients to succeed,' *Auto Express* declared after testing the cars as diesels in April 2013. 'Not only does it look great, it offers a classy interior, plenty of space and a composed driving experience. However, it can't quite match the VW for refinement, comfort and premium appeal. So it's another win for the Golf, then? Not quite. Even if you take into account its long kit list, the VW struggles to justify a £2,010 premium over the £18,490 SEAT. In 1.6 TDI SE guise, the Leon is a very desirable family car.'

GTI – overdeveloped?

The 2013 Geneva Motor Show saw the performance and practical Golfs ready for sale, the GTI having been previewed in Paris the previous year. As well as much all-new hardware the seventh GTI created more than the usual excitement because Volkswagen let it be known that it had called on the expertise of Porsche to fettle its suspension and handling. The GTI was still very important, taking between 10 and 12% of Golf customers.

Aside from special editions, for the first time Volkswagen offered the turbocharged 2.0-litre GTI with two power levels: the standard 220PS (up 10 on the Golf 6) and the GTI Performance Pack with 230PS, larger brake discs and a mechanical front limited-slip differential (lower-powered Golfs had the XDS electronic differential). Even though this GTI was lighter the headline performance improvements were relatively small; the standard car claimed 62mph in 6.5 seconds rather than 6.9 and a top speed of 152mph, the GTI Performance 155mph and 6.4 seconds.

Both versions also had the stop-start system to meet 2014 EU-6 emissions standards and with combined fuel economy of 47mpg an 18% improvement compared to the previous model.

Unlike the XDS system where individual wheels were braked, the Haldex limited-slip differential on the Performance GTI consisted of a multi-plate coupler between the differential cage and right driveshaft, which controlled torque electro-hydraulically. It was intended to provide more 'neutral and agile' driving behaviour through bends, which meant the car was even less inclined to run wide at the front or spin from the rear. It was very difficult to come unstuck in a GTI.

The GTI and GTD both had a 'progressive' version of the electro-mechanical power steering, which varied the steering ratio so it became faster acting, winding on lock the quicker you went round a bend and then releasing it more quickly. On a standard Golf the wheel took 2.75 turns lock-to-lock and on the GTI Performance this was reduced to 2.1.

In mid-2013 a UK three-door standard GTI was

↓ *Autocar* judged the seventh GTI to be hugely competent but not greatly different from its predecessor. (LAT)

£25,845 or £26,825 with the Performance Pack, a premium which the road testers decided was well worth the money. The premium over other cars was still present though – about £5,000 more than the highly-regarded five-door Ford Focus ST. 'We'd certainly never suggest that it is in any way overkill,' wrote Neil Birkitt in *Volkswagen Driver* after sampling the Performance Pack, 'but you do need to be a driving enthusiast to fully appreciate and exploit its advantages, something which can only be done properly on a track day.'

Autocar rated the standard GTI hugely competent but third behind the Renault Mégane and Focus ST for thrills.

The Golf GTD continued to offer the same combination of looks as the petrol car and a performance jump from 170 to 184PS although it was the usual different kind of performance, with peak torque available between 1,750 and 3,250rpm and maximum power between 3,500 and 4,000rpm (petrol 4,700–6,200rpm) and 0–62mph in 7.5 seconds. There was no Performance Pack option but then there was a potential 67.3mpg.

↑ With 184PS the GTD was the closest it had ever been to matching the output of the petrol-engined GTI and in the UK was priced slightly lower.

← As before, muted greys for the GTD interior. This has the optional six-speed DSG automatic gearbox fitted, and the car still claimed to return 51.4mpg in town.

↑ The neatly-styled new estate was also available with 4Motion four-wheel drive for the first time, but not for the UK.

↓ Fastest-ever soft-top Golf: the R cabriolet had all the right details but its initial high price drew most attention.

The fifth estate

Accepting that the last two generations of Golf estates had arrived late in the day and that the Golf 6 was a heavy facelift of the fifth, Geneva 2013 saw the first all-new Golf estate in six years. With the hatchback already boasting an increased boot capacity and longer wheelbase, the estate's boot volume expanded from 505 to 605 litres and loaded up to the front seat backrests 1,620 litres (versus the 1,495 litres of the Golf 6). It looked better too with the distinctive C-pillar close to the design of the hatchback model and similar rear light clusters. The engine range started with the 1.2TSI 105PS petrol and for the first time it was available as a full 1.6 TDI BlueMotion model, with a claimed combined fuel consumption of 85.6mpg (87g/km of CO_2).

Two Rs

The GTI safely into the price lists, the enthusiasts' attention turned to the next Golf R and spy shots of cars testing started to appear in summer 2013. Meanwhile the Golf cabriolet – based on the now redundant platform of the Golf 5/6 – continued on sale and spawned an 'R' version, which met a somewhat mixed reception. Presented as a concept at Wörthersee in 2011, but only announced for production at the March 2013 Geneva show, its 2.0-litre engine produced 265PS. Connected to a standard six-speed DSG gearbox it had an electronically limited top speed of 155mph, with the benchmark 0–62mph sprint taking just 6.4 seconds. Of course this made it comfortably the fastest ever factory-produced Golf cabriolet with the very necessary XDS differential to stop the front wheels from steering themselves under hard acceleration.

It was lavishly equipped but what everybody noticed was the initial price of £38,770, some £8,000 more than a GTI cabriolet and almost double the differential that had ever been asked between the hatchbacks. This was Porsche Boxster money. Not long after delivery had started in June Volkswagen UK dropped the price by £5,600.

A spokesman said the original price had been set by the factory in Germany mid 2012, before the product team had its annual chance to negotiate the prices charged in the UK. 'The new cost is the price we'd have liked it to be, and where it should have been.' The 'handful' of customers who bought the R cabriolet at the earlier asking price were refunded the difference.

The 'proper' new Golf R was revealed at the October 2013 Frankfurt Motor Show. With its modified EA888 TSI engine it was now producing 300PS (296bhp), more than some contemporary Porsches and a very long way from the 50PS people's car of 1974. Having shed a claimed 45kg in three-door guise, 0–62mph (100kph) was claimed to be possible in an impressive 5.1 seconds.

The R's four-wheel-drive system had been seen on the 4Motion (once more not UK-bound), the fifth-generation Haldex system. Under low loads or when coasting, the rear axle was decoupled, helping to reduce fuel consumption. An electro-hydraulic pump was claimed to improve its engagement time. It also offered the Driver Profile Selection of other Golfs but with an extra setting: 'Race', which attenuated throttle response and altered the shift pattern of the DSG gearbox. The

GTI Vision

Five years after the W12-650 (see previous Chapter), Volkswagen yet again created an even more exaggerated GTI for Wörthersee, the 503PS Design Vision GTI. It was reported to have cost 4 million Euros (£3.4m) to build.

Based on the seventh-generation GTI, every styling element was pulled out and stretched to cartoon proportions, notably the C-pillar appearing to be detached. The only shared component was the windscreen. Future-looking and yet retro, beneath all the scoops and vents there was the straight line underneath the door handles from the first Golf whilst the rear three-quarter section was lifted from the fourth.

It was, however, closer to a real Golf than the W12-650, retaining the front engine position and highlighting how the MQB platform could be adjusted. Sitting on the same wheelbase, it was 15mm shorter than a production GTI, 57mm lower but 71mm wider with specially designed 20in wheels and suitably large 15in ceramic-disc brakes.

In the spirit of the VR6 a 3.0-litre V6 TSI with twin turbos sent drive to all four wheels via a 4Motion system and the unit was reported to be destined for the next-generation Passat. Although its headline power output was less than the 2007 car, a claimed 300kph (186mph) top speed with 0–62mph (100kph) in 3.9 seconds was – in relative terms – respectable.

Like the W12-650, it could be driven by the press to an accompaniment of glorious noise, albeit largely in a straight line because the wheels were not allowed to go onto full lock.

Volkswagen playfully suggested that it could form the basis of a racing series, and the interior was finished in Alcantara (fake suede) trimmed plastic panels. Rear seat space was taken by an X-shaped cross-member with stowage for two crash helmets.

The number of switches in front of driver and passenger was reduced to an artistic minimum while a large display in the centre console was said to be able to show the circuit the car was racing on and information about the times driven. It could communicate with other vehicles on the course and calculate the status of the race in real time.

↑ Its 3.0-litre twin-turbo V6 (a new generation under development) was in the front and transversely mounted. The neatness of the mouldings in the engine bay shows the vast cost expended in its construction.

← Looking like it had emerged from a comic book, the 2013 Design Vision GTI was still closer to a real Golf than the W12-650 had been, showcasing styling and the possibilities of the MQB system.

➔ **First driven by the press in January 2014 on a frozen lake in Sweden, the Golf R was again distinguished by a subtler approach to the GTI with a new front bumper design with larger air ducts.**

engine sound was tuned to appeal to the driver and for the first time for Europeans enhanced by a sound synthesiser under the bonnet.

The first press drives in January 2014 were in snowy Sweden, so more of a preview of the R's abilities. But it looked like being highly skilled on tarmac. 'There is a new-found agility and responsiveness to the whole car,' wrote *Autocar*'s Greg Kable, 'making it both terrific fun and, thanks to its outstanding traction and the fast-acting differentials, supremely secure, even at –26 deg C on a frozen Swedish lake.'

In June 2013, Golf production had reached 30 million. In December the 500,000th seventh-generation Golf was delivered, one year after the car had been launched. Production started in Puebla, Mexico in January 2014 and it was set to debut in China, the United States and be built in Brazil. The summer promised a new Golf Plus, the e-Golf and the Golf plug-in hybrid. There were rumours of a Golf Alltrack, a high-riding variant of Golf estate and a four-door 'Golf CC' coupe similar to the Passat CC.

The world's favourite car was showing no signs of slowing as it hit 40 in May 2014 having been Europe's best-selling car of 2013 with 470,229 sold. It had taken the concept of continuous improvement started by the Beetle to a far greater scale. The history of the modern motor car was the Golf: the front-drive five-door hatchback class; the diesel-engine revolution; the hot hatchback; safety; refinement and environmental awareness. That it appeared to never change its looks belied the fact that it was always changing the automotive world.

🡻 **Frankfurt 2013 saw the likely shape of the all-new Golf Plus, the original having survived in face-lifted and re-engined form since 2005. Called Sportsvan, it was unclear whether the Plus name would be used in production.**

Thoughts of Golf: what's its secret?

Stephen Bayley, design critic, 2013:
'Every new generation of Golf just enhances its Golfness. Like a living organism, it contains inherited and predictive genes. Like a Porsche, or a Leica, you need only look at a small detail to be able to understand the whole. That's one definition of a masterpiece.'

Carl Hahn, former Volkswagen chief executive, 2013:
'When you drive a VW it's like in the old Beetle days, nobody knows whether you are a billionaire, a millionaire but you must be a well-to-do guy. And you enter a certain club. You could belong to a certain class. This is why everybody pays a little more and finds by experience that he gets a little more, not only prestige but engineering.'

Ray Hutton, motoring journalist and author, 2012:
'Because they didn't change it very much and because it evolved rather than having revolutions, Volkswagen managed to achieve this kind of semi-premium status with the Golf. It became the solid benchmark for cars of that kind, and somewhere along the way, probably through the 90s, VW were able to achieve 10% or more premium over what should be exactly equivalent cars like Ford Escorts and Vauxhall Astras. None of the others could do it.'

Jeremy Clarkson, *Sunday Times*, January 2013:
'I sometimes wonder why anybody ever buys anything else. You want a fast car? Buy a Golf GTI. You want an economical car? Buy a Golf diesel. You want a cheap car? Buy a Golf from the second-hand columns. You want a big car? Buy a Golf Plus. You want a convertible car? Don't buy a Golf convertible. It's terrible. But do buy a Volkswagen Eos. Which is a Golf.'

Jay Nagley, automotive industry analyst, 2014:
'Rather prosaically, it is the right size – it is big enough for most people's needs, so it does not look like a car someone bought because they could not afford something bigger. If you see someone in a Polo, you might assume they would have preferred a Golf, but you do not tend to assume a Golf owner would have preferred a Passat.'

Prof. Dr Martin Winterkorn, Chairman of the Board of Management of Volkswagen AG, as the 25 millionth Golf was produced in 2007:
'To this day it is the only vehicle that has given its name to a whole class of vehicles...The Golf is and remains the heart of Volkswagen.'

← A Golf 7 awaits its public at the 2012 Paris Motor Show. The shape is already familiar. (Author)

Appendix 1: The hybrid and electric Golf

After decades of watching and waiting, in 2014 Volkswagen was finally ready to sell both an electric and a hybrid (petrol/electric) Golf in (hopefully) large numbers.

Experimental electric and hybrid Volkswagens had come and gone for decades while the company watched and weighed up the market for what it considered the right time to bring both of these choices into the mainstream. At the same time it tested alternative fuels such as methanol, biodiesel or hydrogen. Depending on the priorities of the day, electric and hybrid Golfs would be presented to the press as two possible answers to the problems of inner city pollution, dependency on fossil fuels, rising prices and latterly carbon dioxide emissions.

Electric cars were as old as the history of the horseless carriage but constrained by the weight and bulk of their batteries and small range. The internal combustion engine took over and dominated the 20th century. Every now and then when there were fuel shortages, electric vehicles would receive renewed attention, but range and speed would hold them back for decades.

During the 1950s and '60s a cottage industry grew up in the United States producing very small runs of electric cars and vans. Enterprising individuals made their own – the Volkswagen Beetle and Karmann Ghia were popular donor cars.

However, it was the American drive towards better safety and environmental standards for cars that really

➔ **An electric company backed the first small-scale trial of electric Golf 1s. (RWE Archiv)**

set the ball rolling, with Congress recommending in 1966 that electric cars were a way of tackling public concern about how to limit smog in towns and cities. Anti-pollution legislation followed. The immediate effect for European engines was to either have power-sapping emissions-control equipment bolted on or – as Volkswagen pioneered – fuel injection. Ford and General Motors showed a sudden enthusiasm for electric-car research towards the end of the decade as well but lost it with equal rapidity. No smaller company could withstand the unprofitable risk of mass electric-car production, so it remained in the background.

Towards the hybrid Golf

The idea of the hybrid has a distinct Volkswagen heritage. In 1898 Dr Ferdinand Porsche developed and built the first petrol-electric hybrid, the Lohner-Porsche Mixte Hybrid. It used an internal combustion engine to spin a generator that provided power to four 2.5–3.5bhp electric motors located in the wheel hubs. The car was said to have had a range of 40 miles on battery alone and the top speed was 30mph.

Once it had made its massive investment in research in the late 1960s Volkswagen devoted energies into alternatives to the traditional 'otto cycle' internal combustion engine such as rotary engines and gas turbines, and electric drive was an early subject.

Because of their range and bulk, electric and hybrid drives were only thought suitable for city-bound commercial vehicles at first and the Type 2 Transporter with its large underfloor compartments and rear drive was an ideal base. In the early 1970s German power company Rheinisch-Westfälisches Elektrizitätswerk AG (RWE) worked closely with Volkswagen and Daimler-Benz, and a company was set up to establish a network of electric 'filling stations'. You would remove flat batteries hidden beneath the load platform with a forklift truck and insert a fresh pack. A fleet of 200 Type 2s were planned for field testing and the electric Type 2 went on in various forms throughout the 1970s.

A Type 2 minibus was the basis of Volkswagen's first hybrid, the 1976 City Taxi, with a small electric motor fitted with a drive into the gearbox. The driver could choose pure electric or hybrid drive, but inefficiency in charging and a 265kg battery weight meant fuel consumption increased by 25%. Volkswagen didn't consider it a suitable basis for a passenger car, but nonetheless the City Taxi clocked up over 100,000 test kilometres (62,000 miles) and was shown throughout the world. At the same time Bosch was working on a hybrid Ford Escort estate.

The first hybrid Golf was created in 1983 – its drive system called EVW2 – on the basis of a 1982 first-generation Golf. Fitted with a four-speed manual gearbox with no clutch pedal, it would start under petrol power, which a control unit would favour for bursts of rapid acceleration and high speeds, but when stationary switch to electric power from a 200kg lead-acid battery and run on that alone for up to 22 miles. EVW2 featured regenerative braking, charging the battery from the energy under braking, a feature to be used in BlueMotion Golfs over 20

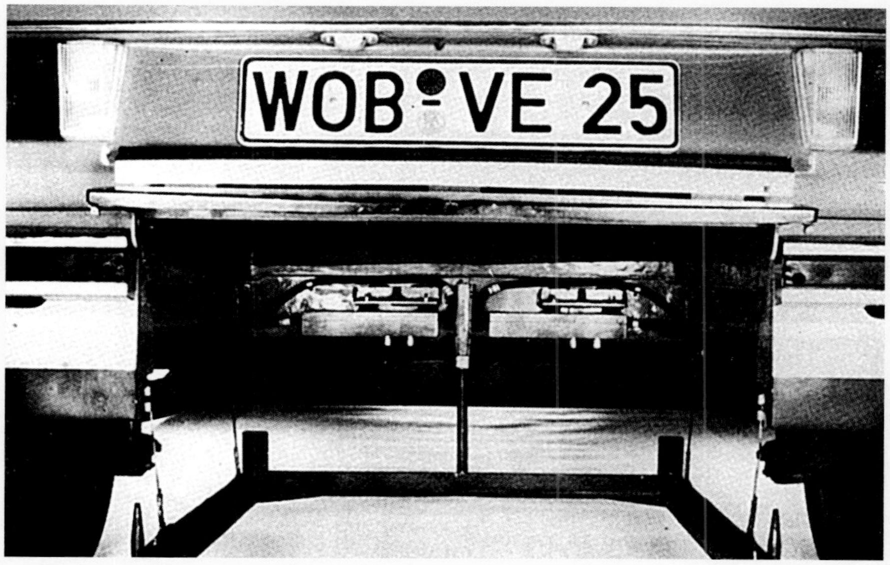

↑ Volkswagen's own early electric Golf received various combinations of battery, loading beneath the rear floor. (Author's collection)

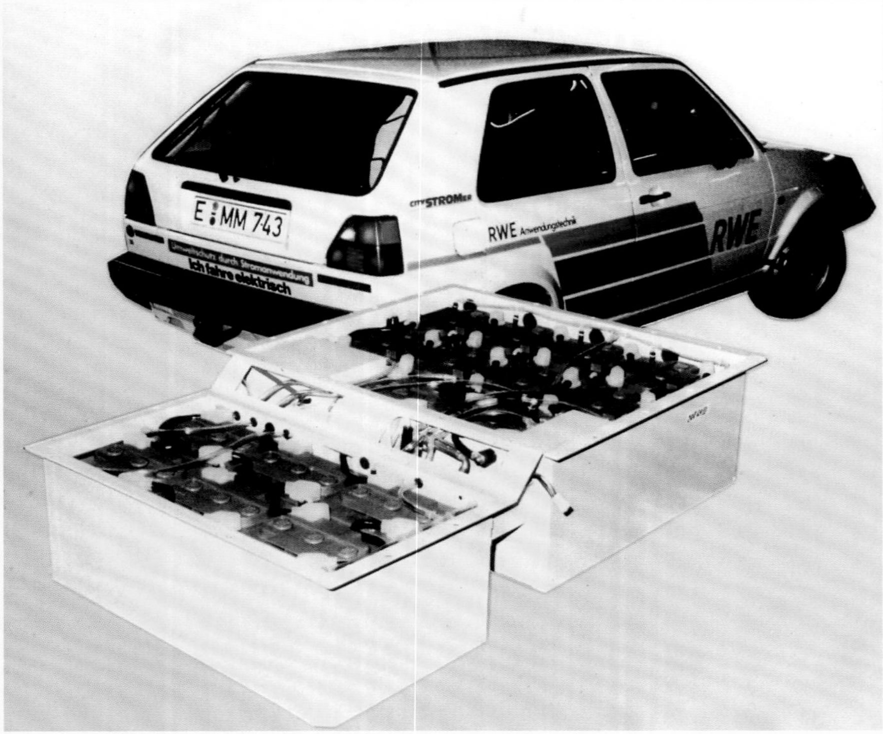

years later. However, the petrol engine didn't charge the battery, so for holidays Volkswagen engineers suggested that it could be removed for extra luggage space.

The next stage hybrid drive – EVW1 – was developed towards the end of the 1980s in conjunction with Bosch and integrated an electric motor/generator (replacing the alternator), which combined with the gearbox drive and took up only two inches more space than a regular Golf's combination. In this 'single shaft hybrid' the electric motor unit replaced the flywheel and a secondary clutch was used to isolate the engine. It would run on diesel, electric or shut itself down when coasting and use neither. The flywheel kept spinning when stationary in readiness to start the engine again when needed. A socket was provided for 'topping up' the battery, but a long motorway run would now also be capable of recharging.

It was tried in Golfs with petrol and diesel engines and in 1990 a 1.6-litre/diesel hybrid Golf 2 in rainbow colours was displayed at the Geneva Motor Show and Ulrich Seiffert, head of research and development, showed it at a technology conference that May. Built in collaboration

↑ RWE's 'compact' battery pack was a relative term for the 1980s electric Golf. (RWE Archiv)

→ The layout resembled a conventional car, with the electric motor up front and batteries taking the place of the fuel tank and spare wheel. (Volkswagen Classic)

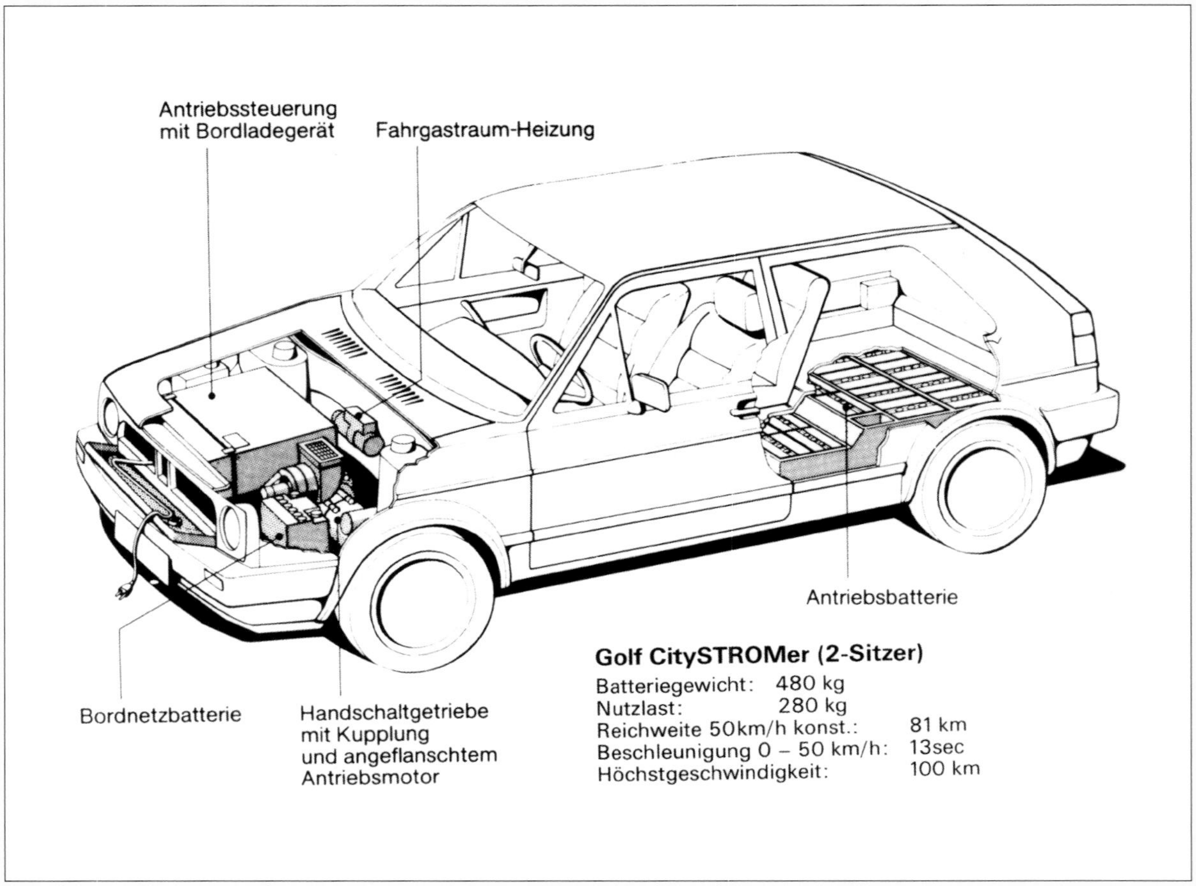

One of Volkswagen's early hybrids from the late 1980s. A number of companies sponsored the Swiss field tests. (LAT)

with Bosch and Swiss electrical company ENSA it would automatically cruise at 30mph in town on electric power and switch to diesel under acceleration. Under braking the electric motor became a generator and charged relatively small batteries under the boot floor. It was said to be capable of 113mpg, of going into immediate production and could sell for the price of a Golf GTI.

Between 1991 and 1993 a fleet of 20 Golf hybrids were tested by 40 private drivers in Zurich, and by December 1992 90% said they liked the automatic changeover system.

Autocar drove an example in early 1992 but was not impressed, finding that despite development since the previous year it was 'agonisingly' slow in electric-only mode (max 35mph) and the diesel engine would jolt back into life: 'Much work remains to be done if this type of drive is to be acceptable to the everyday driver.' The market for such a car was far from clear as Volkswagen engineers had admitted in a 1989 research paper, predicting an additional DM 10,000 premium, which would take ten years to claw back through fuel savings. It concluded: 'So the hybrid drive will hardly be able to find a market for itself today, just like the pure electric drive.'

Although it said correctly in 1992 that hybrid vehicles were more flexible than electric-only so more likely for full production, Volkswagen became increasingly sceptical about hybrid drive into the decade. It could have brought a purpose-built hybrid to the market with the innovative 1991 Chico city car project, its 6kW electric motor working with a two-cylinder 34bhp petrol engine but got cold feet about the Chico with any engine and hybrids in general. Under the direction of Ferdinand Piëch, Volkswagen poured its energies into fuel-saving techniques applied to conventional engines and fuel-sipping concepts with the 'one-litre' car philosophy (1 litre/100km = 282.5mpg). In real life the ill-fated Golf

This was an early example of a plug-in hybrid; the engine did not charge the battery pack – the owner did. (LAT)

↑ **The 2008 Golf TwinDrive was a further plug-in hybrid, its electric motor built into the transmission of a diesel engine and a smaller lithium-ion battery unit (below) in place of the boot.**

Ecomatic and the 94mpg Lupo 3L paved the way for BlueMotion Golfs.

Audi carried out hybrid research with the diesel/electric 1989 100 Avant duo, which applied electric power to the rear axle of the Quattro system. It was a simpler modification in response to an anticipated ban on internal combustion engines in towns. The 1997 A4 Avant duo was the first European hybrid to go into very limited production at a very high price. Just 60 were reported sold. Like the earlier Golf, the Audi studies previewed the plug-in hybrid concept in that the battery could be charged from a socket so could be consequently smaller.

Also in 1997 the automotive world was turned on its head with the arrival of the dumpy-looking Toyota Prius saloon, the first mass-produced petrol hybrid and gaining mass acceptance when it became a fashion accessory for Hollywood celebrities in the early 2000s. A completely new Prius arrived in 2003 and Toyota and Honda took the lead in affordable hybrid cars. By 2013 Toyota had sold over 5.5 million hybrid vehicles.

In 2008 Volkswagen publicly re-engaged with the hybrid Golf with the Golf TDI Hybrid design study at the Geneva Motor Show, combining a TDI diesel, electric-drive and a seven-speed DSG gearbox. Signalling that it was to enter the market, Volkswagen partnered with government for its four-year 'Fleet study in electric mobility' analysing the usage behaviour of drivers of cars with hybrid/electrical charging and providing that charge from renewable energy sources. Twenty Golf estates were dubbed TwinDrive research vehicles. Once more the entire drive unit was housed in the engine compartment: a 1.4 TSI petrol engine, generator, and electrically actuated clutch between the engine and one-speed transmission.

Pressure for a hybrid Golf was now irresistible. *Autocar* wrote at the launch of the sixth Golf in 2008 that 'Environmental pressures have fast-tracked plans for a Golf hybrid, being developed under the codename Leonardo. It is expected to pair a 102bhp 1.2-litre petrol engine with an electric motor driving the rear wheels.' However, 2010 saw the large off-roader Touareg become the first Volkswagen hybrid and in 2012 the Jetta hybrid followed (see Golf 6 chapter).

Finally, in 2014, thirty years after the first experiments, the Golf entered mass-production hybrid territory with a plug-in hybrid to complement the all-electric e-Golf. The press had been allowed to drive prototypes the year before, so the only thing that was somewhat of a surprise was the decision to market it as the Golf GTE, an environmentally-friendly sports model in the vein of the GTI.

Being a plug-in hybrid the Golf GTE differed from the Jetta in that the battery allowed all-electric drive for a greater distance because it could be supplemented by the owner charging the battery pack as well as the engine. It was an alternative to full electric if you had 'range anxiety' and Volkswagen had long stated this would be the most popular choice. 'Over the mid-term, the plug-in hybrid offers great potential, because it combines the best of two worlds in one vehicle,' said Martin Winterkorn in 2001. 'The plug-in hybrid offers precisely what many customers expect: unlimited internal combustion engine performance combined with attractive electric mobility ranges in everyday driving.' When the GTE completed the group of Golf power plants (including Compressed Natural Gas) a traditional hybrid Golf was absent as the Jetta provided that option.

By arriving late in the day, the hybrid and electric Golfs had benefitted from lithium-ion battery technology derived from mobile phones, which made them smaller, lighter and more powerful, combined with complex electronic control systems and a body structure (the MQB platform) designed for multiple power units across the brands. The GTE's fuel tank was relocated beneath the boot floor. There was still, however, a weight penalty. The battery weighed 120kg, giving the GTE a total kerbweight of 1,520kg compared to 1,270kg for a 1.4 GT.

The GTE had a 150PS 1.4-litre TSI petrol engine coupled to an electric motor within the gearbox rated at 75kW/102PS. Drive was channelled to the front wheels through a six-speed DSG gearbox designed for hybrid drive. When energy ran low, the engine management system engaged the engine and used the electric motor as an alternator to generate some energy for the battery.

When used together a combined maximum power of 204PS was quoted, a near-GTI figure for this heavier car, with a claimed 0–100 kph (62mph) figure of 7.6 seconds.

Volkswagen claimed the 350Nm maximum torque available from standstill of the Golf GTE set it apart from competitor plug-in hybrids (although that was not a very big field). For comparison, a diesel 184PS 2.0-litre Golf GTD produced 380Nm of torque from 1,1750rpm and made 100kph in 7.5 seconds.

The driver could interact/fiddle with all this technology via the largest 6.5-inch dashboard display in the Golf range, which could, like the Toyota Prius, show range and energy flow. With the 'e-manager' he or she could preset vehicle charging, as well as interior cooling or heating. These functions could also be operated remotely using a smartphone application.

To go fully electric you pressed an 'e-mode' button. Unlike the Jetta hybrid, which could only run for about a mile on electric power, the GTE was claimed good for 31 miles depending on conditions. The driver could choose to drive on pure electric power for weeks, with a recharge from a standard mains outlet taking about three-and-a-half hours. If you wanted all the performance you pressed the 'GTE' button.

Based in the European test procedure a provisional combined fuel consumption figure of 188mpg (using a great deal of electric power) was quoted, but press tests of pre-production cars in December 2013 saw 70mpg displayed.

The electric Golfs

Volkswagen's first electric drive research in the Golf started in 1976. A first-generation Golf was equipped with a 20kW electric motor and used as a test bed for different battery types and electric motors until the mid-1980s.

↑ The Golf 3 CityStromer had 16 battery blocks in the engine compartment (neatly covered) and some underneath, so boot space was freed up. (Author)

Later sodium-sulphur batteries were considered as they had twice the energy of lead-acid units but operated at 300 degrees C.

In 1981, one of the electric vehicle development companies set up by RWE presented the first Golf CityStromer (Strom being German for electrical current) based on a standard Golf 1. Twenty examples were tested by private drivers, but they were never likely to buy them. Each cost DM 50,000 to build in 1983 when a basic Golf 2 cost DM 13,490 and had they ever gone into production would still have been DM 25,000.

Volkswagen worked with RWE to produce a second-generation Golf CityStromer (there was also a Jetta) between 1984 and '85. With an 18.5kW AC motor and 16 lead-gel batteries installed under the boot floor, it had a claimed range of about 50km. There was a diesel-fuelled heating system to save energy and it could be charged on a domestic socket. Only about 100 left-hand-drive and two right-hand-drive versions were made. One of the latter was tracked down and bought back by Volkswagen UK for restoration in 2010.

↓ A Golf 3 CityStromer tops up. The charging cable was stowed behind the front number plate. (Volkswagen Classic)

A total of 120 third-generation CityStromers were then built in a joint venture with Siemens between 1993 and 1996 and was available to buy, albeit at nearly DM 50,000 (25,000 Euros at 2014 rates) – about twice as much as a basic Golf 3.

The design featured braking energy recovery (battery regeneration), which would appear on regular Golfs over ten years later, and had a five-speed manual gearbox instead of a continuously variable automatic. The range was gradually creeping up to a claimed 90km. The electric Golf programme tailed off somewhat as development energies were put into TDI diesels. Although at first bought by companies, Golf CityStromers have gradually found their way into the hands of enthusiasts who continue to rescue, cherish and upgrade them with better equipment. Eighty Golf 3 CityStromers are said to survive.

Electric cars shot back into the news with the 1996 General Motors EV1, an advanced two-seater designed from the ground up as an electric car, anticipating Californian laws requiring zero-emissions vehicles, and as a corporate technology showpiece. Up to 1999 1,117 were recorded as having been made and were only available to lease. However, in 2003 the support programme was cancelled, General Motors recalled the majority of the lease cars and controversially crushed them. The electric car looked to be dead, or as some would have it, murdered by a conspiracy from the oil industry.

Meanwhile Volkswagen's hybrid and battery studies and concept cars continued, but by 2010 they risked looking behind the times as major manufacturers leapt into the uncertainty of the fledgling electric car market. The five-door hatchback Chevrolet Volt (also an Opel or Vauxhall) used a small petrol engine to recharge batteries but not drive the wheels, so it never needed a top-up. The same year the Nissan Leaf appeared, a car designed purely for electric power. Nissan's affiliate Renault announced its intention to launch four electric vehicles from 2011. BMW held trials of electric Minis and in February 2011 announced a new sub-brand BMW i, to launch the all-electric i3 and i8 in 2013.

As more and more manufacturers felt obliged to chase this very small and uncertain market two approaches emerged: you either built an electric car from the ground up with no compromises in packaging and made it look futuristic (Nissan Leaf, BMW i3, Renault Zoe), or you adapted an existing model, which wouldn't frighten the neighbours, like the Renault Fluence, or for that matter, a Golf. In 2013 it was reported that Volkswagen internal studies revealed potential electric car buyers were more interested in overall everyday practicality and ease of use than standing out.

No sudden surprises then from Volkswagen but a long-term exercise in customer reassurance. In 2011 a fleet of 500 prototype electric Golfs called the Golf Blue-e-motion (based on the sixth-generation car) began testing in real-world conditions for production scheduled for 2013 with the Golf 7. By the time the real thing arrived the public would be very familiar with the idea of an electric Golf. Companies and private motorists became development testers and visitors to Wolfsburg could test drive an electric Golf from the car park. 'It allows us at this stage to secure all aspects regarding technical detail, everyday drivability and user requirements ahead of series production," said Rudolf Krebs, VW group chief for electric traction.

In the wake of the 2011 nuclear disaster at Fukushima, Japan, the 'Fleet study in electric mobility' assumed greater importance as the German government vowed to close its nuclear power stations. It wanted the number of pure electric vehicles to reach one million in Germany alone by 2020 and they had to be run from renewable energy sources.

The compromises of CityStromers had gone. For the first time there was an electric five-door Golf with very little loss of interior space and a workable range. The batteries were still located in the boot and under

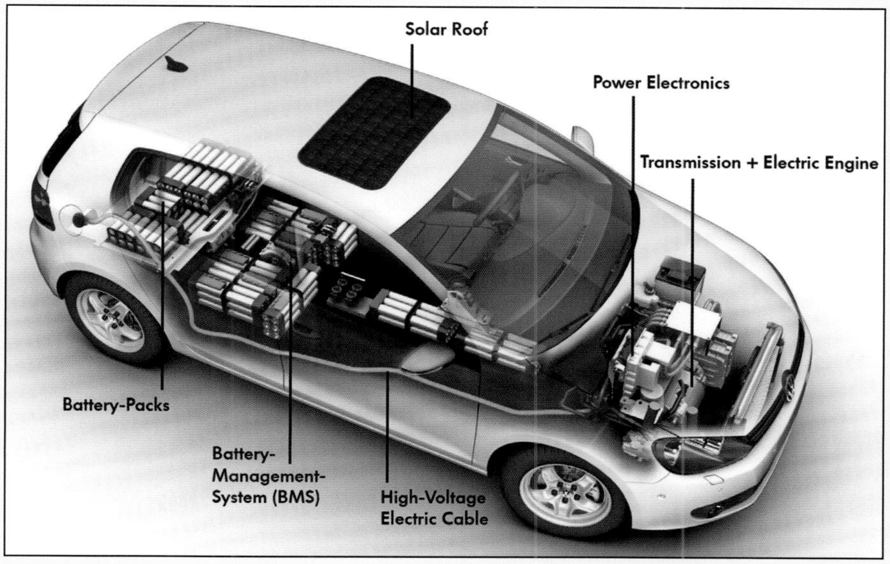

Based on the Golf 6, the Golf Blue-e-motion was used in a large-scale test, its packaging transferred to the Golf 7 for production.

A test car waits on the plug in Wolfsburg. Test drives were also offered at the Phaeton factory in Dresden.

↑ **More than a decade in development, the 2013 Volkswagen XL1 was a corporate hybrid technology showpiece capable of over 200mpg. It went into limited production at £100,000 per example.**

the rear seats but also in the transmission tunnel to leave a boot capacity of 279 litres. They were kept at the best temperature by a secondary cooling system.

Mounted in the engine bay, the 115PS (85kW) electric motor, transmission and differential, along with control systems, accounted for a claimed rise in overall weight of 205kg compared to a conventional diesel Golf. The performance was claimed to allow a respectable 0–62mph in 11.8 seconds before reaching a top speed of 86mph with a potential range between charges of 93 miles, which Volkswagen claimed suited the 46% of German commuters who travelled less than 10km (6 miles) each way.

To eke out the range, the Blue-e-motion had three power profiles. 'Comfort+' gave the full 85kW, 'Normal' reduced it to 65kW, and 'Range+' chopped power to 50kW and turned off the air conditioning.

Back in the marketplace though, electric car sales remained stubbornly low despite government subsidies to bring the purchase price down. The Nissan Leaf sold 12,000 worldwide in the first half of 2012 against a forecast 40,000 units (1,051 of them in the UK). A revamp and price cut in 2013 saw sales improve, with 3,000 total by the end of the year in the UK, where it was market leader in electric car sales. To put this in perspective though, in just one month regular UK Golf sales were about 4,000. Purely or partly battery-powered vehicles accounted for 4,157 new car registrations in Germany in 2012.

Volkswagen continued to keep itself in the public eye with fleet trials, symposiums and workshops for journalists, and made sure nobody thought it was lacking in innovation by putting the 2013 XL1 'hybrid supercar' into limited-scale production. It was clear though that its electric cars would look more or less the same as the petrol/diesel versions, which some commentators concluded was the right approach. Ford followed this route with the 2013 Focus Electric.

In September 2013 the Volkswagen Group, as well as aiming to be number one car producer, had set its sights on global market leadership in electric vehicles. Electric motors, gearboxes and lithium-ion batteries were developed in-house, and manufactured in Germany at Volkswagen plants.

Step forward the e-Golf (now shorn of its BlueMotion tag) and the e-Up! at the 2013 Frankfurt Motor Show. The e-Up! went on sale first and the e-Golf was set for summer 2014 sale and would be available in Europe and the USA for the first time.

The e-Golf offered tangible improvements on the previous generation development cars. There was still an 85kW/115PS electric motor but it now reached 100kph (62mph) in 10.4 seconds. Off-the-line performance of electric cars was always striking because the motor developed maximum torque straightaway (flying starts though were not really the point). Top speed was electronically limited to 140kph (87mph).

The 24.2kWh battery was claimed to give a potential range of 190km (118 miles). There were now two driving modes, 'Eco' and 'Eco+', and regenerative braking modes D1, 2, 3 and 'B' helped to extend maximum ranges. The battery packaging had reached the point where the only loss of space was the boot floor being set on the upper level where other owners could lower it an extra few centimetres. A full charge took 13 hours on a standard 240 volt household socket but like other carmakers Volkswagen offered an optional faster high-power charging system to get the battery up to 80% charged in half an hour.

There was an extensive amount of pre-sale publicity with motor show tours and press drives of almost-production-ready examples. The emphasis was on familiarity with the regular Golf, ease of use and refinement, although if you were interested you could toggle between driving modes. In December 2013 *Autocar* endorsed the e-Golf's prospects of success if the end price (helped by a £5,000 UK government grant) could undercut the £25,000 BMW i3: 'Signs are the e-Golf could be the car to get the long-predicted electric car revolution rolling.' But was the GTE hybrid the future?

↑ Prior to sale the e-Golf toured the motor shows of the world. Its German price was 34,900 Euros in spring 2014 (about £28,000) with an eight-year battery guarantee.

↓ Like the e-Golf, 2014 Golf GTE featured blue trim highlights and LED lighting. The 16 to 18in aluminium wheel rims were designed especially for the GTE.

↑ The GTE plug-in hybrid could be recharged by a bonnet socket and retained a fuel filler flap for the regular petrol tank.

Appendix 2: The Golf in motor sport

Even if it's not always been top of the motor-sport tree, every weekend there will be a group of Volkswagen Golfs racing against each other somewhere in the world. There's another book to be written here, but essentially the peak of the Golf's factory-backed competition success was in the 1970s and 1980s on the rally circuits of Europe.

Pre-Golf there had been no history of company racing. With the Beetle selling in millions without the help of motor-sport publicity, Volkswagen did not have a motor-sport department and Heinrich Nordhoff would not sanction any official works sports activities. Yet the Beetle was out there in vast numbers, was tough, cheap and could be tuned to some degree. It was rallied with success across the world, notably in African safaris.

Formula Vee, using Beetle running gear in single-seat racing cars, started in America in 1963 and spread to Europe, eventually using the water-cooled engines. It was a series that brought on Formula 1 World Champions including Jochen Rindt, Keke Rosberg, Nelson Piquet and Niki Lauda. The Formula Vee Association of Europe was wholly financed by but independent of Volkswagen and Volkswagen's Motorsport division in Hannover was established under Klaus Peter Rosorius in 1972.

The potential of the water-cooled front-drive cars was first exploited by private teams and tuners. In 1975 mighty Audi 50s were worked over by the noted engine tuner Shrick, bored out from 1,093 to 1,150cc with twin carburettors for 115bhp. Nothelle tuning offered an all-out racing version.

↓ Early competition Golfs had to establish the car's new name: here one competes in the 1979 Hunsrück Rally. (Volkswagen Motorsport)

In 1974 VW Motorsport at Hannover created a 1,500cc Group 1 rally Golf for Freddy Kottulinsky, a private BMW and Audi driver. What is said to be the world's first circuit racing Golf was created by former NSU race tuner Rolf Nothelle in 1975 and it notched up its first win at Hockenheim driven by Bernd Lielier. The 'red racer' became somewhat of a legend.

For track racing Volkswagen Motorsport began to support single-car championships, which used near-showroom-spec cars. Its first one-specification cup was based around the first-generation Scirocco in 1976 and from 1977 to 1982 the first-generation Golf was the base vehicle.

With all of its competitors boasting factory rally teams Volkswagen then reconsidered its decision to shun official activities and the 1976 Golf GTI – which had been sanctioned on the basis of 5,000 for motor sport – was sold in a 'basic configuration' for racing.

Volkswagen left engine preparation of the cars it backed to specialists and the Hannover University Science department. At first the 1,600cc GTI engines produced 120bhp (up from 110), but in 1978 a Group 2 version with a special cylinder head and Zenith fuel injection produced 180bhp, Jochi Kleint securing second place in the opening stages of the 1978 Hunsrück Rally. Kleint was the first rally driver with an official Volkswagen contract and in winter 1978 as an experiment he and Andreas Hänsch entered a turbocharged 1500 Golf diesel in the Monte Carlo Rally and caused a stir when they managed to finish 13th out of 270.

The Golf's first outright rally win was the September 1979 Sachs Baltic Rally, where a Group 2 version was driven by Swedish rally star Per Eklund, who was famous in the 1970s as a Saab driver. A works-backed GTI was then entered for the 1980 Monte Carlo Rally fitted with a Pierburg CS racing fuel-injection system and painted yellow, the colour of its sponsors. Eklund and co-driver Hans Sylvan drove into fifth place despite particularly icy conditions.

The team colour changed from yellow to green between 1981 and 1982 when throat lozenge manufacturer Rheila became an additional sponsor. The green Golf became known as the Rheila-Frosch (from the slogan Gegen Frocsh im Hals 'I have a frog in my throat') and despite a notable write-off when their car landed in a tree, the Alfons Stock/Paul Schmuck team were crowned German Rally champions in 1981. Per

↑ The 162bhp 'Red Racer' Nothelle Golf of 1975 pre-dated the GTI. It was restored by Marcus Nothelle, son of its creator Rolf and first shown in 2012. (Volkswagen Driver magazine)

↓ Famous British Golf GTI circuit racer Richard Lloyd in action in 1978. Power was the standard 110bhp, but a lot of work was done to improve the braking and balance of the car. (LAT)

↑ **A modern re-creation of the 1981 Pierberg Golf active on the classic rally scene. (Volkswagen Classic)**

↓ **The 'Rheila Golf' competing in the 1982 San Remo Rally, by then powered by a 16-valve engine. (Volkswagen Motorsport)**

Eklund once more drove for Volkswagen in the 1982 San Remo Rally and at Group 4 specification with a 16-valve Oettinger engine was now giving 193bhp and was in the top ten before clutch failure.

With the rally success of the first-generation Golf behind it, Volkswagen Motorsport invested heavily in international rallying with the second-generation Golf, producing specialised road cars such as the Golf Rallye and the G60 (see Chapter 3). In 1982 the classifications changed to Group A for fairly standard road cars and Group B for specials without many limits, which gave rise to short-lived cars such as the Ford Escort RS200 and monster Lancia Deltas.

Another Swedish driver had rallied a Golf 1 as a privateer and caught the attention of the company. Kalle Grundel marked a notable start to the Golf 2's Group A career in 1984, his car producing 160bhp from its 1.8-litre engine. With co-driver Peter Diekmann he scored category wins in the Portuguese and San Remo rallies.

'You had to do a lot of work with the old car, both with the steering wheel and the pedals, just to hold a line through a corner because it jumped around so much,' Grundel was quoted as saying at the time. 'The new car

gives you far more warning. It's much more forgiving, so it can be made to go much faster. The longer wheelbase gives it more stability and the suspension has longer travel – those two things make it completely new, and far better.'

Volkswagen Motorsport's team was tiny compared to the likes of Toyota and when it secured its best success in 1986 it had just 15 mechanics compared to about 100 for the big names. Kenneth Eriksson and the German champion Peter Diekmann as co-driver entered the World Rally Championship (WRC) with a 194bhp Golf GTI 16-valve. Three class wins, four second-place and two third-place finishes were enough to secure the Golf's only WRC win for Group A.

From 1987 to 1989 the GTI continued to have reasonable Group A results and the company determined it would be replaced by the supercharged Golf Rallye G60, taking on the mighty Lancia Delta Integrale and attempting to win the WRC top class. To be homologated, a limited run of at least 5,000 Golf Rallye road cars had to be built (see Chapter 3). The Rallye G60 had four-wheel drive like its rivals but 280bhp was not enough for its 1990 season, the only notable result a

↑ Here on the 1986 New Zealand Rally stage where it scored a first, the Group A Golf GTI 16-valve was branded with Triumph Adler typewriters – a Volkswagen investment that backfired expensively. (Volkswagen Motorsport)

← ↙ To promote the Golf in the US, Volkswagen expended a lot of effort on Pikes Peak International hill climb in Colorado. A twin-engined Jetta and Scirocco were followed by a Pikes Peak Golf with two 1.3 Polo engines for 500bhp in 1986, then this car in 1987 with two turbocharged 1.8 litre 16-valve engines for 652bhp. The front suspension collapsed on the climb. (Volkswagen Classic)

↑ **Golf G60 Rallyes being prepared at Volkswagen Motorsport in Hannover in 1989 or 1990. It was an ambitious project which failed to produce notable results. Its structure was however used for other projects. (LAT)**

↓ **A Rallye G60 in action during its sole 1990 WRC season. Although not a competition success it was the first of many rapid four-wheel-drive Golfs. (Volkswagen Motorsport)**

third place in the New Zealand Rally. It did, however, win the German Rally Championship the following year.

There was idea to create a sophisticated Golf 3 rally special for 1994 and the prototype A59 (see Chapter 4) was created but cancelled in 1992 in the wake of a financial crisis. However, rally versions of the third-generation Golf GTI 16-valve made some forays into the WRC in the Formula 2 (two-wheel drive) class, which ran from 1993 to 1999. Although it was overshadowed by the SEAT Ibiza Cupra F2 kit car, the overall class winner between 1996 and 1998, in 1997 Alister McRae and Tapio Luakkanen took the manufacturer's title for Volkswagen in the Mobil 1 British Rally Championship in a 280PS GTI 16V. In the final year of the F2 class fourth-generation Golf kit cars appeared in only three events.

The major days of the Golf rally cars were over but although the factory no longer fielded competition Golfs for international rallies, the following decades saw support for touring car and one-make series across the world.

With thanks to the history section of www.volkswagenmotorsport.com and Chris Eyre.

↑ Volkswagen UK has a long association with domestic motor sport, teaming up with tuning companies near its Milton Keynes base. The third-generation Golf was rallied domestically from 1994.

↑ A July 2007 scene from the British Volkswagen Racing Cup, in association with Hankook tyres, with a fifth-generation Golf leading a fourth.

↓ Germany's annual 24-hour race at the Nürburgring has often attracted teams of Golfs and in 2011, the 35th anniversary of the GTI, Volkswagen Motorsport built three 450bhp Golf24 cars, each with a 2.5-litre five-cylinder turbo engine and four-wheel drive. One had an accident and two retired with mechanical problems.

WJE 172T

RESTAURANT
HOTEL
Fam.
Rosmann
DN T 795

DubShack Racing
forge
VIDETTE UK LTD

GTI 35 JAHRE
DUNLOP
BILSTEIN
Castrol

Million
173

GTI 35 JAHRE
DUNLOP

Pimp my Golf!

Millions have appreciated the discreet looks of the Volkswagen Golf but others have used it as a blank canvas to be painted, lowered, re-engined and re-created to their own tastes. Just as happened with the Beetle, a whole industry soon emerged to provide Golf embellishments and upgrades.

The Golf GTI was the true catalyst for mass Golf-worship. In 1981 an Austrian GTI enthusiast decided to organise a meeting or Treffen just for fellow GTI owners in the village of Maria Wörth on the edge of the alpine lake Wörthersee. That year 80 turned up. The following year Volkswagen itself helped send the invitations out and 754 GTIs appeared. By 1981 there were 3,000 people attending over four days in May and by 2013 around 150,000 Volkswagen group fans were converging on the two villages of Maria Wörth and Reifnitz from all over Europe for a weekend of cars, beer and mayhem.

It was a mini motor show by then. All the brands showed off modified versions of their sporting cars and Škoda, SEAT, Audi and Volkswagen began to create concept cars or heavily modified sports versions just for the event. Then there was the 1983 See-Golf, or Lake Golf, a cabriolet with hydraulically operated pontoons, which lowered as it entered the water.

Golf customisation was booming in 2014 as this book was finished, with a buoyant magazine and online sector explaining anything from how to give a minor power boost to a diesel to sticking a VR6 in a Golf 1.

The UK's equivalent of Wörthersee, GTI International is organised by Volkswagen Driver magazine and was marking its 27th year in 2014. Held over the first weekend in July at Shakespeare County Raceway, near Stratford-upon-Avon, the main focus of attention had become a quarter-mile sprint track where visitors to the event can test the acceleration of their cars against the clock on a proper drag strip, watched by a potentially huge crowd from the 3,000-seater grandstand.

For those who prefer to polish their cars, the Show 'n' Shine and concours competitions attract a great many of the best-kept VWs in Britain and Europe, from original and restored concours classics to highly modified custom cars.

www.gtiinternational.co.uk

Images courtesy of Neil Birkitt, Editor *Volkswagen Driver* magazine (www.volkswagendrivermag.co.uk) and MadebyBear/Flickr, with thanks.

Bibliography

Books

Road & Track on Volkswagen 1968–1978 road tests (Brooklands Books 1986)

Road & Track on Volkswagen 1978–1985 road tests (Brooklands Books 1986)

VW Golf GTI Limited Edition Extra 1976–1991 (compiler Clarke, R. M.; Brooklands Books)

Abbott, David and Marcantonio, Alfredo: *Remember those great Volkswagen ads?* (First published 1982, reprinted 1993 Boot-Clibborn Editions, London)

Copping, Richard: *VW Golf – Five Generations of Fun* (Veloce Publishing Ltd. Kindle Edition)

Dymock, Eric: *The Audi file, all models since 1888–1995* (Haynes)

Hahn, Carl: *Mein Jahre mit Volkswagen* (Signum Verlag 2005)

Hopfinger, K B: *The Volkswagen Story* (G.T. Foulis and Co. Ltd, Third edition 1971)

Hutton, Ray (editor): *Volkswagen Golf GTI, the enthusiast's companion* (Motor Racing Publications 1985)

Kuch, Joachim: *VW Golf 1 1974–1983, Schrader-Typen-Chronik* (Motorbuch Verlag 2007)

Ludvigsen, Karl E: *introduction to 'People's car, a facsimile of B.I.O.S final report no.998 investigation into the design and performance of the Volkswagen or German people's car*, first published in 1947 (HM Stationary Office, 1947 and 1996)

Marek, Bjorn: *VW Golf, Meister Aller Klassen* (Komet Verlag 2008)

Meredith, Laurence: *VW Golf, Sutton's photographic history of transport* (Sutton Publishing Ltd 1999)

Meyer, Jens: *Kult Klassiker VW Golf 1* (GeraMond Verlag 2010) – recommended for its detail.

Paxton, Phil: *Bug, the strange mutations of the world's most famous automobile* (Simon & Schuster, New York 2002)

Seidler, Edouard and Wilkins, Gordon: *Ole Toledo!* (Editions JR, J. – R Piccard 1991)

Steiger, Christian and Wirth, Thomas: *Audi 1965–1975 Die Entscheidenden Jahre* (Edition Oldtimer Markt, HEEL Verlag GmbH)

Wagstaff, Ian: *Golf GTI, first and finest of the hot hatches* (Windrow & Greene Ltd, 1992)

Wood, Jonathan: *The new Beetle, the creation of a twenty-first century classic* (Quadrillion Publishing 1998)

Ruppert, James: *VW Golf with Scirocco, Corrado and Karmann convertible derivatives* (Crowood Autoclassics, Crowood Press 1996)

Academic papers

Walzer, P and Kalberlah, A: *Electric hybrid drive systems for application in road vehicles* (Part of New developments in power train and chassis engineering, 2nd international conference, Strasbourg, 14-16 June 1989 Institution of Mechanical Engineers).

Reitmayer, Morten and Rosenberger (Hg.), Ruth: *Unternehman am Ende des 'goldenen Zeitalters' Die 1970er Jahre in unternehmens und wirtschaftshistorischer Perspektive* (Klartext Verlag, Essen 2008)

Specific magazine articles

As well as the magazines quoted from, these particular articles provided good reference:

Autocar 25 November 1971: Upheaval of an empire by Edouard Siedler

Motor 26 May 1975: Electric cars – nearer than you think? by Karl Ludvigsen

VW Classic no 6 2013: 40 Jahre Passat. (Delius Klasing Verlag GmbH)

Harvard Business Review: 1991 interview with Carl Hahn.

Websites and specific online articles for research material

www.stern.de

www.spiegel.de

www.auto-motor-und-sport.de

www.volkswagenclassic.de for its excellent magazine features on many aspects of Golf history

Volkswagen corporate history timeline at: www.chronik.volkswagenag.com/

The archived road tests and news at www.autocar.com, including: A brief history of hybrid and electric vehicles 25 August 2013

www.fortune.com: Getting The Bugs Out At VW: In six years, Ferdinand Piëch has turned VW into one of the world's strongest car companies. Can he sustain it? Janet Guyon

www.fortune.com 29 March 1999

www.ft.com various London *Financial Times* news stories

www.reuters.com Insight: Has Volkswagen discovered the Holy Grail of carmakers? Laurence Frost, Andreas Cremer and Paul Lienert Berlin/Detroit 11 February 2013

Acknowledgements

I was greatly assisted in writing this book by the following people, whom I'd like to thank for their time and patience. Sorry if I've forgotten anybody over the past two years.

Volkswagen AG/Wolfsburg/Vienna

Thanks to Leslie Bothge for facilitating introductions, Rolf Trump for his time for interview and Dr Ulrike Gutzmann at the historic archives. Also Walter de Silva for his interview time.

Special thanks to Eberhard Kittler of Volkswagen Classic, who understood what the book was all about and helped with many images.

Also Dr Kaese and Alexandra Lucka at the Zeithaus museum and Volkswagen Autostadt.

It was a pleasure to spend time with Dr Ernst Fiala and Dr Carl Hahn. Many thanks also to Peter Hofbauer (www.ecomotors.com), Gert Hildebrand, Anton Konrad and Alfons Löwenberg.

Volkswagen South Africa

Thanks to Andile Dlamini and John Lemon for answers and images of the CitiGolf.

Volkswagen of America

Mark Gillies for fielding questions and generous provision of images.

Italy

Special thanks to Mr Giugiaro for his interview and Lorenza Cappello at the Italdesign Giugiaro press office.

France

Thanks again to Patrick Le Quément for his insider accounts. Merci Eric Foléa pour tes archives!

United Kingdom

In the Volkswagen UK press office, thanks to Paul Buckett, Allison Eden, Rory Lumsdon and Louise Ray for answers, access to archive press material and images.

Robin Davies at Audi, Mike Orford and Nick Perry at Porsche, Frank Laville at DDB. Kevin Wood at LAT photographic archive. The library staff at the Institution of Mechanical Engineers, London, especially Rhonda Grantham.

Thank you to Ray Hutton, as always, for his perspective and encouragement. Thanks too to Mark Hughes for commissioning my idea whilst at Haynes Publishing and to Derek Smith for staying with it.

Stephen Bayley www.stephenbayley.com
Neil Birkitt, *Volkswagen Driver* magazine
www.volkswagendrivermag.co.uk
Giles Chapman www.gileschapman.com
Jay Nagley, Redspy automotive analysis
www.redspy.co.uk
James Ruppert www.jamesruppert.com

Last but not least thanks to Paul Havill for many German translations and much morale boosting!

The majority of images are by kind courtesy of Volkswagen UK, Volkswagen AG Media Services, Volkswagen AutoMuseum and Volkswagen Motorsport unless specified.

Index

Page numbers in *italics* refer to illustration captions.

H

I

J

K